MURDER TRIALS

CICERO

MURDER TRIALS

IN DEFENCE OF SEXTUS ROSCIUS OF AMERIA · IN DEFENCE OF AULUS CLUENTIUS HABITUS · IN DEFENCE OF GAIUS RABIRIUS · NOTE ON THE SPEECHES IN DEFENCE OF CAELIUS AND MILO · IN DEFENCE OF KING DEIOTARUS

*Translated with an Introduction by
Michael Grant*

DORSET PRESS
New York

This translation first published 1975

This edition published by Dorset Press,
a division of Marboro Books Corporation,
by arrangement with Penguin Books Ltd.
1986 Dorset Press

Distributed in the United Kingdom by Bibliophile Editions

ISBN 0-88029-075-7
(Formerly ISBN 0-14-044-288-X)

The paper used in this book meets
the minimum requirements of the
American National Standard for
Permanence of Paper for Printed
Library Materials Z39.48—1948.

Printed in the United States of America
M 9 8 7 6 5 4 3 2 1

CONTENTS

INTRODUCTION

MURDER first became a conspicuous feature of the public life of Rome in 133 B.C., when the aristocratic but radical and reformist (*popularis*) tribune of the people Tiberius Sempronius Gracchus was clubbed to death by the senators he had defied, and by their friends.[1]

In the senate, Publius Cornelius Scipio Nasica Serapio[2] demanded that the consul Publius Mucius Scaevola must now act to protect the state and put down the tyrant. The consul answered in conciliatory fashion that he would not be the first to use violence, and would put no citizen to death without a regular trial. On the other hand he declared that, if Tiberius should incite or oblige the people to pass any illegal resolution, he would not consider it to be binding. At this, Nasica sprang to his feet and shouted, 'Now that the consul has betrayed the state, let every man who wishes to uphold the laws follow me!' Then he drew the skirt of his toga over his head and strode out towards the Capitol. The senators who followed him wrapped their togas over their left arms and thrust aside anyone who stood in their path. Nobody dared to oppose them out of respect for their rank, but those whom they met took to their heels and trampled down one another as they fled.

The senators' followers were armed with clubs and staves, which they had brought from their houses. The senators themselves snatched up the legs and fragments of the benches which the crowd had broken

1. See List of Terms, p. 333: Assembly, Senate, Tribunes of the People. The terms *populares* and *optimates* gradually came into increasing use as self-descriptions of the radical and conservative elements in the ruling class, though these never formed units as clearly defined as modern political parties. It was the policy of the *populares*, and of the tribunes of the people who represented them, to try to arrange direct action through the theoretically sovereign Assembly instead of passing measures through the theoretically advisory senate. Cf. P. A. Brunt, *Social Conflicts in the Roman Republic*, Chatto & Windus, 1971, pp. 93ff.

2. Consul 138 B.C., and chief priest. See Genealogical Table, I.

in their hurry to escape, and made straight for Tiberius, lashing out at those who were drawn up in front of him. His protectors were quickly scattered or clubbed down, and as Tiberius turned to run, someone caught hold of his clothing. He threw off his toga and fled in his tunic, but then stumbled over some of the prostrate bodies in front of him. As he struggled to his feet, one of his fellow-tribunes Publius Satureius, as everybody agrees, dealt the first blow, striking him on the head with the leg of a bench. Lucius Rufus claimed to have given him the second blow, and prided himself upon this as if it were some noble exploit. More than three hundred men were killed by blows from sticks and stones, but none by the sword.[1]

Whichever side must be allotted the initial share of blame for these events – and that is very uncertain – the arrival of the evil moment had been inevitable. For one thing, the Roman governing class, although it was the creator of jurisprudence and civil law, had always been willing, as A. W. Lintott has recently pointed out, 'to tolerate and exploit techniques of violence in public life – which led to their own destruction'; and the previous decades had provided ominous signs that this catastrophe of 133 was on the way. Lintott finds the seeds of this hazardous attitude in the Roman tradition of holding and tolerating public demonstrations, stirred up by appeals for help from persons claiming that they had suffered private wrongs or damages.

Such demonstrations ended with a mob howling round a man's house and firing his door, assailing him with stones, or even burning him alive. So too in civil law the element of self-help and permitted violence can be detected in procedures of arrest, enaction of judgement and vengeance (including capital penalties) and forceful assertion of rights. Lack of a civil police necessarily left much scope for private action. Hence direct assertion of certain private and public rights was taken for granted. ... Cicero's writings reveal the ambiguous and

1. Plutarch, *Tiberius Gracchus* (translated by Ian Scott-Kilvert), p. 19. For discussions of the rights and wrongs, see H. H. Scullard, *From the Gracchi to Nero*, O.U.P., 3rd edn, 1970, p. 390 n. 16; A. W. Lintott, *Violence in Republican Rome*, O.U.P., 1968, pp. 175ff.

contradictory attitudes towards the concepts of law and of self-help to which he and other Romans were reduced when they found themselves in the no-man's land where the city-state fails to control partisan violence.[1]

Once unleashed, the monster could not be kept quiet for long. Eleven years after the events that have just been described, further violence was employed to kill Tiberius Gracchus' brother Gaius (122 B.C.), again the occupant of a tribuneship, and on this occasion an attempt was made to justify the murder on the grounds that the senate had previously issued an emergency decree (*senatusconsultum ultimum* or *de republica defendenda*), the first of its kind.[2] The extent and limits of the authority which such decrees conferred will be discussed in connexion with the third speech translated in the present volume, *In Defence of Rabirius* (p. 267). The subject-matter of that case (though thirty-seven years elapsed before it came up) was another outbreak of violence which occurred in 100 B.C., when a third reformist tribune of the people, Lucius Appuleius Saturninus, was murdered in his turn, again after the passing of the emergency decree. The amount of guilt that requires to be attached to his senatorial, conservative killers, although Cicero is all on their side, remains, once more, an intricate and debatable point (p. 257).

On another aspect of policy, however, which now became

1. A. N. Sherwin-White, *Journal of Roman Studies*, LIX, 1969, p. 286, reviewing A. W. Lintott, op. cit., pp. 6ff., 23ff. Sherwin-White quotes the relevant Latin terms. Cf. also R. E. Smith, *The Anatomy of Force in Late Republican Politics*, Studies Presented to V. Ehrenberg, Blackwell, 1966, pp. 257–73.

2. In 132 B.C., after the murder of Tiberius Gracchus, a step had been taken in this direction by the appointment of a special commission which rested on the senate's assertion of its own power to release the consuls from the normal limits of their authority, but this was not yet a *senatusconsultum ultimum*: cf. J. Ungern-Sternberg von Puerke, *Untersuchungen zur spätrepublikanischen Notstandsrecht*, Vestigia XI, Munich, 1970.

9

politically urgent, there is no doubt at all that the senate was at fault: its attitude towards Rome's Italian subjects or 'allies' was far too illiberal. The result was a terrible war, lasting from 91 to 87 B.C.[1] Cicero served in this war at the age of seventeen and was able to see for himself the widespread devastation which increased the likelihood of sudden death throughout numerous areas of the Italian peninsula. Then came a bloody series of confrontations between the *popularis* Gaius Marius (and his successors) and the right-wing, pro-senatorial Lucius Cornelius Sulla (88–86, 83–81 B.C.). The leaders indulged freely in murders, sometimes, though not always, thinly disguised as official executions. The climax of these horrors was the massacre introduced by the proscriptions of Sulla, who, fresh from spectacular though inconclusive victories over King Mithridates VI of Pontus (N. Asia Minor), established himself as dictator[2] in 82 B.C. Plutarch writes that

Sulla now devoted himself entirely to the work of butchery. The city was filled with murder, and there was no counting the executions or setting a limit to them. Many people were killed because of personal ill-feeling; they had no connexion with Sulla in any way, but Sulla, in order to gratify members of his own party, permitted them to be done away with. . . . He also condemned anyone who sheltered or attempted to save a person whose name was on the lists. Death was the penalty for such acts of humanity, and there were no exceptions in the cases of brothers, sons and parents. . . . The lists were published not only in Rome but in every city of Italy. . . . And those who were killed in the passion of the moment or because of some private hatred were as nothing compared with those who were butchered for the sake of their property.[3]

With such gains at stake, 'official' proscriptions – or the vindictive and fraudulent insertions of names in proscription lists – led to a further great increase in private acts of violence

1. The Marsian or Social War.　　2. See List of Terms.
3. Plutarch, *Sulla*, 4 (translated by Rex Warner).

and assassinations,[1] and that is the theme of the first speech translated here, Cicero's oration *In Defence of Sextus Roscius of Ameria* (80 B.C.). It is true that those of Sulla's measures which possessed a more constructive character succeeded in launching the Republic on another forty years of uneasy life. Nevertheless, the dislocations for which he was responsible, including the almost total ruin of central Italy, created an atmosphere in which murder became almost normal. No earlier period, one feels, could have witnessed the shocking series of events at the small town of Larinum (whatever their exact extent and interpretation) reflected by the second of our speeches, *In Defence of Cluentius* (66 B.C.). This and the defence of Roscius are unique documents for the seamy side of life in Italian towns of the period. The historian Sallust, writing in the later forties B.C., analyses the moral collapse which brought about such a situation. He uses extreme terms, and although for our taste his enumeration of vices strikes rather too abstract a note, he is surely not exaggerating very wildly. When he comes, for example, to that typical product of the age, Lucius Sergius Catilina, he points out that the followers of this man of violence included a considerable array of cut-throats and assassins;[2] and there is little doubt that this was true.

Cicero claimed great credit for putting down Catilina, but the backlash caused his own eclipse and exile (pp. 264ff.). When he returned, he was no longer in the middle of the political scene. Nevertheless, his speeches of these years once again include defences of clients, Caelius and Milo, accused of the murders which had become such a feature of the age. Indeed, as life became even cheaper, the rusty machinery of the Republic was on the point of breaking down for ever. Revolutionary tribunes had been superseded by the far more dangerous phenomenon of great warlords, who not only felt

1. Cf. P. A. Brunt, *Italian Manpower 225 B.C.–A.D. 14*, O.U.P., 1971, Appendix 8 (p. 551), 'Violence in the Italian Countryside'.
2. Sallust, *Catiline*, 14, 3.

a total disrespect for the senate, but commanded sufficient force to intimidate its members. Two of these men, Pompeius and Caesar, came to blows in the Civil War of 49 B.C., and it was in the private house of the victorious Caesar, now dictator, that Cicero delivered the last of the speeches in this book, *In Defence of King Deiotarus* (45), a prince in Asia Minor who was accused of planning to murder the autocrat himself.

In the following year that result was duly achieved, by Roman traditionalists who found his autocracy intolerable. This time, Cicero did not have to defend the murderers – strongly though he applauded them – for they were never brought to court. Instead, they fled to the Balkans, where they met their deaths at Philippi. But before that, Rome was stricken by a further series of proscriptions (43 B.C.), drawn up by Antonius and Octavian (the future Augustus). The list included the name of Cicero himself, and this was the end of him.

In the earlier centuries of the Roman Republic (which traditionally began in 510 B.C.), all criminal jurisdiction had been a matter for the officers of state – principally the consuls and praetors[1] – and for the Assembly of the Roman People. Every sentence had to be pronounced by an officer of state in the first instance. But if the sentence was capital (p. 17), or imposed a fine above a certain limit, it could not be carried out – provided that the defendant was a Roman citizen – until it had been confirmed by the Assembly on appeal.

But then in the second century B.C. certain types of investigation, particularly those relating to derelictions of public duty, began, from time to time, to be vested in specially appointed tribunals or commissions (*quaestiones*), presided over by a praetor and composed of a number of senators. The first

1. Dictators, too, possessed this power, and so did tribunes of the people (see List of Terms), especially in relation to political offences. In fact, though not in law, they too were officers of state.

permanent tribunal of this kind (*quaestio perpetua*) was established in 149 B.C., when the tribune Lucius Calpurnius Piso Frugi passed a law setting up a standing court (the *quaestio de repetundis*) to deal with offences of extortion and misgovernment by officials in the provinces. The chairman of this court was a praetor, and the other judges who served with him, too, were at first still drawn from the senate.[1] But in 123–122 B.C. the tribune Gaius Sempronius Gracchus, concluding that the court was corrupt and unwilling to convict senators, arranged for legislation which resulted in its membership of the court passing to the knights, the second order in the community after the senate, consisting of men with a minimum property qualification of 400,000 sestertii.[2] This was almost certainly the first time that non-senators had sat as judges in such trials; and for reasons of gain, advancement and prestige alike, the measure of Gaius Gracchus played a predominant part in giving identity to the knights as a political force, and setting them corporatively against the senate.

During the next forty years several other permanent courts of the same type were established to deal with specific crimes of frequent occurrence. Then the practice was reduced to a system by the dictator Sulla, who, as part of a general overhaul of state institutions, brought the number of standing courts up to at least seven, possibly more – including a court for

1. I prefer to call these *iudices* 'judges' rather than 'jurymen' (though when Cicero addresses them I sometimes render the term 'gentlemen', for the sake of variety).

2. See List of Terms (Knights, Sesterces). For the court, see J. P. V. D. Balsdon in R. Seager (ed.), *The Crisis of the Roman Republic*, Heffer, and Barnes & Noble (reprint of 1938 article), pp. 98ff. The idea that the knights were mostly businessmen is incorrect: many of them were agriculturalists and landowners, like the senators. But it was the businessmen among them, the *publicani* (possessing resources that permitted them to bid for the public contracts and to farm taxes), who made them a political force. Cf. P. A. Brunt in *The Crisis of The Roman Republic* (reprint of 1962 article), pp. 122ff.; *Social Conflicts in the Roman Republic*, pp. 70ff.

murder.[1] In pursuance of his policy of re-establishing senatorial control over the state, Sulla reversed the measure of Gaius Gracchus, entrusting the judgeships of these courts wholly to members of the senate,[2] which at the same time he increased from 300 to 600 members. Out of this total, a general panel was drawn up of those senators who were qualified to serve in the courts, and from this panel, which probably numbered something over 450, the judges were selected for individual trials, 75 in each of the more important courts and 51 in the rest. (When the senators, in 70 B.C., lost their monopoly of the judgeships once again [p. 116], 75 became the standard total.)

The machinery by which these figures were reached was elaborate. At first a large number of judges was chosen from the panel for each court, and then this total was reduced by a complicated process of rejection and counter-rejection in which both prosecution and defence took part; though, even so, corruption was by no means eliminated.[3] Vacancies among the judgeships of a court were filled by its chairman on the authority of the senior praetor (*praetor urbanus*). The chairmen of all these *quaestiones* were still, if possible, to be praetors, of whom Sulla increased the total number from six to eight. When praetors were not available, other senators, generally men who had served as aediles,[4] were assigned to the courts as their chairmen, or in some cases were chosen by the judges of the court in question.

Rome possessed nothing resembling a public prosecutor or attorney general; and it was not the duty of any state official

1. The procedure of these courts was subsequently completed by further statutes.

2. A *Lex Servilia* of Quintus Servilius Caepio in 106 B.C. had begun the process of reversal by giving senators a share (perhaps a majority) of the judgeships, but the tribune Gaius Servilius Glaucia restored the courts to the knights, probably in 101; cf. A. H. M. Jones, *The Criminal Courts of the Roman Republic and Principate*, Blackwell, 1972, p. 53.

3. Cf. *Cicero: Selected Political Speeches*, Penguin Classics, 1969, p. 28.

4. See List of Terms.

to initiate prosecutions. Every citizen was at liberty to make a charge against another, and then the court's chairman, if he thought there was a *prima facie* argument – or was advised in this sense by a committee of his judges – could put the case down for trial. Prosecutions were often motivated by personal enmity, and even more frequently by greed, since the law promised large rewards to victorious prosecutors. When a defendant was convicted on a capital charge, they even obtained part of his confiscated property.

It was the responsibility of the two parties concerned to produce the evidence, though the accuser might have the assistance of state officials in preparing it. On the other hand, the accused was given impressive opportunities for his defence.[1] He might, on occasion, have as many as six counsel, and they were normally allotted half as much speaking time again as the prosecution. Cicero, whose astonishing mastery and versatility made him outstanding among Roman advocates,[2] did not believe in prosecuting frequently (p. 73) – in spite of his famous successes against Verres (70), Catilina (63) and Antonius (44–43).[3] On the contrary, he considered it very much less invidious to act as counsel for the defence,[4] and that was his role in all the four speeches translated in the present volume.

A trial included not only the set speeches of the advocates, but sharp cross-examinations as well. The latter have not survived, but their substance is often incorporated, in continuous form, in the published (and amended) versions of Cicero's speeches that have come down to us.[5] The judges

1. Cf. W. Kunkel, *Introduction to Roman Legal and Constitutional History*, O.U.P., 1966, p. 65.

2. *Cicero: Selected Political Speeches*, p. 18.

3. *Cicero: Selected Works*, Penguin Classics, 1960, pp. 35ff. (Verres), 101ff. (Antonius), *Selected Political Speeches*, pp. 71ff. (Catilina), 295ff. (Antonius).

4. Cicero, *On Duties*, II, 14, 48ff.

5. For the differences between the two versions see *Cicero: Selected Political Speeches*, pp. 29ff.

listened in silence, and were forbidden to speak to each other. Finally, they voted – guilty, or not guilty, or (as in Scotland) not proven. The chairman did not vote, but pronounced judgement and sentence, to which the traditional Roman right of appeal (p. 12) did not apply. The carrying out of the punishment was likewise his responsibility.

From the very earliest known times, the state had possessed some judicial machinery for dealing with murders. Under the designation *parricidium*, meaning the intentional murder of a free man (and only later narrowed down to the murder of a parent or close relation; see p. 26), the crime already appears in a law attributed to the mythical second king of Rome, Numa Pompilius, to whom many ancient Roman laws and other institutions were traditionally ascribed.[1] Officials described as 'quaestors for parricide' were mentioned in the venerable Twelve Tables,[2] a collection of various penal provisions attributed to the mid-fifth century B.C., not long after the primitive monarchy had been superseded by the Republic. It subsequently became normal for a special board of two to be appointed or elected afresh for every murder case that arose.

When permanent commissions to deal with the various most important crimes were gradually appointed from 149 B.C. onwards, this antique murder procedure became obsolete (though it was archaically revived for the case of Rabirius, p. 258). At some time between the death of Gaius Gracchus and the dictatorship of Sulla, a special court was set up to deal with cases of murder,[3] and perhaps it took cognizance of other sorts of assassination as well. Whether this court was set up on

1. M. Grant, *Roman Myths*, Weidenfeld & Nicolson, 1971, p. 137.

2. *Twelve Tables*, IX, 4, cf. *Digest*, 1, 2, 2, 23. For the quaestors, see List of Terms.

3. Cf. E. Badian in *The Crisis of the Roman Republic*, p. 207 and n. 38; P. A. Brunt, ibid., p. 143 and n. 1. There had been special murder courts before, e.g. in 142 and 138 B.C. (cf. Jones, op. cit., pp. 54ff., who tentatively suggests 98 for the introduction of the permanent court).

a permanent basis straightaway is not clear, but in any case it became permanently established by one of the laws of Sulla which created standing courts. Moreover, the terms of reference covered by the court thus established, the *quaestio de sicariis et veneficiis*,[1] were extended to cover other kinds of killing as well as poisoning. In particular, one of the crimes the court dealt with was judicial murder, by one 'who has given false witness to compass a man's death or has been responsible for causing it', though only senators were affected (p. 117).[2] Roman law, for all its admirable qualities, was often harsh. Yet the treatment of murderers, provided that they were Roman citizens, displayed a leniency which would generally be regarded as excessive today. For with the exception of the most atrocious forms of the crime, such as the slaying of one's parents (of which more will be said in connexion with the speech *In Defence of Roscius*), a Roman citizen convicted on a 'capital charge'[3] was not only, according to the usual course of events, exempted from the death penalty, but was also extremely likely even to avoid detention.[4] Indeed, the detention of Roman citizens for a term of imprisonment was not even a legal possibility.[5] There remained the question of a death penalty. Now, it is possible, according to one view, that the theoretical punishment laid down by

1. It operated in three sections (p. 217).

2. This measure, and its limitation to senators, went back to a measure of Gaius Gracchus.

3. Latin *caput*, the legal status or personality of a Roman. According to the *Lex Sempronia de provocatione* of Gaius Gracchus, a Roman citizen could only be prosecuted on this charge with the consent of the Assembly (cf. p. 12).

4. Nor was he normally arrested between accusation and trial, cf. Jones, op. cit., p. 77.

5. When Caesar proposed the indefinite imprisonment of Catilina's conspirators in 63 B.C., he only meant that they should be imprisoned until it was safe and expedient to bring them before a court of law: cf. R. Syme, *Sallust*, C.U.P., 1964, pp. 111ff., n. 38.

the new courts was sometimes death.[1] Yet executions were extremely rare. This was because accused persons could remain at liberty until their sentence and penalty had been pronounced, with the consequence that during the interval between conviction and sentence (or sometimes even before conviction) they almost always left Rome, and hastened towards non-Roman territory. Indeed, from about the beginning of the first century B.C. onwards, state officials were actually precluded from arresting the accused man, even after the pronouncement of the verdict, without first giving him time to depart.[2] It was only after the convicted man had made his escape in this way that a decree was generally passed excluding him from legal protection, threatening him with death if he returned, and depriving him of his citizenship and property.

It was because of this situation that Milo, after his fruitless defence by Cicero, was able to leave Rome without awaiting condemnation, and thereafter to contemplate the scene with equanimity from Massilia (p. 296). But Cicero's incomparable oratory usually got his clients off. It is true that the unusual cases represented by the shorter speeches in this book (*In Defence of Rabirius* and *Deiotarus*) came to indeterminate conclusions, for special reasons. But his long and superb speeches *In Defence of Roscius* and *Cluentius* were triumphantly successful. So was his defence of Marcus Caelius Rufus against accusations including multiple murder charges (p. 293). Yet at least some of these clients were undoubtedly guilty of murder. Milo almost certainly was, Rabirius may have been, Deiotarus and Cluentius, whatever they may or may not have done, were extremely far from being the paragons so fulsomely

1. Cf. E. Levy, *Die Römische Kapitalstrafe*, 1931, pp. 14ff., against the more usual view of D. Daube, *Revue d'histoire du droit*, XV, 1936, p. 64.

2. This position gradually arose as a result of the power of the tribunes to thwart executive action by preventing arrest or enforcing release from custody. Cf. J. L. Strachan-Davidson, *Problems of the Roman Criminal Law*, O.U.P., I, 1912, pp. 160–64; D. Stockton, *Cicero: A Political Biography*, O.U.P., 1971, pp. 136ff.

presented by Cicero, and Caelius, even if he had not, perhaps, tried to poison his mistress, surely had a hand in the massacre of a number of envoys who had come from Egypt to complain about their king.

We need not, of course, suppose that Cicero was ignorant of the likelihood that some of his clients were guilty. Indeed, after defending Cluentius he felt able to boast, in a private letter, that he had thrown dust in the eyes of the judges (p.119). Moreover, in his treatise *On Duties*, he explicitly seeks to justify his willingness to defend guilty men. To make oneself the prosecutor of an innocent person on a grave charge he describes as inhumane.

But there is no need, on the other hand [he continues] to have any scruples about occasionally defending a person who is guilty – provided that he is not really a depraved or wicked character. For popular sentiment requires this; it is sanctioned by custom, and conforms with human decency. The judges' business, in every trial, is to discover the truth. As for counsel, however, he may on occasion have to base his advocacy on points which *look like* the truth, even if they do not correspond with it exactly. But I must confess I should not have the nerve to be saying such things, especially in a philosophical treatise, unless Panaetius, the most authoritative of Stoics, had spoken to the same effect. The greatest renown, the profoundest gratitude, is won by speeches defending people. These considerations particularly apply when, as sometimes happens, the defendant is evidently the victim of oppression and persecution at the hands of some powerful and formidable personage. That is the sort of case I have often taken on. For example, when I was young, I spoke up for Sextus Roscius of Ameria against the tyrannical might of the dictator Sulla.[1]

Thus Cicero defends his practice partly on moral or compassionate grounds of 'human decency', that is to say because it would be indecent to deny assistance to any man confronted by all the sources of organized society. But he also justifies

1. *On Duties*, II, 14, 51, translated in *Cicero on the Good Life*, Penguin Classics, 1971, p. 147. For Panaetius (*c.* 185–109 B.C.), ibid., p. 27.

himself on grounds of expediency, because popular sentiment is on the defence counsel's side – and because if he can show that the defendant was a victim of oppression, as Roscius had been, it will be good for his own career.[1] This almost cynical frankness has earned Cicero raised eyebrows from moral purists. But his critics are usually people unacquainted with the practical requirements of the lawcourts. For English legal practice today, without needing to have recourse to Cicero's arguments of expediency, fully endorses his willingness to defend guilty persons, and indeed goes even farther. 'In a criminal trial,' wrote Sir Patrick Hastings, 'the prisoner is entitled to be represented whether he be innocent or guilty, and the question of his innocence or guilt is no concern of the advocate who appears for him. ... It is no part of the duty of a barrister to form any opinion as to what verdict a jury should return; his task is to place before the court, with absolute honesty and to the best of his ability, the defence which the prisoner desires to raise.'[2]

I am indebted to the Society for the Promotion of Roman Studies for the excerpts I have quoted from *The Journal of Roman Studies*; to Penguin Books Ltd and Mr Rex Warner for a quotation from Plutarch's *Life of Sulla*; and to Penguin Books Ltd and Mr Ian Scott-Kilvert for a passage from

1. He might have qualified this, however, by saying that a reputation for low professional *ethos* will diminish his usefulness in the eyes of potential clients.

2. Sir Patrick Hastings, *Cases in Court*, Heinemann, 1949, p. 237. Hastings adds that all any court has to do is to decide, not whether the prisoner is innocent or guilty, but whether the prosecution have succeeded in proving his guilt, and his guilt, moreover, of the actual offence with which he is charged – until which time he is presumed innocent. He might also have pointed out that another reason why a barrister is bound to help even a killer is because an English court, if he can persuade it to do so, has the power to reduce a murder charge to the lesser offence of manslaughter.

Plutarch's *Life of Tiberius Gracchus*. I am grateful to Mrs Bezi Hammelmann, Mr Thomas Owtram and Mrs Gunilla Rathsman for their assistance, and to Mrs Betty Radice and Miss Julia Vellacott and Miss Alex MacCormick for editorial services. I also want to thank my wife very much for her help.

Gattaiola, 1973   MICHAEL GRANT

I

IN DEFENCE OF SEXTUS ROSCIUS
OF AMERIA

Introduction to Cicero's Speech

SEXTUS ROSCIUS THE ELDER *was a well-known and prosperous citizen of the hill-town of Ameria in southern Umbria, fifty miles north of Rome. The imposing polygonal walls of this ancient place, now known as Amelia, are still to be seen. It was very much the same sort of town as Cicero's own birth-place, Arpinum, sixty miles south-east of Rome. The local notables of such municipalities were carefully cultivated by Roman noblemen and politicians, and Roscius of Ameria was often in the capital, staying with distinguished hosts.*[1]

But one night in 80 B.C. – when Sulla had just retired from his dictatorship, but was still consul and still dominated the 'Restored Republic'[2] *– this Sextus Roscius the elder was returning from a dinner-party at Rome when unknown men attacked him and he was murdered. Subsequently his son of the same name, said to be a retiring individual of rustic tastes, was prosecuted for the murder by a certain Erucius, perhaps a Sicilian Greek by origin. The case came up before the court established by Sulla to deal with poisoning and murder (p. 17). Cicero was briefed for the defence, and as usual, since the speeches of his opponents have never survived, it is through his eyes that we are obliged to form our opinion of the case.*

It possessed a grim significance because of the peculiar detestation in which Romans, very naturally, held the murder of a parent or close relation. In the first century B.C. the term for such a murder was parricidium. *Earlier, this had meant murder in general (p. 16), but in due course, perhaps owing to an etymological association with*

1. Cicero's father, too, who belonged to the same kind of rich, respectable local family as the Roscii, possessed a house on the Esquiline hill at Rome, where Cicero spent part of his early years.

2. The usual statement that he was still dictator is incorrect; cf. E. Badian in R. Seager (ed.), *The Crisis of the Roman Republic* (reprint of 1962 article), pp. 230ff. and n. 117. For the date of the speech, see bibliography in T. E. Kinsey, *Mnemosyne*, 4th series, XX, 1967, pp. 61–7.

25

'father' (pater) *which may or may not be correct, it became restricted to the narrower significance, which the word 'parricide' preserves in our language today. For this crime the death penalty was retained, even during the last centuries of the Republic when citizens convicted of other sorts of murder were allowed to escape (p. 17). And the penalty that was imposed took a form which throws a lurid light on the sadistic nature of some traditional Roman punishments, often designed in accordance with the requirements of religion.*[1] *The interpretation of the various details of the punishment is disputed.*[2] *Its first known employment is comparatively late,*[3] *because retribution in earlier periods had been left, to some extent at least, in the hands of relatives.*[4] *But thereafter the penalty involved was by no means solely theoretical, for it was invoked by Cicero's own brother Quintus, who executed two Mysians (from northern Asia Minor) at Smyrna (Izmir) in this way.*[5] *We learn from other works (one by Cicero, and the other by a contemporary writer) of the gruesome nature of the punishment. First, the culprit had his face covered with a wolf's skin, and wooden shoes were put on his feet.*[6] *Then, as Cicero indicates in a florid passage of the present speech, the victim was sewn up naked in a sack and cast into a running stream to drown (p. 66). We learn from later legal writings that a preliminary scourging had first taken place, and that into the sack, along with the parricide, were crammed a dog, a cock, a monkey and a snake.*[7] *It is*

1. Cf. M. Grant, *Gladiators*, Penguin edn, 1971, pp. 106ff.; cf. pp. 14, 10.

2. See editions of this speech by E. H. Donkin, Macmillan, 1879, pp. xxiiff., and J. J. Freese, Heinemann and Harvard (Loeb edn), 1930, pp. 119ff., For *parricidium* in general see A. Pagliaro, *Studi in onore di L. Castiglioni*, II, 1960, pp. 669ff., W. Kunkel, *Abhandlungen der Bayerischen Akademie der Wissenschaften*, Neue Folge, LVI, 1962, pp. 37ff.

3. *c.* 102 B.C. according to Livy, *Periochae*, 68.

4. Cf. Lintott, *Violence in Republican Rome*, p. 38; cf. pp. 25ff.

5. Cicero, *Letters to his brother Quintus*, I, 2, 5.

6. Cicero, *On Invention*, II, 50, and unidentifiable writer *To Herennius*, I, 13, 23.

7. Modestinus, *Digest*, XCVIII, 9, 9.

surprising that these further horrors were not exploited by Cicero. But he had dwelt heavily on the theme already, and evidently he felt he had said enough.

To save Sextus Roscius from the terror of this fate, or at the very least from exile and outlawry, he decided to divide his speech into three parts. In the first, after the usual introductory passage, he attempts, as he must, to show that the charge is baseless, and he particularly points out the lack of corroborative evidence. His methods will come as a shock to modern readers. This, to our way of thinking, must surely be the nucleus of the case for the defence. And yet the subject is handled in a manner very remote from the legal procedures we should look for today. J. C. Nicol writes:

We should expect details as to the place, the date, the hour of the crime, the sifting of the testimony of eye-witnesses if possible, or failing that the argument from circumstantial evidence. If the younger Sextus Roscius was not in Rome at the time, it would surely have been easy to prove an alibi; if it was alleged that he employed assassins, the onus of proving his complicity would rest with his accusers. It is true we have not got the speech of Erucius to refer to, but if we may trust Cicero he made no attempt to prove anything. No witnesses to the fact were called; the slaves who might have told the truth were withheld, and the court had no power to enforce their attendance. Erucius based his charge on arguments of motive, arguments which were of the flimsiest character. Cicero's defence in like manner rests upon arguments of motive, and it must be admitted that he turns the tables upon his opponents with crushing effect.[1]

This he does in the second section. Here, although his speech is supposed to be a defence of the younger Sextus Roscius, he passes to the attack and tries to fasten the murder specifically upon two other persons, his client's kinsmen Magnus and Capito.[2] Magnus had been at Rome at the time of the elder Sextus' murder, and Cicero declares that it was his doing or at least was done at his instigation. As for Capito, it was deeply suspicious, says Cicero, that he, at Ameria, was the very first man to whom the news of the death was

1. J. C. Nicol, in his edition of the speech (C.U.P., 1954), p. xxiii.
2. Both were called Titus Roscius.

reported. And then the orator goes on to unfold a melodramatic tale. Magnus and Capito, he suggests, were both acting for a very important personage behind the scenes, who wanted to get his hands on the considerable property of the dead man, whose son he proposed to disinherit. This sinister planner, his argument goes, was no less a figure than Chrysogonus, an influential freedman and favourite of the all-powerful Sulla himself.[1] For Cicero, whose introduction, early on in his speech, of one of Sulla's own henchmen must have been an unexpected sensation,[2] now goes on to explain in detail how the freedman had arranged for the name of the deceased Sextus Roscius the elder to be inserted fraudulently and belatedly into the list of Sulla's proscribed (p. 41), with the result that his property then came up for auction and Chrysogonus himself bought it for a nominal sum (since no one dared bid against him), sharing the loot with Magnus and Capito. Next, Cicero declares, Capito prevented an Amerian deputation, which favoured the case of the younger Roscius, from gaining access to Sulla, whereupon the disinherited man, feeling that his life was in danger, fled to a Roman friend, Caecilia Metella, member of an immensely powerful family which enjoyed unique influence with Sulla (p. 44). And this, according to Cicero's version, was the juncture at which the young Roscius' enemies concluded that the time had come to get rid of him altogether, so as to be sure of keeping hold of his property in safety. They decided that the way to do this was to arrange for him to be accused of his father's murder, which they themselves had committed.

Many of Cicero's speeches are full of fiction and special pleading, and these elements are not lacking here either; yet for the most part his story has a convincing ring. We cannot, admittedly, tell what arguments the prosecutor may have put forward, but all the same

1. Whose family name, according to custom, he took when he was freed: he was Lucius Cornelius Chrysogonus. See List of Terms (Freedman).

2. Though W. V. Harris (*Rome in Etruria and Umbria*, O.U.P., 1971, p. 272) suggests that Cicero deliberately makes Chrysogonus seem more formidable than he really was.

the circumstances described sound all too painfully typical of the chaotic, violent times that reached their climax with Sulla. This was the first case of public concern in which the twenty-six-year-old Cicero had ever been engaged,[1] and its triumphant result, the acquittal of his client, was a source of satisfaction to him in later life. It is true that he subsequently disapproved of a certain youthful verbosity in his speech, and felt rather ashamed of that highly emotional, declamatory passage about the parricide penalty (p. 66). But he remembered with pleasure how well his effort had been received.[2]

He was also extremely proud of the way in which he had ventured to attack Chrysogonus, declaring that this meant standing up against the formidable tyranny of Chrysogonus' master, Sulla himself (p. 19). However, it will be seen that in fact he is extremely careful not to offend Sulla by any shadow of personal criticism whatever, a precaution all the more necessary because, through his family and his teachers alike, Cicero was connected with the dictator's late enemy Marius;[3] and very probably the speech, as delivered, was even more careful in this respect than the version that has come down to us.[4] Moreover, his criticism of Sulla's satellite Chrysogonus was calculated very carefully. For all his protestations of love for Greek culture, Cicero makes it clear from innumerable passages in his works how much he detested most living Greeks;[5]

1. Cicero's earliest speech, *In Defence of Publius Quinctius*, dating from the previous year, dealt with a complex partnership dispute; the result is unknown.

2. Cicero, *Orator*, XXX, 107; *Brutus*, XC, 312 – although he was at this time a lanky man with a long thin neck, speaking in a nervous monotone.

3. For these connexions (including the Marian links of his Roman mentors Quintus Mucius Scaevola Pontifex, Quintus Mucius Scaevola Augur, Lucius Crassus and Marcus Antonius), see D. Stockton, *Cicero: A Political Biography*, p. 5, and for Cicero's admiration of Marius, G. B. Lavery, *Greece and Rome*, 1971, pp. 133ff.

4. Cf. W. V. Harris, op. cit., p. 271 n. 5 and p. 272; cf. below, p. 98.

5. With the exception of some of those who worked under him, and (at any rate momentarily) Archias whom he defended in court (*Cicero: Selected Political Speeches*, pp. 146ff.).

and here he was, as it happened, on fairly safe ground in making Chrysogonus look like a Hellenistic ruler's untrustworthy and arrogant slave. For Sulla was now taking pains to pose as the founder of a Restored Roman Republic, and could not fail to disown any behaviour of such a kind as out of place in the new order.[1]

It is true that Cicero left for the east in the following year, and spent the next two years completing his studies at Athens and Rhodes; and it has often been said that he left because his speech for Roscius had made it politically unhealthy for him to remain in Rome. But that seems unlikely, since, after this case, and before leaving for the east, he delivered another speech in the capital, In Defence of the Woman of Arretium *(Arezzo)* *(79* B.C.*)*. This further oration is now lost, but it is perhaps rather more likely than his defence of Roscius to have hastened his departure,[2] since we learn that it directly criticized Sulla – who was still alive at the time, though he died shortly afterwards – for acting ultra vires *by the* disfranchisement of Italian communities.

In any case the two speeches, even if they did not involve Cicero in any great danger, stood for a policy which required a certain amount of bravery, and provided a good example of the creditable manner in which Cicero, although by nature a hesitant and timid man, was able at critical moments of his career to screw up his courage and speak out in support of his ideals – among which hatred of any sort of tyranny figured very prominently.[3]

1. E. Badian in R. Seager (ed.), *The Crisis of the Roman Republic*, p. 230.
2. Cf. A. Afzelius, *Classica et Medievalia*, VIII, 1946, pp. 209ff.; doubted by W. V. Harris, op. cit., pp. 274ff.
3. Cf. *Cicero: Selected Works*, pp. 7ff.

CICERO'S SPEECH

1. The Innocence of Sextus Roscius

You must find it very surprising, judges, to see all these notable orators and eminent citizens firmly rooted in their seats, whereas I, on the other hand, am standing up here and addressing you. For, after all, I cannot compare with these seated personages in age, and still less in influence. It is true enough that every one of them – every single man you see here today – is utterly convinced that the charge on which this case is based is an unjust one which it is imperative to refute, a charge which only an unprecedented act of criminality could ever have concocted. Nevertheless, they do not actually venture to undertake the refutation themselves – owing to the hazardous times in which we live. They are here, that is to say, because they consider it their duty to be here. But they want to stay out of danger, and that is why they are keeping so quiet.

Do I imply by these words that I am a braver person than they are? Far from it. Or do I mean that I am more conscientious? No, I certainly don't covet that sort of praise – if it means diverting it from someone else! You may well ask, then, my real motive in undertaking this defence of Sextus Roscius, which the others were so reluctant to touch. Well, my motive was this. These men I am speaking of are important, authoritative figures. Now, if any of them had made a statement, and if anything in this statement had possessed political implications – a thing which would have been inevitable in a case like the present one – then people would have made out that he was meaning a great deal more than he had actually intended to. But I, on the contrary, can say every single thing that needs to be said, and say it with the most complete

31

freedom, without there being the slightest question of my speech becoming known or achieving publicity to anything like the same degree. For the others are men of rank and position, and nothing they say can pass unnoticed; besides, they are of such ripe age and experience that no allowances will be made for the smallest indiscretion they may commit. But my case is quite different. If I speak out of turn, either nobody will ever hear of it, because I am someone who has not even started his public career, or, if they do hear of it, they will pardon the lapse on the grounds of my youthful years – though the term 'pardon' has lost its real significance these days, when the custom of holding judicial inquiries, to which the word ought exclusively to apply, has virtually been swept out of existence.[1]

And another reason why I accepted the commission is this. For all I know, the circumstances in which the others were requested to take on Sextus Roscius' case may have been such that they felt at liberty either to accept or to refuse such pleas without violating any obligation. Whereas the approach to myself came from men whose friendship I regard as carrying enormous weight; I cannot forget all the services I have received from them, not to speak of the high positions they occupy in the state. The kindness they have done me, as well as the importance of their rank, seemed to me too great to disregard; and so I felt that I could not possibly ignore their wishes.

Those are the reasons why I agreed to undertake Roscius' defence. It is not a question of having been singled out as the most talented pleader. No, the point was that I was the person left over, the person who could plead with the least danger. To say that I was chosen in order to guarantee that Sextus Roscius should have the best possible defence would not be the truth. I was chosen in order to ensure that he had any defence at all!

1. i.e. by the proscriptions of Sulla.

You may well feel inclined to ask for further information about this fear and terror which induces all these distinguished figures to abandon their usual code of behaviour to such an extent that they actually decline to defend a man whose life and property[1] are at stake. And yet if this puzzles you I am hardly surprised, since the prosecutors have deliberately failed to mention the real motive which lies behind the accusation they are bringing.

Well, what is the motive? It is this.

The father of my client Sextus Roscius possessed property worth six million sestertii.[2] But a certain young man claims that he has bought it, and he has to admit that the sum he paid for it was only *two thousand* sestertii. The young man is Lucius Cornelius Chrysogonus, whose position in our country today is exceptionally powerful. And the alleged seller was the valiant and glorious Lucius Sulla – whose name, of course, I mention with all due respect.

What Chrysogonus seems to be asking you, judges, is this. Quite illegally, he says, he has seized an extensive and magnificent estate which is not his at all but belongs to someone else: and since this is so, and since the life of my client, Sextus Roscius, may be regarded as an obstacle standing in the way of his enjoyment of that estate, it is up to you to take steps to eliminate the worries and anxieties that this situation causes him. For while Sextus Roscius remains at large, Chrysogonus feels serious doubts whether he can contrive that this ample and wealthy patrimony, belonging to a wholly blameless individual, shall remain in his own clutches. But if Roscius can only be convicted and thus forced to depart from the scene, Chrysogonus looks forward to the prospect of being able to retain the proceeds of his crime, to squander and dissipate as extravagantly as he pleases. This, then, is the anxious longing which nags and torments him day and night. What he is doing, therefore, is to entreat you to set his mind at rest by

1. i.e. *caput;* see above, p. 17.   2. See List of Terms.

pronouncing yourselves his accomplices in these ill-gotten gains.

Well, if that seems to you a fair and honourable demand, gentlemen, then please allow me, without taking up too much of your time, to put forward a counter-request which seems to me to be a good bit fairer.

First of all, I request Chrysogonus to make one concession. Let him be content with the whole of our property, with all that we possess. He must not demand our life-blood as well. And of you, judges, too, I have certain requests to make. I ask you to resist the evil deeds of evil men and to believe the distresses of the innocent. And I beg you to save us all from a terrible peril, because the peril to which Sextus Roscius is exposed in this trial is one which casts its menace over the entire community. If inquiry brings to light even the slightest corroboration of the charge, even the smallest suspicion of my client's guilt, if it reveals even the most minute trace of any point that could make the accusation look justified, if you can detect in the prosecution's case even the faintest sign of any motive whatsoever other than the simple desire to acquire loot, then by all means let Sextus Roscius' life be sacrificed to the malignant pleasure of these individuals, and I have no objection to raise. But if the one and only issue is to satisfy the lust for gain in creatures who are incapable of ever being satisfied, if the entire object they have in mind is that the rich and massive plunder they have laid their hands on shall be topped up and crowned by the conviction of Sextus Roscius, then surely out of a great many deplorable aspects of the situation the most infamous of all is this: the fact that you yourselves, whose legal verdicts are given on oath, should now seem, in their eyes, to be suitable instruments to achieve the purposes they had formerly employed methods of brutal violence to attain.

After all, gentlemen, the reason why you were elected from

the citizen body to be members of the senate was because of the noble qualities of your personal characters. Then you were called from the senate to become members of this court – and that was because of your inflexible incorruptibility.[1] How on earth, then, can you be the right people for this set of assassins and gladiators to think that they can impose their demands upon? And what they are demanding is not just exemption from the punishment which their iniquities give them every reason to fear and dread at your hands. They are actually claiming permission to leave this court still enriched and loaded with the spoils they have seized without a shred of legality.

The crimes they have committed are wicked and horrible. Nothing I could say could ever be bad enough to describe them. No words that I could find to utter would do justice to the appalling character of these deeds; no superlatives would be sufficient to brand them with the condemnation they demand. To assail such actions as they deserve would exceed my powers; the necessary gravity would be beyond my years, and the necessary outspokenness is discouraged by our times. Moreover, I have special, personal, reasons for feeling nervous. For one thing, I am retiring by nature. And then you are important people; and my opponents are formidable; and the fate that threatens Sextus Roscius cannot fail to inspire terror.

For all of these reasons, judges, I particularly implore you to listen to what I shall have to say not only with great care but with indulgent sympathy. I know I have undertaken a burden in excess of my capacities. But my reason for doing so is because I have such complete and limitless trust in your integrity and understanding. If you will lighten the burden in some degree, then I, for my part, will endure it as well as I can, with all the diligence and determination I am able to muster.

---

1. To make up for the reduction of senators by the civil wars, Sulla drafted 300 knights into the senate. He also returned the function of the judges in criminal trials from the knights to the senate (p. 14).

And indeed, even if you desert me – though this is a fate I cannot bring myself to think about – even then I shall not lose heart. I have taken the job on, and I propose to carry it through to the best of my ability. If it proves to be beyond me, I would rather be crushed by the weight of the duty I am trying to perform than be accused of disloyalty or irresolution for shirking the task which my friends have entrusted to me.

And I most solemnly urge you, Marcus Fannius,[1] to prove to us and your country today that you are the same man whom the Roman people admired once before when you were presiding over this court. Take a look at the enormous crowd that has come to listen to this trial. You can see very well their air of eager expectancy. Their earnest desire that the proceedings should be just and impartial is unmistakable. This is the first murder case that has been heard for a very long time – although in the meantime there has been no lack of abominable murders. But now that you have become praetor,[2] everybody fervently hopes that this court over which you are presiding will really rise to the responsibility of dealing appropriately with the frightful bloody crimes that recur again and again every day.

In most trials it is the accusers who offer up vigorous appeals for severity. Today it is we, the accused, who make the appeal! We appeal to you, Fannius, and to your fellow-judges, to punish criminal acts with unswerving determination. We entreat you to be adamant in your resistance to malefactors. And we urge you to take careful note of one point: if you fail to take advantage of this opportunity to make your policy abundantly clear, then we have indeed, beyond any shadow of doubt, reached a point when all the limits set to human greed and malpractice and outrage have broken down. From this

1. The chairman of the court. On the previous occasion, to which Cicero refers, it had probably been meeting as a special commission.
2. See List of Terms.

time onwards – if you fail to do your duty – the slaughter will no longer be in secret. No, henceforward it will take place here in the very Forum itself, here, Fannius, in front of your own platform. Judges, the massacre, from now on, will be committed right here in front of your faces, right here among the benches where you are sitting!

For quite obviously that is the only reason why this charge has been brought: to clear the way for anarchy of such a kind, anarchy total and unrestricted. On the one hand you have the prosecutors, who have seized my client's property. On the other hand you have my client, whom they have left with no possession in the world except utter ruin. The people who gained by the murder of Sextus Roscius are the men who are bringing the charge today. To my client, on the other hand, his father's death has given nothing but grief and destitution. Yet, even so, his enemies have displayed the most horrifying determination to finish him off by putting him to death as well. That is why, even when he appears before this court, he has to be accompanied by an escort. Otherwise he would be killed on this very spot before your own eyes.

And so these are the people whose punishment the people of Rome demands – the prosecutors in this case! As for the defendant, he has escaped, so far, the dreadful massacre they conducted: and he is the only man who has succeeded in escaping.

But no description of mine, gentlemen, can begin to deal adequately with all the horrors of which they are guilty; and this is something I want you to understand fully. I propose, therefore, to set before you the whole story of what happened from the very beginning. Then you will have a better appreciation of all the misfortunes that have fallen upon my blameless, innocent client. You will also be in a position to realize the full gravity of the crimes committed by his opponents. And you will see, at the same time, the truly lamentable condition of our country.

My client's father, named Sextus Roscius like his son, was a citizen of Ameria. By birth and rank and wealth alike, he was easily the most prominent man not only of his own town but in the entire neighbourhood. He also enjoyed extensive good-will among the greatest personages of Rome, and was con-nected to them by close relations of hospitality.[1] He possessed links of this kind with the Caecilii Metelli[2] and the Servilii and the Cornelii Scipiones. These are houses which I name, as I should, with a keen sense of their splendid character and reputation. And Sextus Roscius knew the members of these families personally, and enjoyed intimate relations with them.

Well, out of all his many assets this was the only one he managed to leave to his son. His inheritance he failed to bequeath, since robbers in the heart of his own family used violent means to seize it for themselves. And so now the former hosts and friends of Roscius' father are compelled to come to the defence of his innocent son, in order to protect his honour and his life. The father had always favoured the cause of the nobility, notably during the recent civil war.[3] During this crisis, when the entire position and safety of every noble was threatened, he was conspicuous throughout his home country for the energy, enthusiasm and influence he exerted in defence of the aristocrats and their cause. For it was to them he owed his exceptionally honourable position among his own people. When, therefore, their honour was at stake, he felt it only right to come to their help.

Then victory was won, and we laid aside our arms. Yet it

1. The tie of *hospitium*, guest-friendship, was an important element in Roman social life. Those linked by the tie, which was hereditary, were received into one another's households and enjoyed all their domestic privileges.

2. See Genealogical Table 1.

3. The war between the Marians and Sulla, 83–82 B.C. 'The cause of the nobility' (see List of Terms, Nobles) is the conservative cause of Sulla.

was a time of proscriptions, and people suspected of having favoured the opposite side were being arrested on all sides. But Sextus Roscius, the father of my client, appeared constantly at Rome. Every day he went to the Forum, for all to see. Here was a man, one would say, who was manifestly rejoicing in the victory of the aristocratic party. The very last thing he ever expected was that this victory would actually bring about his destruction!

However, he had a longstanding feud with two other men, also called Roscius, from his own town of Ameria. One of them I see here today, sitting among the accusers. As for the other, I am told he has taken possession of three farms that are the rightful property of my client. Sextus Roscius the elder was always worried about this feud, and if his precautions had been as great as his anxieties he would still be alive today. For his fears, gentlemen, were all too amply justified. I must tell you something about these two enemies of his. Both are called Titus Roscius. The one who has the farms bears the surname Capito, and the other, the one who is here, is called Magnus. Capito may be described as an old, experienced gladiator who has many victories to his credit. Magnus has recently gone into training as his pupil. Before the present contest, as far as I am aware, he was no more than a novice. But now his violent and outrageous behaviour has gone far beyond anything that even his trainer himself could ever achieve.

One evening, my client's father was returning from a dinner-party. When he had reached the neighbourhood of the baths of Pallacina[1] he was struck down and assassinated. His son, at the time, was at Ameria, but Magnus was in Rome. The dead man's son used to spend all his time on his farms. In accordance with his father's wishes, he devoted himself to the management of the estate, and to the various activities of

1. Somewhere near the Circus Flaminius at Rome, north-west of the Capitol.

country life. Magnus, on the other hand, was constantly at Rome. I hope that this very circumstance already makes it perfectly clear that he, rather than Roscius, is the man who ought to be suspected of the crime. Indeed, I feel perfectly confident in adding a further point as well. If the other facts of the case which you are now going to hear fall short, even in the very slightest degree, of transforming this suspicion into a certainty – you are at full liberty, as far as I am concerned, to go ahead, and declare that my client was involved in the murder after all!

After Sextus Roscius the elder had been killed, the first man to bring the news to Ameria was a certain Mallius Glaucia, an ex-slave with no visible means of support, a dependant and friend of this Titus Magnus. However, Glaucia did not select the bereaved son as the recipient of his information, but imparted it instead to the person who most hated the dead man, namely Capito. The murder had only been committed one hour after nightfall. Yet here was this messenger already at Ameria by the first streak of dawn. During the ten hours of the night he had taken relays of light carriages and had sped over a distance of no less than fifty-six miles. Nor was he merely content to be the first to bring the longed-for tidings to the murdered man's enemy: he was also determined actually to show Capito the freshly shed blood of the person he so detested, and the weapon that had only just freshly been pulled out of the victim's body.

Four days after these happenings, news of the deed was reported to Chrysogonus in Sulla's camp at Volaterrae.[1] He was also informed of the great extent of Sextus Roscius' property and the excellent quality of his farms: for Roscius left thirteen farms, nearly all adjacent to the Tiber. My client's helplessness and isolation were also dwelt upon – and it was

1. An Etruscan hill-town (Volterra), in which the remnants of the Marian party held out against Sulla for two years; cf. W. V. Harris, *Rome in Etruria and Umbria*, pp. 257ff.

pointed out that since his father, a distinguished and popular figure, had been killed without the smallest difficulty, it would surely be the easiest thing in the world to dispose of the son, who was merely an unsuspecting countryman quite unknown at Rome. So Magnus and Capito promised their help in getting the younger Roscius out of the way as well. In short, judges, a partnership in crime was established.

This was a time when there was no longer any talk of proscriptions, and when even people who had previously lived in fear of such a fate were making their way back to their homes under the impression that the peril was over. Nevertheless, it was now that the name of Sextus Roscius the father – in spite of all the ardent support he had given to the victorious cause of the nobility – was inserted into the list of proscribed persons. His possessions, in consequence, were sold – and Chrysogonus bought them.[1] Three of the farms, among the best of the whole lot, were handed over to Capito as his own property, and he is occupying them today. The remaining portion of the estate was seized by Magnus in the name of Chrysogonus: Magnus will tell you so himself. The value of this land was six million sestertii. But it was bought for no more than two thousand!

Now, I am perfectly sure, gentlemen, that Lucius Sulla knew nothing at all about any of this. He is kept fully occupied on our national affairs, repairing the past and at the same time anticipating the probable demands of the future. The arrangements by which peace has to be established, the powers needed to wage war, these are the matters to which he devotes himself, and over which he exercises sole control. All eyes are turned

1. A Valerian Law (of Lucius Valerius Flaccus) of 82 B.C., which gave the force of law to all Sulla's previous acts, also authorized him to order the death-penalty, and a supplementary Cornelian Law added that the goods of the proscribed and of those who had fallen in the enemy's ranks should be sold for the benefit of the state, and that their sons and grandsons should be excluded from the official career. The proscriptions were declared to be at an end on 1 June 81 B.C.

towards him. It is he who directs everything. Matters of the utmost importance engross his continual attention, so that he scarcely even has time to breathe. In these circumstances, it is surely not very surprising if, from time to time, there is something or other that escapes his notice. After all, think of the host of people who spend their time watching until he is fully engaged elsewhere, so that at the very first moment when he looks away they can concoct some plan of precisely the kind we are concerned with here. And there is another point as well. We know that he is Sulla the Fortunate.[1] But nobody can be so thoroughly well endowed by good fortune that his large household does not include a single slave, or former slave, who may be dishonest.

Meanwhile this splendid Magnus, this agent of Chrysogonus, arrives in Ameria, and seizes hold of my client's farms. He finds the poor Roscius overwhelmed with grief because of his bereavement; and before he has even had time to complete his father's funeral rites Magnus has expelled him naked from his own house, driven him headlong from his ancestral hearth and home and household gods. And that is how Magnus himself became the owner of these extensive estates. Hitherto, being limited to his own slender means, he had lived very poorly. But now, after he had succeeded in grabbing what did not belong to him, he cast all restraint aside – as happens so often. He carried away a great deal to his own home quite openly, and secretly he removed even more. He lavished large and extravagant presents upon his accomplices. And what was left over he sold by auction.

This was regarded by the people of Ameria as such a scandalous proceeding that there was weeping and lamentation all over the town. Simultaneously, a whole series of tragic events crowded in upon their gaze. They saw their prosperous fellow-citizen, the elder Sextus Roscius, brutally murdered.

1. After the defeat and death of Gaius Marius' son of the same name (81 B.C.), Sulla assumed this designation (*Felix*).

They saw his son reduced to shameful destitution. Out of all his large inheritance that infamous robber had not even left him the right of way to his own father's tomb! And they saw the outrageous purchase and occupation, by someone else, of the property that ought to have been his. It was, indeed, a tale of theft and plunder, and of henchmen well rewarded.

Now the whole population of Ameria would have stopped at nothing to prevent Magnus from gloating and lording it over the property of that good and respected man, Sextus Roscius. And so the local town council, as soon as it possibly could, passed a decree. It pronounced instructions that its ten principal members[1] should go and see Lucius Sulla personally. They were to tell him what sort of a man Sextus Roscius had been. They were to lodge complaints about the iniquitous behaviour of his enemies. And they were to implore him to consent not only to the rehabilitation of the dead father's good name, but also to the restoration of his possessions to his innocent son. I will read you the terms of the decree. . . .

[*The decree of the town council is read*]

The deputation arrived at the camp. It is perfectly clear, gentlemen, as I said before, that all these outrageous crimes were committed without Sulla knowing anything about them. For it was Chrysogonus who now took all the action. He immediately went to meet the delegates himself. He also commissioned certain high-ranking personages to dissuade them from approaching Sulla in person, and told them to guarantee that he, Chrysogonus, would do everything they wanted. For so bad was his conscience that he would rather have died than let Sulla discover about the things that had been happening. As for the delegates, they were men of old-world simplicity who judged other people's characters by their own. When, therefore, Chrysogonus promised them that

1. These formed the executive committee of the council.

he himself would remove the elder Sextus Roscius' name from the list of proscribed and would hand over the entire property to his son, and when Capito, who was actually one of the ten envoys, added his own assurance to the same effect, they believed what they were told, and returned to Ameria without presenting their petition to Sulla at all.

Chrysogonus and Capito, however, continually delayed the fulfilment of the promises they had made, procrastinating from one day to another. Indeed, shortly afterwards they began to display even more uncooperative behaviour, which amounted, indeed, to nothing less than downright fraud. It was easy enough to see what this was leading to: and so it now turned out, for at this juncture they started plotting against the younger Sextus Roscius' life. Evidently they doubted their capacity to hang on to another man's property while the real owner still remained alive.

When this state of affairs dawned upon my client, he took the advice of his friends and relations and fled to Rome. He went to Caecilia Metella, Nepos' sister; her father was Balearicus, a name I mention with respect.[1] She had been a friend of Sextus Roscius' father, and let me add, judges, that she is universally agreed to be a woman blessed with an old-fashioned and exemplary sense of duty. And so Roscius, now destitute, cast out of his house, expelled from his possessions, a fugitive from his plunderers and all their weapons and menaces, was received by Caecilia Metella into her own home. Crushing troubles had overtaken him, and everyone

1. Caecilia Metella's brother was Quintus Caecilius Metellus Nepos, consul 98 B.C., and her father was Quintus Caecilius Metellus Balearicus, consul 123 B.C. Another of her relatives, Quintus Caecilius Metellus Pius, was consul with Sulla (to whom the whole family was very close; J. Carcopino, *Sylla*, p. 161) in 80 B.C., the year of this trial. See Genealogical Table I. (The Caecilia Metella whose tomb is preserved outside Rome is a different person, the daughter of Quintus Caecilius Metellus Creticus.)

regarded his case as desperate. Yet she made him her guest, and came to his help. It is thanks to her goodness and loyalty and energy that he is still alive – that his name can still be entered on the charge-sheet! Otherwise the only list to display it would have been the fraudulent list of the proscribed, for he would have been struck down and put to death.

As it had turned out, however, his life was now protected with the utmost care. His enemies noticed this, and saw that they were not going to be given the opportunity to assassinate him. This being so, they formed an alternative design, and an infamous and horrible design it was. For they decided instead to accuse him of murdering his own father. They planned, for this purpose, to get hold of some prosecutor who was an old hand and could always think up something to say, even when, as here, the defendant was not under the slightest trace of suspicion. Since, however, the charge in itself was clearly lacking in all substance, they proposed to use the circumstances of the times as a weapon. For because, they reflected, there had not been a single trial for parricide for a very long time indeed, it was highly probable that the first person to be brought to trial on such a charge would be found guilty. Moreover, the influence of Chrysogonus, it seemed to them, would be enough to ensure that no one would come forward to act as Sextus Roscius' advocate. For the same reason no one was likely to utter a word about the sale of the property or the partnership relating to its purchase. The mere designation of parricide, they concluded – the horrible nature of such a charge – would be enough to get rid of Sextus Roscius without the slightest difficulty. Indeed, it was certain that no one would come forward to defend him.

Such, then, was the plan of action, the maniacal plot, which they entered upon: with the intention that the man whom they themselves had wanted to assassinate, but could not contrive to, should be murdered by *you* instead, on their behalf.

This is all so terrible that it is hard to know at which of the many points involved one's censure ought to start. But one thing I can say at once – I only wish I knew which way I could turn to find people who would help me. If some names were forthcoming, it would be the greatest possible relief! And whether it is the immortal gods whose protection I should be begging for, or the people of Rome, I really do not know. Or best of all, gentlemen, should it not rather be yourselves? For at this juncture it is you who have been given the supreme power to make the decision. Here is the foul murder of a father; his home besieged and captured by his enemies; his goods grabbed and stolen and looted; his son's life in the gravest danger, repeatedly attacked both by open violence and by secret treacherous snares. Well, that is a list of crimes which might seem to include every category of evil-doing that you can think of. But apparently not. For somehow or other these individuals manage to extend and expand the grim list by concocting a fresh set of crimes altogether. They invent an accusation that totally exceeds belief. Not only do they succeed in procuring false witnesses and prosecutors against my client, but they actually pay them with his own money. And, finally, they confront their wretched victim with these alternatives: either he offers his throat up voluntarily to Magnus, or he dies the most degrading of all possible deaths, with his living body sewn up inside a sack – the penalty for parricide.[1]

When his enemies believed he would be short of defenders, they were perfectly right. But all the same he will have the services of one man who is prepared to speak out freely and defend him with devotion, and in a case as strong as this, gentlemen, that is all he will need. Perhaps, in undertaking the task, I have acted with youthful rashness. Nevertheless, having once accepted the commission, no matter what terrors and dangers may threaten me on every side, by heaven, I am going to save him! Nothing would induce me to let him down. I am determined to bring forward every single point that I believe

1. See pp. 26, 66.

46

to have a bearing on the case – and I shall bring them forward boldly and frankly, without the slightest constraint. Nothing that can possibly happen will frighten me out of doing my duty. For I cannot believe that anyone in this world would be so lacking in moral sense that he could witness these crimes and yet stand by and disregard them and hold his peace. *You* were the assassins of my father, my client tells his foes. In his lifetime, he declares, my father was never proscribed. It was only after he was killed that you people got his name inserted in the proscription list. You drove me out of my own house by force, he says. You seized my entire heritage. What do you want next? Are you actually venturing to brandish your lethal weapons yet again, here in this very court – intent on getting Sextus Roscius condemned to death by legal processes, if you cannot murder him yourselves?

By far the most ferocious personality we have known in politics during recent years was Gaius Flavius Fimbria.[1] He was also, it was generally agreed, the craziest of the whole lot, except in the opinion of people who are lunatics themselves. At the funeral of Gaius Marius it was he who was responsible for the wounding of Quintus Mucius Scaevola Pontifex.[2] Scaevola was the most revered and illustrious figure in our whole national life; though this is not the place to sing his praises, and in any case the people of Rome remember him so well that there is little I could add to their memories. After the deed, when he heard that Scaevola might possibly recover from his wound, Fimbria proceeded to lodge a charge against him. Whereupon someone was reported to have asked him

1. A prominent supporter of Marius, whose soldiers in Asia Minor deserted him in favour of Sulla in 85 B.C., so that he was forced to commit suicide.

2. Consul 95 B.C., chief priest, and a famous lawyer. He survived the attack by Fimbria (86) but was killed by the praetor Lucius Junius Brutus Damasippus in 82. See also above, p. 29, n. 3.

what accusation he could possibly be proposing to bring against a man whose noble qualities were beyond all praise. And Fimbria, like the madman he was, is said to have replied: because Scaevola failed to submit his body to the full thrust of the sword.[1] A more disgraceful thing never occurred in all the history of our country – except Scaevola's actual murder, which followed later. So deplorable were its consequences that one may regard it, without exaggeration, as having brought ruin upon every single citizen of Rome. His whole aim had been to save them. That is why he wanted to bring about a reconciliation between the two sides. And yet it was actually the people he wanted to save who struck him down.

Surely the present case exhibits striking analogies to what Fimbria said and did. You set yourselves up as the accusers of the younger Sextus Roscius. Why? Because he escaped from your clutches, and refused to be murdered. Fimbria's deed may seem the more scandalous of the two, because its victim was the famous Scaevola. But the present atrocity does not become any easier to endure just because its perpetrator was the famous Chrysogonus.

Indeed, heaven only knows how the present trial can really be thought to require any case for the defence at all. I cannot see that it raises a single point demanding an advocate's ingenuity or an orator's eloquence. However, gentlemen, we must go over every detail all the same. When the entire picture has been assembled before our eyes, we shall be able to see where we have got to. My survey will be designed to show you the basis of the whole matter, and the fundamental issues that it raises – and the considerations which, in my opinion, ought to guide the decision you will then be called upon to take.

As far as I can see, there are three obstacles threatening Sextus Roscius today. There is the charge his opponents have brought.

1. When a gladiator was defeated, if it was the wish of the spectators he had to offer his chest for the death-blow.

There is their violence. And there is their power. The prosecutor Erucius has undertaken to concoct the charge. As for the violence, Magnus and Capito have claimed this speciality for themselves. And what Chrysogonus has contributed to the contest, since he is the most powerful, is his power. Now, I can very well see that it is my duty to discuss each of these three aspects in turn. But how had I better proceed? Clearly I cannot deal with all the three points in one and the same way: because the first relates to my own personal duty, whereas the responsibility relating to the other two has been assigned by the Roman people to yourselves. The charge, that is to say, is for me to refute, whereas the repression of violence is your job. And when we come to the third point, what you have got to do, at the very first possible opportunity, is to crush and stamp out the power, the lethal and insufferable power, that has fallen into the hands of scoundrels of the type that we are concerned with today.

The younger Sextus Roscius is accused of having killed his father. God, what a crime! A crime so foul and loathsome that it seems to combine every single kind of guilt that you can think of. The philosophers declare, very aptly, that even a mere facial expression can be a breach of filial duty. Well, in that case, it is impossible to imagine what punishment could be frightful enough for someone who has actually put his own parent to death – that very person on whose behalf the laws of gods and men alike require that he should willingly die himself, if he should be called upon to do so.

In the case of a criminal act so hateful, so unique, so utterly exceptional that whenever it occurs it seems a portent and monstrosity, you will certainly have to think very hard, Erucius, about the arguments that your role as prosecutor demands. Presumably you will have to demonstrate that the man you are charging with such an act is an abnormally violent individual. No doubt you will want to indicate that he is a person of savage and brutish nature, whose whole life is given up to every sort of vicious and infamous behaviour: in short, that his entire character is ruinously perverted and depraved. And yet, strangely enough, you have not attempted to bring a single one of these imputations against my client – not even by way of the usual kind of routine abuse.

Sextus Roscius, you say, killed his father. Well, what sort of a person is he, then? Obviously he must be some degenerate youth, who has been corrupted by men of evil character? On the contrary: he is over forty years old. Well, then, he must be a veteran cut-throat, a ferocious individual thoroughly accustomed to committing murders. But the prosecutor has never even begun to suggest anything of the kind. So I suppose he must have been driven to his criminal act by extravagant habits, or huge debts, or ungovernable passions. As regards extravagant living, Erucius himself has already cleared him of that when he indicated that Sextus hardly ever even attended a party. Debts? He never had any. Passions? Not much scope for these in a man who, as the prosecutor himself critically remarked, has always lived in the country, devoting his time to the cultivation of his lands.

One may well ask, then, what on earth could have prompted the insane act Sextus Roscius is charged with. 'His father disliked him,' explains the prosecution. All right, then, but what was the cause of this dislike? There must surely have been some valid and substantial and unmistakable cause for such a feeling. For a father is not likely to hate his son without numerous well-grounded and cogent reasons – any more than a son is likely to kill his father without motives that are equally weighty, indeed overwhelming. So I return to my point, and ask once again what the grave faults were, in the son, which caused his own father to hate him. However, it is abundantly evident that no such faults existed. So must we assume that the father was out of his mind, if, *without any reason at all*, he conceived this hatred for the son he himself had begotten? But that was certainly not the case; on the contrary, he was an exceedingly stable character. It is perfectly clear, then, that since the father was as sane as a man could possibly be, and the son led a life that was quite the opposite of vicious, the father had no motive for hating his son, and the son had no motive for murdering his father.

'What the reason for the hatred was,' answers the prosecutor, 'I have no idea. All I know is that it existed. Because previously, when the father had two sons living, it was the other one, now dead, whom he always wanted to have with him, whereas he sent this one away to his farms in the country.' Now, although my case is impregnable, in sharp contrast to Erucius' charge which is both wicked and frivolous, it does so happen that the line of argument he puts forward here places the pair of us in a very comparable situation, and it is rather an embarrassing one. For he can find no proof to support his fraudulent charge. And I, likewise, can find no way of disproving allegations that are so utterly silly.

However, I take it, Erucius, that what you are really trying to say is this. Sextus Roscius gave his son all those excellent, productive farms to cultivate and manage merely to get him out of the way and punish him. Yet surely the exact opposite must have been the truth. The fact rather is that heads of households, especially men of the elder Sextus Roscius' rank in the country towns, regard it as highly advantageous to themselves (if they have children) that their sons should devote themselves very thoroughly indeed to the management of their property and lavish the most careful attention upon the cultivation of their farms. You can't expect us to believe that Roscius sent his son away to the country merely in order to segregate him down there at the farmhouse and deprive him of every amenity of life except his bare sustenance! So I want to put this question to you. If it turns out, instead, to be a proved fact that the younger Sextus not only superintended the cultivation of the estates but also, even during his father's lifetime, was permitted the privilege of keeping the full enjoyment of certain farms to himself, will you still, in spite of that, persist in stigmatizing his life as an unfriendly dismissal and banishment to the depths of the country?

You see, Erucius, there is a total discrepancy between the line of argument you are trying to adopt and the actual facts of the case. What fathers habitually and normally do, you attempt to find fault with as a strange innovation. What is, in reality, a sign of affectionate kindness is interpreted by you as a mark of hatred. When the father has been generous to his son in order to show what a good opinion he holds of him, you describe it as a punishment. And all these misinterpretations cannot just be attributed to foolishness on your part. The fact is that you have so exceedingly few arguments to put forward that you cannot merely limit yourself to trying to refute my case. No, you have to try to do more, and so you find yourself constrained to argue against a whole array of definite facts – indeed, against the customs and convictions of all mankind.

However, you still press the point that Sextus Roscius had two sons, and kept one of them always by his side whereas he let the other one stay in the country. Now, Erucius, please do not take offence about what I am going to say next. I assure you I shall not be saying it just in order to be unpleasant, but because you need the reminder. Even if fortune has not given you the advantage of knowing for certain who your father was, which would have given you a better idea of how a father feels towards his children,[1] at any rate nature has endowed you with your fair share of human feelings. And you have a studious disposition as well, so that literary allusions are not beyond you. That being so, let me borrow the question I want to ask you from the comic drama. I want you

1. A double thrust. Erucius as a former slave (freedman) legally had no father; and Cicero uses the opportunity to suggest that he was a bastard.

to consider one of those plays written by Caecilius,[1] and let me know if in your opinion the old man in the play really thinks less of his son Eutychus, who lived in the country, than of his other son whose name, I believe, was Chaerestratus. Please tell me whether, in your opinion, he kept Chaerestratus with him in the city as a mark of respect, and whether he banished the other son to the country in order to punish him.

'But why,' you will say, 'do you have to stray off into irrelevant literary queries of such kind?' All right then, I can equally well assure you that I should have no difficulty whatever, without calling upon any such theoretical illustrations at all, in bringing forward a great many names on my own, living fellow-tribesmen[2] or neighbours who are every bit as keen that their favourite sons should be conscientious farmers. However, I prefer not to quote real, well-known people if I can help it, because one doesn't know whether they would like their names to be mentioned in this way. Another reason why I refrain from doing so is because, in any case, you yourself are not likely to be any better acquainted with such personages than you are with this Eutychus I was speaking about. And, besides, it makes not the slightest difference to the validity of my argument whether I use the name of this young man in the comic play or some actual person, say, from the territory of Veii.[3] After all, the reason why the poets invented these stories was surely just this – so that we should be able to see our own behaviour mirrored in these other, imaginary characters, which thus cast a vivid light upon our own daily lives.

1. Caecilius Statius of Mediolanum (Milan) (died *c.* 166 B.C.) was a leading Latin comic dramatist. The play referred to was an adaptation of the Athenian Menander's *Supposititious Child*.

2. See List of Terms (Tribes).

3. Rome's Etruscan neighbour, north of the Tiber. But the reference to Veii is malicious, because Chrysogonus had moved some of the property he had acquired from Sextus Roscius' estate to a house he was building there; cf. below, p. 98 n. 2.

However, by all means turn your attention back to actual realities, if that is what you prefer, and consider what occupations meet with the greatest approval from the actual heads of country households, both in Umbria and in the surrounding districts, and, for that matter, in the long established municipalities nearer at hand. And there you will certainly find it confirmed that the position of the younger Sextus Roscius, which your dearth of convincing accusations against him has made you present as a fault and a crime, does him, on the contrary, a very great deal of credit.

And it isn't just out of obedience to their fathers' wishes that sons dedicate themselves to agriculture. I have come across a great many people – and so, unless I am entirely mistaken, has everyone present in this court – who are extremely fond of this pursuit, quite of their own accord. There is a widespread feeling that country life, which you assail as a disgraceful slur, is instead the most honourable and enjoyable existence that any man can possibly lead. And just think of the knowledge and skill which Sextus Roscius displays in these agricultural matters. I learn from his excellent relatives here that he is every bit as knowledgeable about such questions as you are about your profession as prosecutor. True, by courtesy of Chrysogonus, who has not left him a single farm, he will now be in an excellent position to forget all this expert knowledge and abandon his interest in the subject. That would be a shame and a tragedy. And yet, even so, he will endure such a fate patiently enough, gentlemen, provided only that your verdict enables him to save his honour and his life. But really, if we are going to have to conclude that he owes his present lamentable situation to the quantity and excellence of his farms, if the care he has taken to develop them is going to count against him more than anything else, then what an insufferable state of affairs we have come to! Surely, it is misfortune enough that others derive the profits from the cultivation upon which he has lavished so much care, without making it a further crime that he ever engaged in this cultivation of his lands in the first place!

I am afraid you would have cut a ludicrous figure in your job, Erucius, if you had been born in the times when men used to be called from their ploughs to become consuls. For since you regard it as such a crime to be an agriculturalist, then obviously the famous Atilius,[1] whom the envoys found sowing the seed with his own hand, would have seemed to you a thoroughly degraded and disreputable personage. But, heaven knows, our ancestors took a singularly different view about Atilius, and about all the others who were like him! And theirs was the attitude that made this country rise out of insignificance and poverty into the imposing and prosperous commonwealth that they handed down to ourselves. The transfiguration was due to the meticulous care they dedicated to the cultivation of their lands. To covet and hanker after properties belonging to other people did not even occur to them. And yet it was their hard work, in the long run, which enabled them to bestow whole territories and cities and even nations upon our Republic and empire, to the greater glory of Rome.

My motive in quoting these instances is not to suggest they are in any way comparable with the matters we are investigating today. But what I want to establish is this. In the time of our ancestors, men of eminence and distinction who might at any time be called upon to guide the nation's affairs nevertheless lavished a great deal of time and trouble upon the cultivation of their soil. Consequently, a person who has spent his life in the country, and therefore defines himself as a countryman, must never be regarded as blameworthy for so doing – especially when it is borne in mind that no other occupation could possibly have been more agreeable to his

1. Probably Gaius Atilius Regulus Serranus, consul for the first time in 257 B.C. (not the better known Marcus Regulus, prisoner of the Carthaginians).

father, or more pleasing to himself, or indeed, speaking generally, more worthy of praise.

So this, Erucius, is how you set out to prove that the father violently hated his son. The proof that he did so, you say, is because he allowed the young man to remain in the country. Or is there something else as well? 'Yes, certainly there is,' declares Erucius. 'His father was proposing to disinherit him.' Now that, if true, is an assertion which would be distinctly relevant. What you are saying now could actually have something to do with the case. Yet I do feel you will have to agree that your corroboration of this statement on the grounds that 'he never went to any parties with his father' is frivolous and beside the point. How on earth could he? He never even came to town, except very rarely indeed. 'People hardly ever invited him to their houses.' Well, that's not very surprising. After all, he didn't live in the city; and in any case he was in no position to ask them back.

But surely you must realize perfectly well how futile these last two arguments are. Let us go back, then, to what we were beginning to discuss, just before, because it would provide the firmest proof of hatred that could possibly be found: 'the father intended to disinherit his son.' I am not asking you why he intended to do this: all I want to be told is how you are so certain it *was* his intention. And yet, I must admit, one cannot help also feeling that it really was your inescapable duty to explain and enumerate *every single motive* that existed in his mind. For it would surely have been expected of any conscientious prosecutor, who was charging someone with a crime of this magnitude, to set out the most meticulous list of every one of the son's vices and misdeeds which could possibly have enraged his father to such an extent that he overcame all his personal inclinations, and banished from his heart every trace of his deeply implanted affections, until in the end he even contrived to forget that he was a father at all. For this remarkable transformation, I am certain, could not possibly ever have taken place unless his son had committed offences of the most outrageous character.

However, leave them undefined if that is what you prefer. It is all the same to me. Nevertheless, if you really have no such offences to point to, that shows you are admitting that they don't exist. But when we come to your statement that the older Roscius proposed to disinherit his own son, this you really do have to prove. Very well, then, what are your arguments? None, certainly, that possess any foundation whatever. But do at least invent something plausible, since otherwise it will be all too painfully clear to everybody what you are, in fact, quite plainly doing. And what I mean is this: you are simply treating the distress of my unfortunate client, and the dignity of this eminent panel of judges, as targets of mockery and ridicule.

So the father wanted to disinherit his son. Why? I still have no idea. Did he actually take this step? No. Who prevented him? Well, he was thinking about it. Whom did he inform of that? Nobody. But charges and imputations of this kind, which you are quite incapable of proving – indeed are not even attempting to prove – are nothing better than an insult to this court, and to the laws of the land, and to the high authority of the judges before whom we are appearing. We are all perfectly well aware, Erucius, that your attack on the younger Sextus Roscius is not motivated by any history of personal enmity. Everyone understands the motive that has brought you into court to speak against him today: it is his money. So why say more? And yet there is one further thing, after all, that still needs to be said. If you had reflected that the opinion these judges form of you might have certain repercussions upon your own future, the thought might have tempered your greed. And surely the stipulations of the Remmian Law are by no means negligible, either.[1]

1. This was a law of uncertain date, by which a penalty was instituted if a prosecutor failed to establish his charge.

The existence, in any city, of a large number of prosecutors has its uses. For this at least means that people are unlikely to commit so many crimes, because they will be afraid to do so. But the existence of these men is only useful on the condition that they do not blatantly make fools of us. Let us imagine a man who is innocent, but has come under suspicion. That, certainly, is too bad. All the same, I can to some extent excuse the prosecutor who brings a charge against such a man. For assuming that this prosecutor has something to say which offers some apparent justification for suspecting and incriminating the man, at least he is not just fooling us quite openly, by the deliberate concoction of charges that are complete fakes. That is why there is no objection to having as many prosecutors as you like. For, after all, it is possible for an innocent man, once he has been accused of something, to secure an acquittal, whereas if a man has really committed a crime you cannot get him condemned for it unless he has first been charged. And, on balance, it does less harm for an innocent man to be tried than for a guilty man to escape. The reason why the geese on the Capitol are provided with food at the public expense, and dogs are kept there too, is in order that they shall give the alarm if a thief should appear.[1] It's true that they don't actually possess the capacity to identify a thief. All the same, they sound the alarm if *anyone* appears on the Capitol during the night. For that is a suspicious occurrence, and if they err they err on the side of caution. After all, they are only animals. But if the dogs started barking during the day, when people come to worship the gods, I am sure someone would give them a broken leg, for making a fuss when there were no grounds for suspicion at all.

Very much the same considerations apply to prosecutors.

1. The sacred geese were fed at public expense because they were supposed by their cackling to have saved the Capitol from capture by the Senonian Gauls (390 or 387 B.C.), while the dogs failed to give a warning.

Some of you are geese who only cackle and can't do any harm. Others are dogs who can bite as well as bark. We arrange for you to be fed. But you, in return, must direct your attacks against the people who really deserve them. That's what the community wants. Certainly, when there is a probability that some identifiable individual has committed a crime, you can show your suspicion by barking, if you feel inclined to. We allow you that much. But if you're determined to go ahead and accuse someone of killing his father without being able to say why or how, if in other words you're just going to bark when there isn't a trace of any suspicion, it's true that no one will break your legs, but if my knowledge of these gentlemen on the bench is any guide, they'll brand your forehead with that letter which you prosecutors regard with such distaste that you even hate the first day of every month because its name, the Kalends, starts with the same initial.[1] And they'll do the job so forcibly that in future you'll not be in a position to bring any accusations against anybody or anything at all, except against the dire misfortune you've managed to get yourselves into.

So let me find out from this marvellous prosecutor just what he is really asking me to defend my client against. It's up to him to specify the *grounds for suspicion* that he hopes to instil in the judges' minds. What he will reply, presumably, is this. The younger Sextus Roscius was afraid he was going to be disinherited. So you say! But nobody has put forward any indication whatever why he should have had the slightest reason to fear that such a thing was going to happen. 'But that *is* what his father intended.' Prove it. There isn't any proof. You can't point to a single person whom the elder Roscius

1. The Remmian Law (see p. 57 n. 1) laid it down that a prosecutor who failed to establish his case should be branded on the forehead with the letter K, the ancient initial of the word *calumniator*. This deprived him of political rights.

either consulted on the subject or informed of any such intention, and you can't even suggest any reason whatsoever why you yourself allegedly began to harbour the suspicion.

In fact, what you are openly confessing, when you produce such an imputation, is this: 'I know what I was paid. But I am rather at a loss about what to say! The only thing that weighed with me was Chrysogonus' assurance that Roscius would not find anybody to defend him, since he believed that in the present national situation no one would dare utter a sound about the purchase of the property or about the partnership.' Yes, that was the misapprehension which induced you to launch the whole fraudulent business. If you had believed that anyone was going to contradict you, you would certainly never have said a word.

It would have been of value to you, gentlemen, if you had happened to notice the casual way in which Erucius embarked on this prosecution. I find it easy to believe that when he saw the occupants of the advocates' benches he inquired whether this or that personage was going to undertake the defence. The idea that I might be going to do so never crossed his mind, because I had never pleaded in a state trial before. When he found that none of the usual, recognized people was going to take the job on, he began to behave in a very relaxed fashion, sitting down if he felt like it, strolling about, and shouting for his slave – to order his dinner, I suppose. In other words he treated you judges, and everyone else who is assembled here today, with as little respect as if there had been no one in the whole place except himself.

Finally he concluded his speech and sat down. And then someone else got up; but it was only myself. Erucius visibly breathed a sigh of relief, because it wasn't one of the others. I began my speech. But at the same time I was able to watch how he went on joking, and made no attempt to concentrate – until I suddenly let drop the name of Chrysogonus. As soon as I uttered that name Erucius immediately started to attend and seemed overcome with amazement. I knew very well what had stung him. Then I mentioned Chrysogonus a second and a third time. After that, people started scurrying about in every direction. I imagine they wanted to let Chrysogonus know what was happening. Here was a man in Rome who had the nerve to speak up against his interests. The case was not going the way he expected. The facts about the purchase of the property were leaking out, and the partnership was coming in for rough treatment. Chrysogonus' influence and power were being handled disrespectfully. The judges were paying close attention – and as the scandal began to come out, the public began to show how deeply shocked they were.

So you miscalculated about the whole thing, Erucius. You can appreciate now that the entire situation has been transformed. Sextus Roscius' case, as you can see, is still perhaps not getting the defence it deserves, but at least *someone* is defending him outspokenly. The men you thought were going to betray him into your hands are to be seen acting as impartial judges instead. So now you had better muster up some of that old ingenuity and sound sense of yours. What you hoped for when you came here was some of the pickings. But instead you have started to find out that what prevails in this court is justice.

The charge is parricide. But the prosecutor has not been able to indicate the motive which supposedly impelled the son to kill his father. Now, even when some minor offence is being dealt with – one of the petty misdemeanours which have become increasingly frequent and are now of almost daily occurrence – the very first thing that is always done is to make the most meticulous inquiry about the motive. But here we have a trial for the very grave crime of parricide, and yet Erucius apparently does not consider such an inquiry to be necessary! Yet in regard to an issue of this magnitude, gentlemen, even when there is a clear combination and multiplication of motives, still an accusation is never lightly believed, still its outcome is not allowed to depend on superficial conjectures, still unreliable witnesses are regarded with due suspicion, still the prosecutor's ability is not conceded to be the deciding factor. Moreover, in such cases it is held to be indispensable not merely to prove that the defendant has committed a whole series of previous crimes and has led a thoroughly dissolute life, but actually that his entire character is degraded to the point of utter frenzy and complete mental derangement.

And even when all this has been demonstrated, it still remains necessary to point to manifest indications of the specific crime itself, where and how it was committed and by whose agency and when. And unless these indications are both numerous and beyond question, surely such a dreadful, unspeakable deed must continue to defy belief. For against it is all the strength of human feeling, all the potent ties of blood relationship. Nature itself cries out against any suspicions of such a horror. It is an utterly unnatural and monstrous phenomenon that a being of human shape and demeanour should so far exceed even a wild animal in savagery that he has malignantly extinguished the light of day for the very person who is responsible for his own enjoyment of its life-giving rays. For the experiences of parenthood and infancy, of bringing up young and being brought up, teach even wild beasts to be at peace with one another. It is the teaching of nature itself.

There is a story that not many years ago a certain Titus Cloelius of Tarracina,[1] a man who was quite well known, finished his dinner one night and then went to bed in the same room as his two grown-up sons. In the morning he was found dead with his throat cut. Investigation pointed to no one,

1. He is Cloelius and not Caelius; cf. T. P. Wiseman, *Classical Review*, 1967, pp. 263ff. Tarracina, formerly Anxur and now Terracina, is sixty miles south-east of Rome on the Appian Way.

slave or free man, against whom suspicion could be directed, while the two sons who had spent the night beside him insisted that they had noticed nothing. However, they were charged with the murder.

The circumstances were certainly most suspicious. It seemed extraordinary that neither of the young men had seen or heard anything whatever, and that someone else had actually had the nerve to venture into the room at the very time when Cloelius' two grown-up sons were both there. One might have thought that they would inevitably have realized what was going on, and offered resistance. Besides, there was no one else at all who could reasonably be regarded as liable to suspicion.

All the same, the judges were struck by the fact that when the door was opened in the morning the young men were both found fast asleep; and so they were acquitted and cleared of all suspicion. For no one could believe that any man was capable, first, of perpetrating such an unspeakable deed which outraged every law that god or man had ever thought of, and then immediately afterwards going off to sleep. Surely, it was argued, people who have committed a horrible crime like that are incapable of sleeping in peace. Indeed, every breath that they draw renews their terror.

The poets have told us of legendary sons who killed their mothers to avenge their fathers.[1] But even when they are supposed to have been acting in accordance with divine commands and oracles, you must have read how the Furies haunt them and never let them rest, because even the fact that they were performing a duty on behalf of their fathers did not exonerate them from the crime they had committed. And that, gentlemen, is true: for such is the power and sanctity of the ties of the blood that link a man to his own father and mother.

1. e.g., Orestes who killed Clytemnestra to avenge Agamemnon; and Alcmaeon who killed Eriphyle to avenge Amphiaraus.

A single drop of that blood creates a stain which can never be washed out, but penetrates deep into the heart, where it plants madness and frenzy. You are not obliged, of course, to believe literally what you so often see in plays, that a man who has performed some impious or criminal act is pursued and terrorized by the blazing torches of the Furies. What really torments him is his own sinful deed and the terror he has inspired in himself. His own guilt is what harasses and maddens him. The panic he feels is caused by his own ghastly thoughts, his own stinging conscience. These are the abiding Furies which live with evil men, and continue every day and every night to avenge the parents of sons who are stained with this fearful sin.

It is because of the very enormity of the crime of parricide that unless it is quite unmistakably proved people are unable to credit it. The charge can only carry conviction if the man's youthful life has been completely debauched, his character utterly corrupt and degraded, his way of living outrageously and scandalously extravagant, his capacity for violence unlimited, his wild behaviour not far from insanity. What is more, he must surely have been the victim of his father's hatred, so that he now stands in fear of repression at his hands. He must have depraved friends, slaves who know about the whole business, a convenient opportunity, a suitable place for the deed. I would almost go so far as to say that the judges must actually see his hands stained with his father's blood before they can believe that so awful, monstrous and loathsome an action has really been committed.

And this very incredibility of the crime means that once it has been decisively proved its punishment must be all the more severe. Now, our conclusion that our ancestors surpassed all other countries not only in military might, but in wisdom and good sense as well, is based on a variety of excellent reasons. And one especially valid reason is this: they devised an altogether singular punishment for those who sinned against their own parents. For nothing could provide a clearer demonstration that they were indeed wiser than any other nation. According to tradition the wisest of all states was Athens, while it was the leader of Greece; and the wisest of all its citizens was said to be Solon, who drew up the laws they still use there today.[1] Well, Solon was once asked why he had not fixed any penalty, in these laws, for a man who killed his own father. He replied that he simply could not believe that anyone would ever do such a thing. He has been praised because he refrained from fixing a punishment for this crime which up to then had never been committed – a decision he took because he was afraid that the establishment of a penalty, far from reducing the likelihood that such a deed be committed, might suggest its possibility to people's minds. But our Roman ancestors were a very great deal wiser still. They realized that there is nothing in the world which possesses a sufficiently eminent degree of sanctity to prevent it from one day succumbing to violence. Consequently, they believed they must think out a punishment for parricide, and a unique punishment it was. For what they wanted to do was to set a penalty so frightful that it would serve as a deterrent even when nature itself proved powerless to enjoin filial conduct. And so they ordained that anyone found guilty of this crime should be sewn alive into a sack and then thrown into a river.[2]

It was a remarkably wise decision, gentlemen. What they did, in effect, was to cut the culprit off and shut him out of the entire sphere of nature. By depriving him, at one single blow, of sky and sun and water and earth, they created a situation in which the murderer of the very person to whom he owed his own life should in turn be deprived of all the elements which have given life to the world. To throw the condemned man to wild beasts did not seem to them the right

1. Solon held the leading office at Athens (chief archon) in 594–3 B.C.
2. For this punishment, see above, p. 26.

solution, in case this contact with such a monstrosity should make the beasts even more savage towards us than they had been before. And the idea of dropping the guilty man naked into a river they likewise rejected, for fear that when his body had been carried down to the sea it would defile that very element which is itself believed to purify every defilement that exists. In a word, they left the criminal wholly bereft of all the things that are most abundantly available to the rest of the world. Breath to the living, earth to the dead, the sea to those who float upon its surface, the shore to those the sea casts up – these are the most universally available things in the world. Yet men condemned for this crime live, as long as they are allowed to go on living, without being able to breathe the air from the sky. They die without the earth coming into contact with their bones. They are tossed about by the sea without its cleansing waters ever reaching them. And, at the end, when they are cast up on the shore, even the rocks do not support their dead bodies to give them rest.

That is the enormous crime you are imputing to Sextus Roscius, and that is its horrifying punishment. Do you really imagine, Erucius, that you can convince judges of this calibre that such a crime was committed, in spite of your complete and total failure to demonstrate any motive whatever? If the case was actually being pleaded before the purchasers of the property themselves, if Chrysogonus himself was presiding over the trial, even so it would surely have been advisable for you to have come more carefully prepared! There are two things that you have apparently failed to appreciate; first, the extremely solemn nature of this trial, and secondly, the impeccable integrity of the judges who are conducting it. For the case concerns parricide, a crime which it is inconceivable that anyone could commit without motives of the most serious possible kind. And it is being tried by judges of the utmost shrewdness, who are very well aware that the idea of someone committing even the most trifling offence, without any motive whatsoever, is inconceivable.

All right, you cannot produce a motive. Then in that event I ought to be adjudged the winner straightaway. However, I won't insist on that right. Indeed, I shall concede to you a point which I should never be prepared to concede in any other case; and this is a manifest proof of my conviction that my client is wholly innocent. That is to say, I won't even ask you *why* Sextus Roscius killed his father. I only ask *how* he killed him. Yes, Erucius, that is all that I insist you should explain. And I'll tell you how I am going to deal with you. Although it is my time for speaking, and not yours, I'll give you the fullest possible freedom to answer me, or interrupt me, or even ask me questions if you want to, at any moment that you like.[1]

How did he kill his father, then? Did he strike the blow himself, or did he get others to do the job? If you are trying to maintain that he did it himself, let me remind you that he wasn't even in Rome. If you say he got others to do it, then who were they? Were they slaves or free men? If they were free men, identify them. Did they come from Ameria, or were they some of our Roman assassins? If they came from Ameria, I ask again who they were – I want to be told why we are not allowed to learn their names. If they were from Rome, on the other hand, how had Roscius got to know them? For after all he himself had not been to Rome for many years, and had never on any occasion stayed there for more than three days at a time. So where did he meet them? How did he get into conversation with them? What methods did he use to persuade them? He gave them a bribe. Who did he give it to? Who was his intermediary? Where did he get the money from, and how much was it?

1. It was customary to leave the *altercatio* (interposition of questions, i.e. cross-examination) until counsel had completed his speech.

Surely those are the sort of matters one always has to follow up in order to get back to the origins of a crime. And meanwhile don't forget how you yourself described my client's way of life. He was a boorish and savage fellow, you said, who never talked to anyone and just stayed in Ameria. Now, there's a point in this assertion of yours which might be regarded as a very powerful argument in favour of his innocence. I don't propose to stress it unduly, but it is a fact that country habits, a plain routine, a rough uncivilized manner of life, don't usually produce crimes of this sort. You don't find every variety of crop and tree on every soil, and by the same token you don't see every sort of crime coming from every type of existence. It's the city that creates luxury. And out of luxury, inevitably, comes greed, out of greed bursts forth violence, out of violence proliferate all the various kinds of crime and iniquity. Whereas this country life, which you describe sneeringly as so rustic, is the teacher of economy, honest work and fair dealing.

But I will leave all that aside. What I want to ask you instead is this. You yourself emphasize that my client was not accustomed to see very much of his fellow human beings. Then I must insist that you identify the men who were his instruments in this terrible crime that you allege he committed, apparently in conditions of total secrecy, and while he himself was far away. I concede that there can, on occasion, be charges which, although unjustified, are at least based on facts that have given genuine grounds for suspicion. But in the present case it is so wildly unlikely that you could find grounds for the smallest suspicion that, if you managed to do even as much as this, I really believe that I should be prepared to admit at once that my client was guilty.

The elder Sextus Roscius is murdered at Rome when his son is in the neighbourhood of Ameria. I suppose we are asked to believe that the younger Roscius, who knew no one at Rome, conveyed instructions to some assassin there. Yes, you tell us, he sent for an individual to carry a message. But who did he send for, and when? He dispatched a messenger. But who was it, and who was supposed to be the recipient of the message? He persuaded someone, using bribery, influence, expectations, promises. But really, such imputations are so implausible that it is hard to see how anyone can bother to produce them at all, even as blatant fabrications. And yet this is a terribly serious matter, involving nothing less than the dread charge of parricide.

The other alternative would have been for my client to employ slaves to commit the crime. But when this allegation is made, in pity's name, it places him in a truly lamentable and catastrophic situation. For what has happened is this. Usually, when charges of this kind are brought, an innocent man is allowed to save himself by offering his slaves for examination by torture.[1] But Sextus Roscius has not been permitted to adopt such a course. And the reason why this has not been permitted is perfectly clear. It is because you, his prosecutors, have seized possession of every one of his slaves. Out of all that large household of his, the younger Sextus Roscius has not even been left with so much as one single boy to bring him his daily meals.

Publius Scipio, Marcus Metellus,[2] I appeal to you both to help me! When your support had been enlisted on Roscius'

1. Except in special circumstances such as the Catilinarian conspiracy (63 B.C.), or for crimes against the divine law (*Cicero: Selected Political Speeches*, p. 252 n. 36), it was forbidden to examine slaves in order to elicit evidence against their masters. The master, however, could offer his slaves voluntarily for examination. The examination of slaves could only be conducted under torture.

2. Two of the supporters of Sextus Roscius (*advocati* as opposed to the *patronus* who did the speaking in court) when, before the trial took place, he had requested the praetor Marcus Fannius to authorize the examination of his slaves. The first-named is possibly Publius Cornelius Scipio Nasica (praetor, 93 B.C.). If the reading 'Marcus' for Metellus is correct, which is not certain, he may have been the man of that name who was praetor in 69 B.C. See Genealogical Table I.

behalf and you were giving him your assistance, you can confirm that he several times requested his opponents to provide two of his father's slaves in order to put them to the torture. And do you not remember that Roscius refused? Well, where are those slaves now? Gentlemen, they are on Chrysogonus' staff. That is where they are. And he thinks a lot of them and values them highly. Yet, even now, I again put forward a demand that they should be examined; and my client begs and entreats that this demand should be granted. It seems to me incomprehensible that you can bring yourselves to reject such a request.

All right, go on feeling uncertain, gentlemen, about who killed Sextus Roscius – if you can bring yourselves to believe that this is a tenable attitude! Ask yourselves if the culprit is really likely to have been the man whom his father's death plunged into poverty and peril, the man who is actually being prevented from inquiring into the circumstances in which his father died. Or should the guilt not, rather, be attached to the people who shun the investigation, the individuals who are in possession of the dead man's property? There are the murderers – living on the proceeds of murder! But I will come back to this point again quite soon. For it concerns Magnus and Capito, and I promised to speak of their monstrous doings once I had finished refuting the charges put forward by Erucius.

However, Erucius, I have not quite finished with you yet. If my client is really implicated in the crime, you will no doubt agree with me either that he committed it with his own hand (though in fact you admit he didn't) or that he got other people to do it for him; and if so they must have been either free men or slaves. So let us first consider if they could have been free men. But it is completely beyond your powers to explain how he can have managed to meet them, or how he persuaded them, or where, or through what intermediaries, or by raising what hopes, or by offering what bribes. I, on the other hand, am able to prove not only that Sextus Roscius did none of these things, but that he could not conceivably have done them, since he had not been in Rome for many years and, indeed, had never even left his farm at all unless there was some pressing reason to do so. So the only course left to you, clearly, was to begin saying he acted through slaves. At first this looked like a haven where you could find refuge after all your other attempts to raise suspicion had ended in enforced retreat. But instead you have struck a rock. And so now you see the charge rebounding off Sextus Roscius altogether. Indeed, something else is happening as well: for you are beginning to realize that all the suspicions are recoiling upon yourselves.

Well then, let us see where the prosecutor, embarrassed by his lack of arguments, has gone to earth. 'The times in which we were living,' he says, 'were so hazardous that it was quite common for people to be murdered with complete impunity. Consequently, since there were such a lot of murderers about, it was perfectly possible for Sextus Roscius to have committed the crime without encountering the slightest difficulty.' But sometimes, Erucius, you remind me of the sort of man who tries to obtain a couple of articles for a single payment. Because, on the one hand, you are trying to drown us in a mass of legal proceedings, and then at the very same time you are contriving to make the most damning admissions about the very people who have been your paymasters. For you've just been suggesting that people were being murdered on all sides. Now, if that is so, one cannot help asking who the murderers were, and who were the intermediaries they used. In this connexion I am surprised you don't seem to remember that the people who brought you here were purchasers of confiscated property themselves. And cut-purses of that type, who flourished so exceedingly during the times we were discussing, were very often cut-throats as well.[1] Here were people who,

1. The property of a proscribed person was sold by public auction, the sale being called a *sectio*. This means a 'cutting', though the reason

day after day and night after night, rushed about and brandished swords, never once leaving Rome, looting and killing all the time. It really does seem outrageous that people of this kind should have the nerve to blame the misery and cruelty of the times upon the younger Sextus Roscius, and imagine that the proliferation of assassins, of whom they themselves were the leaders and chiefs, can somehow be made into an argument to encompass his ruin. For one thing he was not even at Rome. And secondly, he did not possess the slightest knowledge of what was happening there, because, as you yourself admit, he was a man who never left the countryside.

However, if I go on elaborating what is perfectly obvious you will begin to find it boring, gentlemen, I am afraid, or I shall seem to be underestimating your intelligence. So may I just express my conviction that Erucius' charge has been utterly disproved. Unless, perhaps, you are waiting to hear me refute his imputations of embezzlement and other purely fictitious charges of the same kind, which were never mentioned at all before today and have now been introduced as complete novelties.[1] Indeed, Erucius seemed to me to be reciting them out of some other speech altogether, concocted against some quite different victim, so wholly were these points irrelevant both to the accusation of parricide and to the defendant who is my client. They are only bare assertions, unsupported by argument – and another bare assertion will be quite enough to deny them! And if what the prosecutor has in mind is to keep something back for the cross-examination of witnesses,[2] what has happened just now will happen again: once more he will find us better prepared than he ever expected.

---

for this description is disputed. The purchaser of such goods, or property broker, was called *sector* – hence Cicero's pun. .

1. It seems to have been suggested that Sextus Roscius had illegally kept back some of his father's confiscated property.

2. For this, see above, p. 15.

2. *The Guilt of Magnus and Capito*

I now come to a matter which it gives me no particular pleasure to talk about; but my duty to my client demands that I should bring it up all the same. If I enjoyed being an accuser, there are other people I should prefer to accuse, engaging in cases that would advance my career. But this I have decided not to do, as long as the option remains open to me. For real respect is earned by improving one's reputation by one's own merits, not by climbing upon the distresses and disasters of someone else.

However, the time has now come for us to cease, for a while, examining baseless slurs. It is necessary, now, to look for the crime where it really exists and can be located. In the process, Erucius, you will learn what a genuine accusation really is. You will find that it is a charge supported by a host of convincing circumstances. However, I do not propose to mention the whole lot of these circumstances, and I shall be quite brief in my treatment of each successive point. Indeed, I would not touch on them at all unless I had to. And I shall prove my reluctance by not pursuing these matters one single step farther than the safety of my client and my own duty demand.

Against Sextus Roscius you found no possible motive. But I find one in Magnus. I am afraid it is against you that I have to turn my attack, Magnus; you leave me no alternative, because you are actually sitting with the prosecutors and declaring your hostility quite openly. We'll see about Capito later on, if he comes forward as a witness; and I understand he is ready to do so. When he appears, he'll be told about some triumphant achievements of his which he doesn't even suspect I have ever heard of.

When the famous Lucius Cassius Longinus Ravilla,[1] regarded by the Romans as a judge possessing flawless integrity and wisdom, was presiding at a trial, he always used to ask the same question: *who benefited by what was done?* And such a question is very realistic. No one attempts to commit a crime unless he is hoping it will do him some good. As president of the bench and as judge, Cassius was avoided and dreaded by prisoners in the dock, because although devoted to the truth he did not seem to show much natural inclination towards mercy, being apparently disposed to severity instead. Today, however, our president is a man whose determined opposition to violence is only equalled by his resolute support for every accused man who is innocent. All the same, I should have felt just as ready to defend my client even before the rigorous Cassius himself or other judges who are described as 'Cassian' after him, a designation which even now strikes defendants with terror.

For this is a case in which the question 'who benefited?' would not seem to such judges worth asking at all. For they could see with their own eyes that our opponents are in occupation of vast properties, whereas my client is reduced to penury. That being perfectly clear, they would be disposed to attach guilt and suspicion to those who had secured the loot rather than to the man who had lost everything he possessed. Besides, Magnus, you can't contradict me when I assert that, hitherto, you were poor, you were greedy, you were violent. And you were on extremely bad terms with the man who was murdered. Surely we don't have to look for any motive beside these to show that the man who committed the horrible deed was not my client but yourself!

All these facts are unquestionable. Your former state of destitution was too glaring to be concealed now; indeed, efforts at concealment make it more conspicuous still. You

[1]. Consul 127 B.C.; famous for formulating the principle of investigation *'Cui bono?'* ('Who profited?')

show your greed by entering into a partnership with a complete stranger in order to gain possession of the fortune of a fellow-townsman and a relation. As for your violence, it can clearly be appreciated – leaving everything else aside – by the brazenness of your appearance here in this court. Out of all the conspirators – in other words out of this entire gang of assassins – you alone have had the nerve to come here and sit right among the prosecutors, and not merely to show your shameless face but to flaunt it before everyone's eyes. And the fact that you were thoroughly hostile to the dead man, and got involved in serious disputes with him about family affairs, is something that you need not try to deny.

So all we have to do is to weigh up these two persons one against the other, and decide which of them is the more likely to have murdered the elder Sextus Roscius. Is it the man who became rich because of his death, or the man whom that event reduced to complete poverty? The man who had been poor *before* it happened, or the man who became exceedingly poor afterwards? The man whose burning greed impelled him to assail his own kinsmen, or the man whose way of life was such that all he knew about was the produce of his own agricultural labours, so that acquisitiveness meant nothing to him at all? The individual who grabbed confiscated goods with unrestrained savagery, or the person whose unfamiliarity with the Forum and the courts causes him to dread the sight not only of these benches but of the very city itself? Finally, gentlemen, and this in my opinion is the most important question of all: the dead man's enemy – or his son?

Imagine, Erucius, that you were defending a case which put you in a position to muster all the convincing arguments that I have at my disposal today. What an immensely long speech you would make! How you would hurl yourself about, gesticulating in all directions! You would run out of time, I am convinced, long before you began to run out of words.

Indeed, the material is so extensive that you might spend whole days on each single topic alone. And I won't deny that I could do the same. I hope I am not conceited, but I am also not modest enough to suppose that you can speak more fluently than I can.

However, the city is full of advocates, and I am prepared to admit that I am only one of the common herd: whereas the recent slaughter of accusers, a veritable battle of Cannae, has left you fairly high up in the ranks of the survivors. We have witnessed a wholesale massacre, not at Lake Trasimene this time but beside the Servilian Lake here at Rome –

Who was not wounded there by Phrygian steel?[1]

There's no need to make a list of them all. There was a Curtius and a Marius, and a Memmius as well, although he was exempted from active service by his age, and finally there was that elderly Priam himself, Antistius, whom not only his years but the law had withdrawn from the battle.[2] And then there were hundreds more men who used to act as prosecutors in murder and poison cases, whose names nobody mentions because of their insignificance. As far as I am concerned, I wish

1. A line from the tragedy *Achilles* by Ennius (died 169 B.C.). 'Phrygian steel' refers to the weapons of the Trojans. Cicero compares the massacres of the proscribed to the two most disastrous defeats inflicted on the Romans by the Carthaginians in the Second Punic War, at Lake Trasimene (217 B.C.) and at Cannae (216). The Servilian Lake was a reservoir beside the Basilica Julia at Rome where the heads of those who had been proscribed and executed were exposed (they were also exposed on the Old Rostra in the Forum).

2. These prosecutors who met their deaths in the proscriptions are not identifiable. Possible candidates include Marcus Marius Gratidianus – a relative of Cicero – and a certain Lucius Antistius. Priam was the aged king of Trojans when the Greeks fought against them. Antistius' removal from the battle of the law courts 'for legal reasons' is attributed to the Remmian Law, under which a man convicted of malicious prosecution could never prosecute again because he lost his civil rights; cf. p. 57 n. 1.

they were all still alive. For when there are a lot of people to be watched and a lot of things to be watched over, it does no harm to have as many watchdogs as possible.

However, as is so often the case, the ferocity and disorder of war means that a lot of things happen without the commanders knowing. While the leader in supreme control was preoccupied with quite different matters, there were other individuals who concentrated on attending to their own private wounds and scores. As they sped from place to place under cover of darkness, as they spread disorder and chaos wherever they went, our country seemed to be enveloped in a night that would never end. I only wonder they did not actually burn up these benches in this very court, so that every trace of due legal process might be utterly eradicated. They certainly struck down judges and prosecutors alike. But fortunately their behaviour was so outrageous that it would have been beyond their powers to eliminate all the witnesses to everything they had done, even if they had attempted to do so. For as long as the human race exists, there will assuredly be no lack of people to indict them: as long as our nation survives, there will still be courts to bring retribution down upon their crimes.

As I remarked earlier, if Erucius, in some case he was appearing in, had been able to avail himself of the arguments I have offered you, he would be very glad to go on talking indefinitely – and I could do the same. But, I repeat, it is my intention to pass them over lightly and merely touch on the successive points they raise, so that everyone may understand that I am not bringing accusations because it gives me pleasure but because I want to do my duty and defend my innocent client.

Well, then, there were obviously many motives which could have impelled Magnus to commit the crime. We must now consider whether he had any opportunity to commit it.

Where was the elder Sextus Roscius killed? 'At Rome.' And where were you at the time, Magnus? 'At Rome – but what has that got to do with it? Many other people were at Rome as well.' Let me reassure you; the fact that I name the place of the murder does not mean that I shall go out of my way to search the whole population of the city for the murderer. Nevertheless, I now have one quite simple question to ask: is it more likely that Sextus Roscius was killed by a man who at that time was constantly at Rome, or by someone who for many years past had not visited the city at all?

It is also worth noticing the other factors which point to Magnus as the culprit. As Erucius pointed out, this was a period when assassins were numerous, when men were struck down with impunity. Well, who were these numerous assassins? They included, evidently enough, the individuals who were purchasing confiscated properties – and the creatures whom they hired in order to do their killings. If you believe that the former category, the people who coveted other people's goods, were responsible for the removal of Sextus Roscius, then you, Magnus, are once again one of those under suspicion, because you've got rich on money that belongs to us. But if you prefer to attribute the responsibility to the second category, the murderous characters who are politely known as bandits, I suggest that you should just inquire who their bosses and protectors are, and I can assure you that you will find one of your partners among their number. Contradict all this as best you can, then compare your contradictions with my arguments on the other side; and the total contrast between the merits of your case and mine will become glaringly obvious.

'All right,' you will say, 'even supposing I was constantly at Rome, what does that prove anyway?' But my reply, in my client's name, will be this: 'I, on the other hand, was never there at all.' 'I admit,' Magnus may say, 'that I bought confiscated properties, but so did many other people as well.' 'Yet I, as you claim yourself,' Sextus Roscius can answer, 'have spent all my time elsewhere, engaged in farming and agriculture.' Magnus: 'Just because I have been associating with a gang of assassins, it doesn't follow that I am an assassin myself.' Sextus Roscius: 'But as regards myself, I could not possibly come under the slightest suspicion at all, because I'm not even acquainted with one single assassin!'

You, Magnus, had every possible opportunity to commit the crime – and with your own hand at that. There is every kind of evidence to prove that this is precisely what you did. Nevertheless, about your actual authorship of the deed I propose to say nothing more. This is partly because it gives me no pleasure whatever to accuse you. But my principal reason is a different one: if I wanted to speak about all the men who, at that period, suffered the same fate as Sextus Roscius, I am afraid it would look as if my speech was aimed not only against my present opponents, but against a number of other people as well.

So let us instead take a look, Magnus, at what you were doing after the elder Sextus Roscius' death. The inquiry can be quite brief, like our glances at all the other points. Indeed, may the god of good faith himself be my witness, your activities were so open and palpable that I feel some embarrassment about even mentioning them. Besides, whatever sort of a man you are, I don't want my eagerness for the protection of my own client to make it seem that I have been merciless in my treatment of you. However, just when I begin to get anxious about this, and start forming the determination to do everything I can, short of neglecting my duty, to spare you, then suddenly I feel impelled to change my mind after all. Because now I remember your extraordinary impudence. For this was a moment when your associates were busy making themselves scarce and going into hiding, so that it would look as if this trial was genuinely concerned with a crime committed, not by themselves as a result of their robberies, but by my client instead. And to think that at this of all times you, of all men, chose to appear in court – and take your seat with the prosecutors! However, the only thing you accomplished by this was to bring home to everyone that there were no limits to your brazen effrontery.

After the murder of Sextus Roscius, let me remind you who was the first man to bring the news to Ameria. It was Mallius Glaucia, whom I mentioned before. He is a dependant of yours, Magnus, and an intimate friend as well. The fact that he should have been the person to bring the news, and news, moreover, which might have seemed, on the face of it, not to concern you in the slightest degree, can only be explained by the conclusion that you were already a party to an arrangement about the elder Roscius' death and possessions, and had formed a partnership with some associate to share the crime and the reward alike. 'Not at all!' you say: 'Mallius brought the news entirely of his own accord.' But what on earth had it got to do with him? Or are we expected to believe that he had come to Ameria for some quite other purpose and that it was purely by chance that he was the first to announce what he had heard at Rome? Well, in that case let us inquire *why* he had travelled all the way to Ameria. 'That I can't guess,' says Magnus. But I will now bring the matter to a head, so that we shan't need to do any more guessing. The person Glaucia selected as the first recipient of his news at Ameria was Capito. But why? The younger Sextus Roscius had a house at the place. He had a wife and children there. He had numerous relations and kinsmen, with whom he was on excellent terms. So one cannot help asking why on earth this henchman of yours, who brought the information about the crime, chose to communicate it to Capito before anyone else.

Roscius the elder was murdered while he was returning from a dinner-party. The news was known at Ameria before dawn. How do we explain this incredibly rapid journey, this unparalleled speed and hurry? No, I'm not asking who actually did the killing. Don't be frightened, Glaucia! I'm not proposing to shake your clothes, or search you to see if you've got a weapon concealed on your person. I don't consider it's my business to do so. Now that I have discovered who *planned* the murder, I will not bother to identify the actual hand that struck the blow. But there's just one question that I do want to put to you, because the plain facts of the case, and your perfectly obvious guilt, have placed it fairly and squarely before us. I mean this: one would indeed like to know where Glaucia learnt of the murder, and from whom – because he certainly learnt of it very quickly indeed! Besides, even if we accept the assurance that he just happened, by mere chance, to hear about it straightaway, we are still entitled to ask why he felt he had to embark so hastily upon this whole extensive journey, and complete it in the course of a single night. Even if we are prepared to assume that no one had asked him to undertake the trip, what on earth was the imperative urgency which compelled him to set out from Rome at so late an hour, and to press onwards without sleeping a wink all night?

When the plain facts reveal so much, any further hunting for arguments or grasping after conjectures becomes unnecessary. Gentlemen, I should like to think that the scenes I have described to you emerge so vividly that you feel they have taken place before your eyes. Picture to yourselves, please, that unfortunate man coming back from his dinner, wholly unaware of his impending fate. And then comes the ambush, the sudden attack. Look, there is Glaucia! He's got something to do with the murder. And isn't Magnus there, too? Yes, there he is, setting his Automedon in the chariot with his own hands, to carry the news of his horrible crime and evil victory.[1] Watch how he urges his messenger to go without sleep all night, to labour indefatigably in his interests, to get the news to Capito at the earliest possible moment.

I still wonder why he wanted Capito to learn it first. I don't

1. Automedon was the charioteer of Achilles, famous for his speed.

know the answer for certain: but I can only believe that it must have something to do with the large slice of Roscius' property Capito had acquired: since out of those thirteen farms three of the very finest have passed into his hands. What is more, this is not the first time – or so I have heard – that Capito has been suspected of the same sort of thing. He is credited with a good many famous victories of very much the same type; though this appears to be the first major decoration that has come his way from Rome.[1]

Indeed, there is not one single method of committing a murder, or so it is said, with which Capito is unfamiliar – for he himself has employed every one of these methods quite a number of times. Sometimes a dagger has been his chosen weapon; sometimes poison. I can even tell you of a man whom he threw off the bridge into the Tiber – contrary to the tradition of our ancestors, because the victim was less than sixty years old.[2] Capito will be reminded, I can assure you, about all these stories if he comes forward as a witness, or rather *when* he comes forward, because I am convinced that he intends to. Well, let him appear, and then please notice carefully how he will unroll the document he'll be carrying with him. It was written for him by Erucius, as I can prove, and it is the same document which Capito is said to have flourished in the face of my client, boldly threatening to disclose all its contents as evidence. You've got a remarkable witness here, gentlemen. He's an authority truly worth wait-

1. Latin *palma lemniscata*, a wreath adorned with hanging coloured ribbons, which were a mark of special honour for a victorious general.

2. There was a saying, 'sixty-year-olds off the bridge'. But this referred not to bridges over the Tiber but to gangways described by the same term (*pontes*) which led to the polling booths, so that the saying referred not to the drowning of old men but merely to their ceasing to vote. However, there was also an ancient custom of throwing wickerwork human images (*Argei*) into the Tiber from the Sublician Bridge every year on 14 May; this was believed to be derived, in origin, from human sacrifices.

ing for – a personage so ineffably noble that you must obviously adjust your verdict to his evidence without the slightest hesitation.

The fact that these men have revealed to us such a glaringly clear view of the crimes they have committed is an astonishing testimony to the blindness which greed and cupidity and violence have cast over their own eyes.

Well then, immediately the murder had been committed one of the conspirators, Magnus, sent a swift messenger to Ameria, to give the news to his associate, or rather, one should say, to his boss. By this action alone, even if the whole world had been determined to conceal Magnus' knowledge of who the murderer was, he himself would have unmistakably exposed his own criminal responsibility before everybody's eyes. As for the other creature, Capito, he actually proposes, as I have said – if the immortal gods will tolerate such a thing – to give evidence against the younger Sextus Roscius! Though I should have thought that the question at issue now is no longer the degree of reliance which can be placed on his words, but the severity of the punishment to which he will inevitably find himself condemned.

Our ancestors established the custom that no one should give evidence in a case in which his own interests were involved, however insignificant the issue may have been and however distinguished he himself was. Even Scipio Africanus the younger, whose surname declares that he conquered a third part of the world, would still not be able to give evidence if any interests of his own were at stake; though when a man of his calibre is concerned I would suppose that, once he had spoken up, no one could possibly have disbelieved him. But observe what a transformation there has been nowadays, and how everything has changed for the worse. Here we have a case involving confiscated property and even murder, and yet evidence is to be given by a man who is both a purchaser of such property and a murderer himself! Indeed, he is the buyer and possessor of the very estates which are at issue today – and it was actually he who arranged the murder of the man whose death is being investigated by this court.

Well, my good Magnus, is anything the matter? Is there some point you want to raise? No? Well, then, pay attention to me. I do feel that you should make absolutely sure that you are doing yourself justice. For you yourself, as well as my client, have a great deal at stake. You have committed many crimes and many deeds of violence and many outrages. And you have also done one thing that was extremely stupid; and it was unmistakably your own idea, and was not prompted by Erucius. For it was very misguided of you to sit where you are sitting today, among the prosecutors. If you propose to say nothing at all, then an accuser who doesn't open his mouth is no use to anybody; and a witness who gets up to speak from the prosecutor's bench is equally useless. Besides, if you had not chosen that particular place to sit, your greed would be a little more effectively concealed and less glaringly obvious, and so you would be that much better off. As it is, I can't imagine how anyone on your side could possibly find what you have to say of the slightest value to themselves, since this behaviour on your part makes it look as if you are deliberately working not for your own client at all, but for ours!

Now, gentlemen, let us observe what took place immediately after the murder. Four days after Sextus Roscius had been killed, the news was taken to Chrysogonus in the camp of Lucius Sulla at Volaterrae. Clearly, there is no longer any need to ask who sent the messenger. It must be perfectly clear that it was the man who had dispatched that other messenger to Ameria. Straightaway, Chrysogonus arranged for Roscius' property to be sold – although he knew neither Roscius nor the facts. We must find out just how it occurred to him to covet the farms of a man whom he didn't know, whom he had never even seen in all his life. When you hear something of this kind, gentlemen, it is usually right to conclude that some fellow-townsman or neighbour must have been the informer; they are the people who generally perpetrate these leakages of information, these betrayals. And here we're not just dealing with suspicions: I'm not reduced to basing my argument on mere probabilities. If I were, I could say how *probable* it is that Magnus and Capito sent the information to Chrysogonus. They were already his friends before this. Originally, it is true, they had inherited many long-standing patrons and hosts of their own from their ancestors. But they had ceased to treat these with the slightest attention or respect, and had instead placed themselves under the protection and patronage of Chrysogonus.

These are points that I could argue, and the arguments would be convincing, too. But in a case like the present one there is no need for any such conjectural material at all. Even the other side, I assure you, can't deny that it was they themselves who incited Chrysogonus to get hold of the property. If you see with your own eyes the man who has received his share of the loot for the information he has given, then surely, gentlemen, you don't have to ask yourselves who the informer was. It only remains, then, to identify the people who were rewarded by Chrysogonus for getting the estates into his hands. They were Magnus and Capito. Was there anyone else? No, there was not. Well, obviously the men Chrysogonus shared the plunder with were the men who had acquired it for him in the first place.

But let us now turn to Chrysogonus, and consider the verdict he himself virtually pronounced upon what Magnus and Capito had done. For if they had not served him as useful allies in the fight, one cannot see why he subsequently gave them such abundant rewards. And they must have done more than just pass on the information, because if that was the sum total of their achievements it would clearly have been enough just to offer them his thanks, or at most – if he wanted to do the thing really handsomely – to show his gratitude by giving some sort of present. But what Capito was given, immediately, was a set of three extremely valuable farms. One really does ask oneself why. And why are all the other farms in the joint possession of Magnus and Chrysogonus? Surely it is perfectly evident, gentlemen, that Chrysogonus gave Magnus and Capito these spoils of war in gratitude for what they had told him.

The ten leading members of the Amerian town council who came as envoys to the camp included Capito himself. His behaviour on this deputation, quite apart from anything else at all, will serve as a perfect illustration of the general conduct and character and morals of this individual. If you wanted to regard him as a good man, you would have to turn a blind eye to the demonstrable fact that there is no duty or right upon earth which has proved solemn or sacred enough to have escaped violation and obliteration at his criminal, treacherous hands. It was he who prevented Sulla from learning what had been done. It was he who insisted that Chrysogonus must keep the whole matter shrouded in secrecy. It was he who pointed out that, if the sale of the property were annulled, Chrysogonus would lose a large sum of money and he himself would risk the capital penalty.

He spurred Chrysogonus on, and at the same time continued to deceive the other members of his own deputation. He repeatedly warned Chrysogonus to be careful, while simultaneously holding out false and treacherous hopes to his fellow-envoys. He plotted intrigues against them with Chrysogonus, and passed on to him all their plans and projects. He came to an agreement with Chrysogonus about his own share of the proceeds, and meanwhile did not allow the deputation as a whole to secure access to Sulla, continually inventing various fictitious reasons why the meeting had to be postponed. In the end, by a combination of encouragement, advice and reassurance, he prevented them from seeing Sulla at all. They trusted

Chrysogonus' good faith – or rather his very bad faith, as you will be able to learn from them in person, if the prosecutor decides to call them as witnesses. And so back they went to their homes, taking with them nothing but unfounded hopes, and having achieved no positive result whatsoever.

In private business, if a man showed even the slightest carelessness in his execution of a trust – I say nothing about culpable mismanagement for his own interest or profit – our ancestors considered that he had behaved very dishonourably indeed.[1] In such cases a trial for breach of trust was held, and conviction on such a charge was believed to be every bit as shameful as conviction for an offence such as theft. This, no doubt, was because, when there is a matter we cannot take part in ourselves, we are obliged to rely on the good faith of a friend instead of our own personal endeavours. That being so, anyone who betrays such a commission attacks a safeguard which is designed to serve the whole community: in so far as it rests with himself to do so, he is undermining the entire basis of our social system. For we cannot do everything for ourselves; a man has his own sphere of useful activity, and cannot go beyond it. That is precisely why friendships are formed, so that joint interests can be promoted by mutual services. It is quite wrong to accept a trust at all if you propose either to neglect it or turn it to your own advantage. Don't offer to help me and then thwart and impede my interests while you are pretending to do me a service. Get out of the way, and I can find someone else to act for me instead! You may genuinely imagine that you are strong enough to carry the burden. But only the very strongest characters will really be able to take such things in their stride.[2]

That is why breach of trust is a disgraceful offence. For it

1. A trust or commission (*mandatum*) was a contract in which one person promises to perform or give something at another's request, without remuneration.

2. The text at this point is uncertain and obscure.

destroys two things that are truly sacred, friendship and good faith. A man normally entrusts a commission only to a friend, and only trusts someone whom he believes to be reliable. Only the most degraded of characters, then, would take an action calculated both to destroy a friendship and to damage a man who is suffering this damage because you were the person he trusted. Isn't that so? Since, therefore, even in quite a minor matter, failure to attend to a trust incurs a legal sentence carrying the maximum degree of disgrace, a case as grave as the present one, in which a man entrusted unreservedly with the good name of the dead father and the fortunes of the living son has brought disgrace upon the dead and destitution upon the living, makes it impossible to think of him any longer not merely as a man of honour, but as a man who has any place among human beings at all. If all were done as it should be, the man who entrusts someone with a commission should be able to afford to relax and be negligent, but never the man who accepts it; and that is why, even in private affairs of no importance, the merest carelessness in administering a trust is made the subject of a charge which carries a sentence involving utter degradation. In the present case, on the other hand, we are speaking of a trust of the utmost importance, arranged and commissioned by public authority. Here we have an individual who has not just injured some private citizen by his carelessness, but his treacherous behaviour has violated and defiled the sacred character of an official delegation. It would be impossible to overstate the severity of the sentence and punishment which ought to be inflicted on such a man.

If Sextus Roscius, as a private person, had commissioned Capito to negotiate and arrange this business with Chrysogonus, granting him the discretion to pledge Sextus' word,[1] and if Capito, having accepted the commission, had derived even the very smallest personal profit from its

1. This is only one of a number of different interpretations of what Cicero was saying.

performance, he would surely have been liable to conviction by an arbitrator,[1] who would have compelled him to make restitution, depriving him of every shred of his reputation in the bargain. What actually happened, however, was not merely that Capito received a commission from Sextus Roscius; there was also something much more serious still. For on this occasion you might go so far as to say that what was entrusted, officially, to Capito's care by the town council was Sextus Roscius himself, and everything that concerned him – his good name, his life, and his entire property, all at one and the same time. And it is not just a question of Capito converting some trifle or other to his own advantage. On the contrary, he has totally bereft Sextus Roscius of everything he possessed. As his own share, he settled for three of the farms. And for the wishes of his town council and fellow-citizens he showed as little regard as he showed for his own pledged word.

Take a look at the rest of his actions as well, judges, and you will see that he has contrived to defile himself with every single kind of villainy that you can possibly imagine. Consider, for example, his deception of the other envoys. Even in trifling matters it is considered a very shameful thing to deceive one's partner, every bit as shameful as the breaches of trust I was speaking about just now. And it is justly so regarded, because a man who enters into partnership with another is entitled to believe that he has enlisted a helper. Where on earth shall he look for good faith, if he has not been able to find it in his own chosen associate? Besides, the offences which deserve the severest punishment are those which are the hardest to guard against. In our dealings with strangers, we can be

1. Lawsuits relating to good faith were decided not by a judge (*iudex*) but by an arbitrator (*arbiter*). While the judge would only reach his verdict in accordance with a formula already prescribed (by the praetor), it was left to the discretion of the arbitrator to decide according to 'fair dealing' (*bona fides*) after weighing the rival claims and any special circumstances.

reserved. But our intimate associates cannot fail to know a great deal more about us than any mere acquaintance does; and against one's own partner, therefore, it is quite impossible to take effective precautions. Even to feel nervous about his integrity almost seems like a breach of obligation in itself. How right, then, our ancestors were to maintain that a man who had deceived his partner could no longer be entitled to a place in decent society!

Yet what Capito did was a good deal worse than just cheating one single financial partner. Even that would have been an extremely serious offence; but still we might have managed to find it just endurable. But he had to do with no less than nine men, excellent men, his fellow-envoys on the deputation, appointed in pursuance of the same mandate and commission as his own. And he ensnared the whole lot of them, leaving them completely in the lurch, depositing them right in the hands of their enemies, and trapping them with every imaginable kind of treacherous fraud. Not the slightest suspicion of his criminal purpose was likely to cross their minds. He had been made their partner in an official duty; to mistrust him would have seemed entirely wrong. They quite failed to see what an evil man he was. They believed his empty words. And, in consequence, it is because of his sinister machinations that these good men now find themselves censured for displaying insufficient caution and foresight. Whereas he, on the other hand, the individual who turned traitor and went over to the other side, the creature who first revealed his associates' plans to their enemies and then joined the enemy ranks himself, still continues to overwhelm us with menaces and intimidations, and in the meantime has become richer by three farms, the rewards for his abominable action. His whole life, gentlemen, has been one endless series of iniquities. The disgraceful deed that we are discussing now is only one of them.

May I venture to suggest the principle on which your

inquiry should be conducted? If you come upon someone
with a general record of greedy, violent, depraved and
treacherous behaviour, you will also inevitably find that some
actual crime is lurking in its midst. However, in the present
case 'lurking' is not the right word, since, in fact, the crime
is openly manifest and exposed to view. This being the case,
we do not need to go through the process of merely inferring
the criminal act from Capito's deplorable past record. Indeed,
the contrary is the case: if anyone chose to query this or that
item on the record in question, we could infer it from the
existence of this crime. So we can hardly say, can we, gentlemen, that the master-gladiator Capito has retired from his
cut-throat profession just yet.

However, it would be equally hard to maintain that his pupil
here, Magnus, is in the slightest degree inferior to him in skill.
The one is as greedy and infamous as the other. Their outrages are well matched, and in respect of violence there is
nothing to choose between them. Well, you have heard about
the trustworthiness of the master. Now you must learn about
the pupil – and see what you think about *his* standards of
behaviour.

As I mentioned before, our opponents have repeatedly been
requested to hand over two slaves for examination. But you,
Magnus, have always rejected this proposal. One must conclude, I suppose, that you considered the applicants unworthy
of a positive answer, that the man on whose behalf the
application was made failed to engage your sympathy, that
the request itself was in your opinion unjustified.

And yet the people who asked this of you, people whose
names I mentioned earlier on, are blessed with as fine positions
and characters as anyone in the whole country. Their way of
living is so honourable, and their reputation at Rome so great,
that no one would ever question the fairness of anything they
said. The man for whom they were acting has suffered such

an unparalleled series of horrible misfortunes that he would be perfectly prepared to offer his own body up for examination by torture, provided only he could be quite sure that the death of his father would be properly investigated. Yet you, Magnus, have not allowed even the slaves to be examined, and your rejection of this request seems to me nothing less than a plain confession that you yourself were guilty of the crime. For it really does seem quite extraordinary that you should have had the nerve to turn the application down. When Sextus Roscius was murdered, the slaves were on the spot. As for them, I neither say that they were guilty nor innocent. But your opposition to the demand that they should be examined is remarkably suspicious. This outstanding consideration they are receiving at your hands shows clearly that they know something which would ruin you if it were disclosed.

You object that it is forbidden to examine slaves for evidence against their masters. But in the present case that would not be the situation. For since the defendant is Sextus Roscius, such an examination would not be directed against their master at all: you yourselves declare that *you* are their masters now. 'Actually,' you will reply, 'they are with Chrysogonus.' Indeed! So we have to suppose that Chrysogonus is so charmed by their learning and accomplishments that he has particularly chosen these labourers trained by a rustic householder at Ameria – which is more or less what they are – to associate with his own array of charming, civilized young boys handpicked from the most elegant homes. No, gentlemen, that can't be the answer. Chrysogonus is most unlikely to have been captivated by the literary ability and culture of these slaves. And he is equally unlikely to have thought they would prove industrious and reliable managers of his household affairs. We are not being told the whole truth. And yet all these endeavours to keep the matter out of sight and mind only have the effect of making it all the more blatant and conspicuous.

The next question which might seem to arise is whether the person who is so reluctant to allow the slaves to be questioned may not be Chrysogonus himself, because he wants to conceal his own crime. But that, gentlemen, goes beyond what I am choosing to assert. One must not be indiscriminate in distributing one's accusations. On this particular subject I, personally, entertain no suspicions whatever concerning Chrysogonus. And this is a point I have always intended to make. You will remember that at the beginning of my speech I divided the case into two parts: the presentation of the charge, a task which was left entirely to Erucius; and the act of violence, which was the role of Magnus and Capito – so that any misdeed or crime or murder that can be discovered will have to be placed at *their* door. As regards Chrysogonus, what we contend is that his excessive influence and power are obstructing our case to an intolerable extent. And we request that you, gentlemen, since this lies within your power, should not only cut this power down to size but should attack it with the full retribution of the law.

My view is simply this. The person who is eager that known witnesses of a murder should be examined is presumably trying to get at the truth. But the man who refuses such an appeal is manifestly confessing his guilt, even if he does not venture to admit it in so many words.

Gentlemen, when I began this part of my speech dealing with Magnus and Capito I declared that I did not want to say one single word more about their criminal deed than the requirements and exigencies of my defence demanded. For the amount of evidence that could be brought forward to prove their guilt is enormous, and each separate piece of evidence could be supported by a mass of varied arguments. If I dealt with every one of these questions, I should be doing so unwillingly and of necessity, and in such circumstances I would not feel able to give them prolonged and detailed attention. But there still remain some points that could not possibly be passed over in silence, and those, gentlemen, I have touched upon – though not in detail. If I once began to deal with all the other pieces of evidence, those which are matters of suspicion – justifiable suspicion – I should have to speak at great length. And so instead I prefer to leave them to your intelligent conjectures.

3. Chrysogonus: The Criminal behind the Scenes

Now I return to that golden name of Chrysogonus,[1] beneath which the whole gang has surreptitiously taken shelter. Gentlemen, here I am in a difficulty. For when I speak of this man, I don't know how far I ought to go. But equally I don't feel I can say nothing at all. If I say nothing, I leave out a very important part of my argument. But if I refer to him I am afraid that not only Chrysogonus himself – I do not mind about that – but others, too, may consider themselves insulted. Fortunately, however, the issues that are at stake in the present case do not require me to deliver any attack on the purchasers of confiscated property as a whole. For the case exhibits quite special and peculiar features of its own.

Chrysogonus bought the estates of the elder Sextus Roscius. So the first question we have to consider is this. On what pretext did they come to be sold, or how was it possible for them to be sold at all? Now by asking this question, gentlemen, I don't intend to link it to any general proposition that the sale of every innocent citizen's possessions is a scandal, because, if a situation could arise in which such problems might be boldly and frankly debated, the late Sextus Roscius was not an important enough national figure for his fate to be singled out as a test case. But what I do want to know is how the actual terms of the law which deals with proscriptions, the

1. *Chrysos* means 'gold' in Greek. There is also a reference to his enrichment by the proscriptions.

Valerian or Cornelian law – because I am not familiar with the measure, and do not rightly know its name[1] – could be claimed to legitimize the sale of Roscius' property. Its text is said to contain the following provision: 'that the property of those who have been proscribed should be sold'. But Sextus Roscius does not belong to that category, for he was never proscribed. And then comes another category: 'the property of those who were killed within the enemy's lines'. But as long as such lines existed, Sextus Roscius was within those not of the enemy but of Sulla. It was only afterwards, when fighting had ended and general peace had been restored, that he was murdered, while returning from a dinner-party at Rome. If his killing was legally justified, I admit that the sale of his property was legal too. But if it is clear that his death was contrary to every single law that exists, ancient and modern alike, then I demand that you should tell me the right, the principle, and the legal provision under which his property came to be sold.

You will no doubt be very eager to ask, Erucius, whom these remarks of mine are directed against. Not against the man you would like to suppose, and in fact *do* suppose. For my whole speech, from the very beginning, has exonerated Sulla; and indeed his own noble character does that for him already. No, I maintain that the person responsible for the whole thing was Chrysogonus. He lied. He made the elder Sextus Roscius out to be a bad citizen. He alleged Roscius was with the enemy at the time when he was killed. He prevented the deputation from Ameria from informing Sulla about any of these matters.

However, gentlemen, I have an extremely strong suspicion that the property was not actually sold at all! And let me explain to you the reasons why I have come to this conclusion. The law which deals with proscription and sales ordained, as

1. See above, p. 41 n. 1. Cicero knew well enough about these laws, but is sarcastically implying ignorance of such autocratic measures.

I understand it, that the last day on which such operations could take place was the first of June. But Roscius' murder only occurred some months after that. How, then, can we be assured that his property was officially sold? Either, one must conclude, the sale was never entered in the state accounts, and so this crook is cheating us even more cleverly than we had realized, or, if it was entered, then the accounts must have been tampered with in some way, since it is quite clear that the sale cannot possibly have complied with the provisions of the law.

Yes, gentlemen, I know it is rather early to develop this line of argument. You may well feel inclined to say that when I ought to be saving my client's life I am merely attending to a hang-nail. And indeed money, property, is the last thing he is worrying about. He refuses to concern himself with his finances at all. If only he can be released from this unjust suspicion, this lying charge, he believes he will find mere poverty endurable enough.

However, gentlemen, I still have a few other points I want to make, and while I hope you will give them your careful attention I also want you to appreciate that I am now speaking partly for Sextus Roscius, but partly also for myself. There are some aspects of the situation which I regard as scandalous and intolerable in a general sense, and I believe they will damage us all unless we take measures to remedy them. These are points that I shall feel obliged to mention to you on my own account, because they cause me a great deal of anger and distress. And then there are, of course, the other matters which relate to my client's cause and vital interests. Later on, at the end of my speech, I will let you know the arguments that he, for his part, wishes to raise, and the terms which he would be prepared to accept.

But first of all, let us just leave Sextus Roscius out of the question for the moment. For I have certain inquiries that I personally very much want to put to Chrysogonus. To begin with, I want to ask why the property of a blameless citizen has been sold – the property of a man who was never proscribed, and who was not, as long as he lived, among the enemies of Sulla, though these were the only people, without exception, against whom the law was directed. Why did the sale take place considerably after the final date fixed by the law for such transactions? And why did the property fetch such an extremely small sum?

If Chrysogonus behaves as worthless, dishonest ex-slaves generally do, and tries to put the blame for all this on his patron, the attempt will be unsuccessful. For everyone knows that numerous people have committed numerous crimes which Sulla either disapproved of or knew nothing about, since his attention was wholly engaged elsewhere, with matters of the highest importance. We are certainly entitled to question whether it is desirable that events such as those we are dealing with today should get overlooked in this manner, and the answer, gentlemen, is that it is no doubt undesirable in the extreme. But it cannot be avoided. We know that Jupiter himself, the best and greatest, whose will and command rule heaven, earth and sea, has often tormented the human race, and ruined its cities, and flattened its crops by violent winds and furious storms and dreadful heat and unendurable cold. But when these disasters occur we do not attribute them to a deliberate destructive impulse on the part of the god. We prefer to ascribe them to the impersonal force and immensity of nature. The blessings, on the other hand, which are ours, and the light of heaven which we enjoy, and the air which we breathe, are favours which we are happy to credit to Jupiter. Well, this was a time when Lucius Sulla, by himself, was ruling our nation and governing the affairs of the whole world – when he had recovered our empire by force of arms, and was consolidating its majesty by new laws. If, at such a moment, there were certain things he could not manage to attend to in person, it is surely not very strange. The human brain cannot be expected to obtain results which even the divine might is incapable of achieving.[1]

But in any case, leaving the past aside, what is happening at this very moment makes it abundantly and universally clear that the man who built up the whole of this intrigue was Chrysogonus. It was he who arranged for the charge to be brought against Sextus Roscius. And it was he to whom Erucius, when he offered his services as prosecutor, hoped and expected to do a service.[2]

The people who live in the lands of the Sallentini and Bruttii[3] consider they have a comfortable, conveniently situated place of residence when news hardly comes their way as often as three times a year. But here you have Chrysogonus making his way down to see us from his fine mansion located on the Palatine Hill itself! And he can relax, when he feels so disposed, in another very agreeable house that he possesses outside Rome. He also has a number of farms which are all first-class properties, and all nice and close to the city.

His Roman home is crammed with vessels of Delian and

1. This somewhat riskily sardonic comparison between Jupiter and Sulla was probably not in the spoken version of the speech; cf. W. V. Harris, *Rome in Etruria and Umbria*, p. 272 (and source quoted there), and above, p. 29.

2. There is a considerable gap in the text here, from which some disconnected words have been preserved with greater or less probability. Cicero apparently went on to stress further the low price at which Chrysogonus purchased the property of Sextus Roscius, and to suggest that Chrysogonus had deliberately dispersed the movable goods to prevent them from being taken away from him. Chrysogonus denied this, claiming that he had transported part of them to the territory of Veii, for a house he was building there. Cicero, however, concluded from this dispersal that Chrysogonus was frightened because his 'purchase' of the property had been illegal; and the orator went on to attack his luxury in detail, explaining that it made him desperately short of money.

3. At the south-eastern and southern extremities of Italy respectively.

Corinthian bronze, including the automatic cooker[1] which he recently bought at such a high price that passers-by, hearing the auctioneer crying out the sum, believed a whole estate was being sold. And the quantity of his embossed silver plate, embroidered coverlets, pictures, statues and marble is beyond all computation. Or rather, it adds up precisely to the amount of plunder from many illustrious families, acquired in times of violence and pillage, which can be contained inside a single building!

His vast household of slaves beggars description, and so does the variety of their skills. I say nothing about the ordinary trades of cook, baker, litter-bearer and so on. But he also disposes of a whole host of individuals whose task is merely the gratification of his mind and ear. So numerous are these artists that the entire neighbourhood rings incessantly with the sound of singing and stringed instruments and pipes, and with the racket of nocturnal debaucheries.[2] In a way of life like his, gentlemen, the daily expenditure and extravagance and lavish entertainment that go on all the time are unbelievable. But when you have seen what a peculiar house he maintains, these excesses no longer seem so incredible after all – if you can call it a house, rather than a factory of vice or a rendezvous for innumerable kinds of misbehaviour.

And look at Chrysogonus himself, gentlemen. Take a glance at his curled and scented hair, as he flutters from one end of the Forum to the other, escorted by a retinue of citizens of Rome, formally arrayed in their Roman togas.[3] Note how contemptuous he is of every single person in the whole world except his own self, clearly convinced that he is the only man who deserves to be called a human being at all, and the most successful and powerful individual on earth.

1. A self-acting boiling apparatus (*authepsa*).
2. If *conviviis* is read. An alternative reading is *conviciis*, 'quarrels'.
3. Roman citizens were regarded as disgracing their togas if they appeared in the retinue of an ex-slave.

Nevertheless, gentlemen, if I cared to go into details about all the activities and projects in which Chrysogonus is engaged, I am afraid that people who were imperfectly acquainted with the facts might think I wanted to attack the aristocratic cause that has proved victorious in our civil wars.

Certainly, if there was something about that cause I didn't like, I should be well within my rights in attacking it. For I am not afraid that anyone is likely to suggest I have ever been un-friendly to the interests of the nobility. Quite on the contrary, everyone who knows me is well aware that what I wanted most of all was an agreement between the two parties, but that as soon as this became impracticable I earnestly laboured for the victory of the side which eventually prevailed. For anyone could identify the issue at stake. It was whether nobility or squalor (and I am thinking from the point of view of people's principles, as well as their rank) should control our national affairs. In such a contest, no one but the very worst of bad citizens would fail to join the side whose success would guarantee both the dignity of our nation at home and its authority abroad.

That this has been accomplished, gentlemen – that rank and office have been restored to the people who are entitled to them – fills me with satisfaction and great joy. And I know very well whom we have to thank for this achievement. We have to thank the will of the gods, the vigorous endeavours of the Roman people, and the wisdom and guidance and good fortune of Lucius Sulla. The punishments that were inflicted upon those who fought against him so determinedly are not for me to criticize; and as for the rewarding of the brave men who performed outstanding public services, it deserves, as far as I can see, nothing but praise. For those were the purposes, surely, for which we were fighting, and my absolute devotion to the party that achieved them is something that I am indeed proud to confess.

But let us just imagine for a moment that the objectives

and war-aims of this cause had been quite different; that they had instead been directed towards the enrichment of the lowest of mankind by other people's wealth, in order to enable these degraded creatures to launch a universal attack on the sanctity of private property. Let us imagine, furthermore, that a total prohibition had been imposed not only on contesting these measures in any way whatever, but even on uttering a single word in their condemnation. If that were so, the war, instead of resulting in the revival and rehabilitation of the Roman people, would merely have succeeded in reducing them to complete ruin and destruction.

However, gentlemen, that is not by any means what happened. By resisting such rascals you will not harm the nobility's cause in any way. On the contrary, you will enhance its glory. For, whereas anyone who merely complained about Chrysogonus' power as an existing fact might well be suspected of criticizing the regime, to declare, on the other hand, that no such power had been granted to him at all, to dispute, that is to say, his *right* to such a power, amounts to a commendation of the current order. And no one, I hope, will be so foolish or disingenuous as to say: 'If only I had been allowed to speak my mind, I should certainly have expressed a strong view about such a matter.' But you can! 'In that case, I should have acted in such and such a manner.' Well, you may; nobody is stopping you. 'I should have passed such and such a decree in the senate.' Pass it, then, provided it does some good; everyone will support you. 'As a judge, I should have given this or that verdict.' Yes, do so, and it will meet with universal applause, if it is really sound and justifiable.

While the necessities of the situation demanded such a thing, control remained in the hands of one man. But after he had made various appointments and passed the required laws, the other people got their legitimate responsibility and authority back. And, what is more, the men who gained these prizes will be able to keep them for good – if they really set about things in the right way. But if they commit or condone acts of murder and looting, or excesses of prodigal extravagance – well, I don't want to speak too harshly against them, if only to avoid the bad omen, but this I do feel obliged to say: if these nobles of ours should by any chance fail to show themselves vigilant and right-minded and courageous and merciful, then they will inevitably find themselves compelled to resign their distinctions in favour of other men whose possession of those qualities is less liable to doubt.

So I will tell these personages what I ask them to do. Stop declaring that a man who has spoken truthfully and frankly has done wrong. Stop making common cause with Chrysogonus. Stop thinking that, if he is injured, you too will have suffered a loss. Consider how scandalous and lamentable it is that men who even found the pretensions of the knightly order unendurable[1] are able to tolerate domination by the most worthless sort of slave. Formerly, gentlemen, it is true, this domination was directed towards other ends.[2] But now you can see it is constructing for itself a different road – preparing to follow an even more sinister route. For it is planning a direct onslaught upon your own good faith, upon the sanctity of your oath, upon the justice of your verdicts. And these are almost the only things in our entire community that still, up to now, remain honourable and inviolate.

Does Chrysogonus really believe that even here, in this court of law, he is not without influence? Does he have ambitions to extend his power into this field as well? What a shameful and cruel indignity that would be! And, heaven knows, it is not because of any fear that he might be justified in such an assumption that the idea fills me with anger. No, what enrages me is his audacity in even venturing to entertain

1. In particular, Sulla returned the office of the judges to the senate from the knights to whom it had been transferred by Gaius Sempronius Gracchus in 123 B.C. (see above, p. 13).

2. Such as the proscriptions, and the purchase of confiscated goods.

the barest hope that he might have sufficient influence to bring about the ruin of an innocent man – when he has to deal with judges of your impeccable integrity.

I cannot believe that the nobility roused itself[1] to take possession of the state by force of arms merely in order that its members' freedmen and petty slaves should be let loose to plunder our goods and our property. If that was the object they had in mind, then I confess I was quite wrong to desire their victory as I did – crazily mistaken to approve, as a non-combatant, what they were trying to do. But if, instead, the victory of the nobility is to be regarded as a glory and a blessing to our nation and to the people of Rome, then every good and patriotic Roman must approve strongly of my criticism of Chrysogonus. For people who choose, instead, to regard any attack upon him as an injury to themselves and to their own cause have totally failed to understand what the cause really is – and they have formed a low estimate, an appropriately low estimate, of their own merits! For the cause, every time it opposes a scoundrel, becomes more and more splendid on each successive occasion; but the man who is degraded enough to give his allegiance to Chrysogonus, to imagine that there is a community of interests between the two of them, is inflicting an irreparable self-injury, because he has cut himself off from all the glory for which the cause stands.

However, I repeat that what I have just been saying was said in my own name. The national situation, my own indignant feelings, and the abominable way in which these individuals have behaved contributed to my determination to speak up. It is I who am declaring how intolerable these things are – not Sextus Roscius. He is accusing no one. Even the loss of his entire patrimony is not enough to make him complain. A

1. Or, according to an alternative reading, 'was eagerly awaited' (*expectata* instead of *experrecta* or *excitata*).

farmer and countryman with little knowledge of the world, he believes that all these actions for which you say that Sulla was responsible accorded perfectly with custom, and law, and the universal principles of equity. All he hopes for is to be allowed to leave this court exonerated of blame and cleared of this dreadful charge. If only he can get free of the baseless suspicion that hangs over his head, he declares himself willing to endure the loss of everything he possessed, and to endure it with complete equanimity.

And what I am going to say next, Chrysogonus, you will not be able to deny. Out of all his father's ample fortune Sextus Roscius has converted not a scrap to his own use. He has defrauded you of nothing whatsoever. He has yielded up to you every single thing that was his, counting it up and weighing it out with the most scrupulous good faith. He has handed over to you the very clothing which covered his back, the very ring he wore on his finger.[1] Out of all his many belongings, he has one thing and one thing only left: his own naked body. If this is all true, Chrysogonus, then my client begs and entreats you to allow an innocent man this one thing at least: that he should graciously be permitted to pass the rest of his life in destitution, supported by the assistance of his friends.

You have taken over my farms, says Roscius; I am living on other people's charity. I raise no objection, he continues, because I am resigned, and I have no alternative. My house is open to you – and closed to myself. Very well, I put up with it. My whole large household is at your disposal, while I lack even one single slave to call my own. This too I tolerate. I shall regard it as endurable. But in this case, he adds, what are all these further demands? Why do you still pursue and attack me so relentlessly? In what way do you claim I have offended against your wishes? How do I stand in the path of your ambitions? If all you were after was to commit an assassination for the sake of the spoils, you have got the spoils already, so

1. The seal-ring worn by every free Roman.

I fail to see what more you can need. Or is it a feeling of enmity that drives you on? But I can't understand how there can possibly be enmity between yourself and a man whose farms you seized before you even knew him. Or is fear, perhaps, your motive? But you can't conceivably need to fear the man whose incapacity to defend himself against these cruel wrongs is so utterly obvious. If, however, it is your acquisition of the property of the late Sextus Roscius that makes you so determined to kill his son, aren't you making it abundantly clear that you are afraid of a contingency which you must have less reason to fear than anyone in the world – that at some future date the children of the proscribed shall be given their fathers' property back?[1]

If you imagine, Chrysogonus, that the validity of your purchase will be more effectively safeguarded by my client's death than by all that Sulla has achieved,[2] you are surely misguided. But if you have no reason in the world for wishing the total ruin of this unfortunate man, if he has already handed over to you everything he possessed except the actual breath in his body, if he has not kept back so much as a single keepsake from his father's possessions, then heaven only knows what is the point of all this savage brutality, this monstrous relentlessness. I have never heard of a brigand or a pirate so utterly devoid of humanity that, when he was in a position to plunder his victim without violence, he preferred nevertheless to tear the spoils by force off the man's very limbs, amid a deluge of blood!

My client, as you know perfectly well, has no possessions at all. He dare not do a thing. He *cannot* do a thing. He has

1. Cicero means that Chrysogonus was especially safe because he was a close friend of Sulla. But in any case Sulla's laws had regulated that no children of the proscribed should ever be able to recover their ancestral property.
2. i.e., Sulla's triumph has been so complete that there is no need to fear a reaction and a consequent revival of the proscription laws.

never harboured the slightest hostility against your interests. And yet this human being, whom it is inconceivable that you should fear and entirely wrong that you should hate, whom you see to be so bereft of possessions that there is nothing left for you to take away from him any longer, is still, even now, the victim of your continued merciless attacks.

I can only assume you must regard it as outrageous that he even has enough clothes to his back to take his seat in this court – since he is the man, after all, whom you drove from his patrimony as bare as if he had come from a shipwreck. And yet you are presumably aware that he is being clothed and fed by Caecilia Metella, the daughter of Balearicus and sister of Nepos.[1] She is a lady who inspires profound respect. Her father was a famous man, her uncles illustrious, her brother highly talented. And she herself, woman though she is, has displayed virtues worthy of a man. The honour she derives from the eminence of her relations is amply matched by the distinction her own noble character confers upon them in return.

However, what you really regard as so infuriating, I suspect, is the fact that Sextus Roscius is being actively defended here in this court. But believe me, if all his friends had felt that the ties of hospitality and friendship linking them to his father made it incumbent upon them to appear today, and if they had ventured to speak out openly on his behalf, he would have enough defenders and to spare. Moreover, if each of them exacted vengeance in proportion to the greatness of the injustice, and in proportion to the damage inflicted upon our national interests by the character of this trial, then heaven knows, it wouldn't be very long before you stopped standing where you are!

As it is, however, the situation regarding the younger Sextus Roscius' defence is surely not impressive enough to kindle our opponents' indignation: they can hardly suggest

1. See above, p. 44, n. 1.

they are being overcome by undue influence. His domestic needs, it is true, are being seen to by Caecilia Metella, as I have said. And Marcus Messalla, you can see for yourselves, is looking after his interests in the Forum and in this court.[1] If Messalla were old and experienced enough, he himself would be pronouncing the defence of Sextus Roscius. But since his youthful years, combined with a natural modesty which does them credit, debar him from speaking, he has entrusted the brief to myself, in the knowledge that I felt both eager and obliged to fall in with his wishes in this way. Yet it was due to Messalla's perseverance, his efficiency, his influence, and his hard work that the fortunes of Sextus Roscius were rescued from the tender mercies of the purchasers of confiscated property, and submitted instead to the just verdicts of you judges.

It was for the sake of members of the nobility like Messalla, gentlemen, that the greater part of our nation was recently up in arms. The aim of the war was to restore to public life the sort of nobleman who would act as you see Messalla acting – who would defend, that is to say, the civil rights of an innocent person, who would stand firmly against injustice, who would show his powers by saving his fellow-men rather than by striking them down. If everyone who had been born in that walk of life were to behave as he does, our country would be suffering less from this class, and they themselves would be suffering less from the criticisms to which they are subjected.

But I must warn you that there is a particular possibility which we have to face. I refer to the possibility that we shall not be able to persuade Chrysogonus to be content with seizing all our property. He may want to make an attempt on our lives as well. Although he has taken from us everything that was

1. Probably Marcus Valerius Messalla Rufus (consul 53 B.C.). He was only about sixteen at the time of this speech – but his family was a very great one, and Sulla married his sister Valeria in this same year.

ours, it is likely enough that he still cannot be dissuaded from seeking to deprive us of that possession which is denied to no one, the light of day itself. Our goods may not be sufficient to assuage his greed; his savagery may demand the sacrifice of our life-blood as well.

If this turns out to be the case, gentlemen, then Sextus Roscius has only one hope left, and it is the same unique hope which our entire country cherishes: I mean, your own traditional kind-heartedness and mercy. If these qualities abide, then salvation may still be ours, even now. But if the cruelty which in these times stalks abroad throughout our nation should harden and embitter your hearts as well – though I cannot bring myself to believe that this will be so – then, gentlemen, we are finished. It would be better to spend one's life among wild animals than to dwell amid the savagery which will then have overwhelmed us.

Don't tell us, gentlemen, that this was the prospect for which our nation reserved your services. Don't assure us that the reason why you were chosen as judges was to inflict condemnation upon a man whom even property-dealers and assassins had not managed to kill!

At the outset of a battle, a good general very often posts soldiers on the likely line of the enemy's retreat, with the intention that they shall fall upon the fleeing foe and take him by surprise. Now, I expect the purchasers of confiscated property are hoping that you will proceed in the same sort of way. They probably imagine that the purpose for which you are sitting here is to catch the victims who have slipped through their own hands. But there they have obviously misjudged your characters. For heaven forbid, gentlemen, that this court, which our ancestors designated by the glorious name of our National Council,[1] should be regarded as positively

1. *Consilium publicum*, a name which could be applied to the court which a public official, i.e. the presiding praetor, had convened. Usually, however, the term is applied to the senate.

assisting these speculators to seize their gains. However, I am sure you understand, judges, that the manoeuvres of these individuals are aimed at nothing less than the complete elimination of the children of the proscribed by any means whatsoever, and that your sworn judgement and Sextus Roscius' trial are to be the first stages in this process.

Surely, the identification of his father's murderer could not possibly be clearer! On one side you see a specimen of these property purchasers, malignantly hostile and murderous: and he has chosen to undertake the prosecution of my client in person. On the other side, reduced to the depths of poverty, you see the murdered man's son, highly esteemed by his own relations, a person to whom not the smallest shred of guilt or even suspicion can conceivably be attached. In the whole case there is one thing and one thing only which places Roscius in peril: the fact that his father's property was sold.

But if, gentlemen, you really propose to support his enemies' cause and enable it to triumph, if the reason why you are sitting here is because of your determination that the children of those whose goods have been sold should be tried and condemned, then I beg you most earnestly to be vigilant indeed: for otherwise you will find that what you have done is to inaugurate another proscription, much more ruthless even than the last. At least that was directed against men who were capable of taking up arms. Even so, the senate refused to take responsibility for the operation, because they did not agree that a measure more severe than anything ever ordained by our ancestors should receive the sanction of our national authority.[1] But the second proscription, which I am now ·forecasting, will fall upon the children of the proscribed – upon their infant sons still in their cradles! Unless, therefore, gentlemen, you show by your verdict in this trial that you find such a prospect entirely loathsome and horrible, then heaven only

1. See last note.

knows the lamentable condition into which you will be plunging our whole country.

It is the duty of wise men like yourselves, equipped with the authority and power that have been entrusted to you, to apply the most effective remedies to the major troubles that afflict our community. Now, you are all very well aware that this state, which used to be regarded as exceptionally merciful to its external enemies, is grievously oppressed by the cruelty with which Romans themselves are being treated. Judges – it is up to you to stamp out this cruelty from our midst. Suffer it no longer to stalk abroad in our land! For it has destroyed many Roman citizens by terrible deaths. And it has had another lamentable result as well: by familiarizing us with evil in all its forms, it has stifled the sentiments of pity in the hearts of a hitherto merciful people. For when, hour by hour, we never cease seeing or hearing about some appalling deed, the constant repetition of horrors drains even the gentlest natures of every feeling of humanity.

II

IN DEFENCE OF
AULUS CLUENTIUS HABITUS

Introduction to Cicero's Speech

IN 66 B.C. *Aulus Cluentius Habitus, who belonged to a leading and ancient family of the small but important town of Larinum (Larino) 125 miles east of Rome,*[1] *was arraigned for murder before the same court that had tried Sextus Roscius fourteen years earlier, and he, too, briefed Cicero to defend him. The orator was now praetor, and was therefore chairman of another court (p. 217). He left this temporarily in order to speak on behalf of Cluentius, whom he defended in this outstandingly brilliant and enormously admired speech. Already in ancient times it was held in the highest esteem. For example, Pliny the younger (c. A.D. 61–112), in a letter written to the historian Tacitus, remarks that it is not only the longest of Cicero's orations but is generally regarded as the best.*[2] *In addition to its historical significance (p. 120), it contains, in the words of H. Grose Hodge, 'a sustained interest, a constant variety, a consummate blend of humour and pathos, of narrative and argument, of description and declamation; while every part is subordinated to the purpose of the whole, and combines, despite its intricacy of detail, to form a dramatic and coherent unit'.*[3]

Cluentius was accused of killing his stepfather Oppianicus,[4] whose

1. For the strategic importance of the roads and trails leading to Larinum, cf. E. T. Salmon, *Samnium and the Samnites*, C.U.P., 1967, p. 390 n. 2. Larinum belonged ethnically to the Oscan-speaking tribe of the Frentani but was politically separate from them.

2. Pliny the younger, *Epistles*, I, 20, 4. In spite of the length of the speech, Pliny also rightly points out that the spoken version had probably been considerably longer, like those of Cicero's other speeches.

3. H. Grose Hodge (ed.), *Cicero: the Speeches: Pro Lege Manilia etc.* (Loeb edn), Heinemann and G. P. Putnam's Sons, 1927, p. 211.

4. His full name (and his son's) was perhaps Statius Abbius Oppianicus, rather than Albius as is generally supposed, cf. P. Boyancé, *Cicéron: Discours*, Tome VIII, 1953, p. 9, n. 1.

fifth wife had been the defendant's mother Sassia.[1] *Oppianicus had met his death in about 72 B.C., and now, six years later, his son Oppianicus Junior, with Titus Attius as his spokesman, was charging Cluentius with the murder, relying to a large extent, it would appear, upon the testimony extracted from slaves.*

In order to get his client off, Cicero employs the methods of surprise – without much regard for strict relevancy – which had stood him in such good stead at the trial of Roscius. But now the shock tactics are employed more boldly still. For in the earlier speech he had at least dealt with the charge against his client, however superficially, before seeking to fasten the guilt on other relatives of the dead man. But in his present oration he does not even reach the murder charge against Cluentius, which was what the court was supposed to be hearing, until the very last of the three sections of his speech. And when he does finally come to the charge he begins, in order to distract the judges' attention, with an elaborate disquisition about the law governing the court – in apparent contradiction of his client's wish to rest his case on his innocence, and not on legal technicalities. Next follows an equally strange passage, in which it becomes clear that Cluentius is accused of two other cases of poisoning as well, his intended victims allegedly being a certain Gaius Vibius Capax and the present prosecutor, Oppianicus Junior. But Cicero dismisses both charges with extraordinary briskness and brevity (one can only assume that this was all that was expected of him), and in the former case on the basis of only the vaguest of arguments.[2]

Then, in dealing with the main charge, Cicero asks: why should

1. For the various relationships involved, see Genealogical Tables, II–V.

2. The only 'witness' produced in this part of Cicero's defence, Lucius Plaetorius (p. 230), is described in terms that suggest he was not a formal witness at all, and so could hardly substantiate Cluentius' plea. As regards the alleged attempt to poison Oppianicus Junior, however (in which, again, a witness of a kind is produced, p. 231), W. Peterson (ed.), *Cicero: Pro Cluentio*, Macmillan, 1899, p. xvi, describes Cicero's argument as 'the only satisfactory piece of evidence in the whole speech'.

Cluentius kill Oppianicus, who was already a ruined man anyway? So what reason had Cluentius either to fear him or hate him? But in reality, it would appear, Oppianicus was nothing like as badly ruined as all that,[1] and in his reference to fear and hatred Cicero has executed another of his devastating, illogical shifts, for in describing the assassinations supposedly committed by Oppianicus he had attributed the motive to greed, whereas now he describes fear and hatred as the only motives worth considering for such crimes. In dealing with this main charge Cicero does not even trouble to produce a witness at all.

Before this, the second and middle section of the oration had dealt with a number of earlier trials: these had resulted in adverse verdicts which, although the defendants were different, had caused damage to Cluentius' case in advance – quite unfairly according to Cicero.[2] But this middle section is preceded by a very long, and, it would appear, technically irrelevant 'preamble' – not much less than half the entire speech – discussing an earlier trial of 74 B.C. in which Oppianicus, some two years before his death, had himself been prosecuted by Cluentius and convicted (by the margin of a single vote) for the attempted murder of Cluentius, as well as for a variety of other crimes.[3] Like his wife Sassia, Cluentius' mother, Oppianicus had lived, if we are to believe Cicero, a life of quite appallingly murderous criminality: so complicated, in its domestic repercussions and slaughters, that the reader will find reference to the genealogical

1. The evidence is collected by G. S. Hoeningswald, *Transactions of the American Philological Association*, 1962, pp. 114ff. The alleged intended victim was probably called Capax, not Cappadox, as some manuscripts prefer.

2. On the other hand Cicero himself lays great stress on earlier trials of other defendants which (rightly, he claims) prejudiced the chances of Oppianicus in this trial of 74 B.C. (p. 149) (though it was embarrassing for him that he had defended one of them in court.

3. Cf. W. Peterson (ed.), op. cit., p. xx. For the margin, see Cicero, *In Defence of Caecina*, 29. He claimed that his vast digression about Oppianicus' trial was necessitated by the prosecutor's concentration on the same theme (p. 121).

tables unavoidable. Without such tables, the judges must have been completely at sea, and no doubt Cicero was only too glad that they should be, since, in spite of his assertions to the contrary he seems to have spread mystification quite deliberately (p. 119).[1]

The trial of 74 B.C., known after its chairman Gaius Junius as the Junius Case (iudicium Iunianum), had fallen into deep disrepute, perhaps deeper disrepute than any other legal proceedings in Roman history, since it was perfectly clear that a large number of the judges had been bribed. This, therefore, was an explosive area in which Cicero, who wanted to urge that the court's conviction of Oppianicus was correct, had to tread somewhat delicately. Moreover, there was a constitutional and political point involved. For the judges in 74 had all been senators, in pursuance of the monopoly of the judgeships granted to the senate by the dictator Sulla seven years earlier (p. 14). Since that time, however, the pro-senatorial measure of the dictator had been partly reversed by a compromise law of 70 B.C.[2] ordaining that in future only one third of the judges should be senators, the remaining two thirds being divided equally between the knights and a class which came immediately beneath them in property qualifications. So the judges whom Cicero was now addressing, in 66, came from all these three categories.

It was clear enough that he did not want to offend the senators, whose support he needed for a consulship in the near future. And,

1. These complications caused the historian J. A. Froude, *Short Studies on Great Subjects*, vol. III, to damn the speech as 'knotted, twisted and entangled'.

2. This was the Lex Aurelia of Lucius Aurelius Cotta. He himself was *nobilissimus*, and would have considered himself not so much a reformer as a Restorer of the Republic, i.e. the boundaries between *optimates* and *populares* were not always fixed or clearly defined (p. 7, n. 1). For the third class in the revised court (the *tribuni aerarii*) see A. H. M. Jones, *The Criminal Courts of the Roman Republic and Principate*, pp. 87ff.: an obsolete term may have been revived. For the lower social level of the new Bench, requiring Cicero to enter into some slightly elementary explanations, cf. M. I. Henderson in R. Seager (ed.), *The Crisis of the Roman Republic* (reprint of 1963 article), p. 71 n. 22 and p. 74 n. 42.

*in consequence, he refrained, in the present speech, from siding too
openly with the reformers, as he had, by implication, when he
criticized aspects of the Sullan regime in his speech for Roscius, and
as he had once again, this time quite outspokenly, in his famous
attack on the corrupt governor Verres in 70 B.C. which had made his
name.[1] Yet at the same time Cicero was also anxious, as part of a
lifelong policy, not to alienate the knights from whom he himself had
come. As regards the present trial, there was one point on which his
opponents the prosecutors were attacking the knights. For they were
urging, in order to be able to ruin the knight Cluentius, that one
clause of the law governing the murder court favoured the knights
unfairly. This was the provision that charges of judicial murder (of
which Cluentius had been thought guilty owing to the bribery he had
allegedly instigated at Oppianicus' trial in 74) could be lodged
against senators only, and not, that is to say, against knights.[2] Cicero,
in the interests of Cluentius, and in pursuance of his friendship with
the knights, was obliged to dissociate himself from this prosecution
view, but he does so with considerable tact; and he engages in other
balancing tricks as well.[3] For this speech came at a time when he was*

1. *Cicero: Selected Works*, pp. 35ff. This, too, was (in part) a murder
trial with Cicero as prosecutor, for his speech *Against Verres*, II, v, is
largely concerned with unauthorized executions and judicial murders
in Sicily.

2. Judicial murder figured in Sulla's law governing this court and
trial, the *Lex Cornelia de sicariis et veneficiis* (p. 17): but the reason why
it only operated against senators was because Sulla had given them a
monopoly of the judgeships, and although that had been changed (see
p. 116, n. 2), this particular clause had remained untouched. W. Peterson,
op. cit., p. xxxi, is therefore probably wrong in believing that, although
Cluentius was a knight, judicial murder was somehow made to form
part of the present formal indictment in 66 B.C. For possible deliberate
misinterpretations of the law (or charge) by Cicero, see H. Grose Hodge
(ed.), *Cicero: the Speeches: Pro Lege Manilia* etc., p. 212.

3. For example, Cicero, anxious not to make living enemies un-
necessarily, tries not to annoy the prosecutor Oppianicus Junior, a
knight, though he equally refrains from stressing the knightly origins
which he himself shared with his client and the prosecutor alike.

unwilling to commit himself to either side.[1] *And, meanwhile, his discussion of Sulla's law provided another opportunity to get involved in technical complexities which would divert the judges' attention from such awkward political issues.*

Nevertheless, Cicero could not get away from the fact that this trial of 74, when his present client, Cluentius, had prosecuted Oppianicus whom he was now accused of murdering, had been thoroughly corrupt. Since Oppianicus had been convicted on that occasion, the prosecution naturally maintained that the corruption in question was the work of Cluentius. Cicero paints Oppianicus in the blackest possible colours, and argues that it was he, Oppianicus himself, who had bribed the court that was trying him, though without success. Then he goes on to say: we agree that the court was bribed: all right then, either Oppianicus or Cluentius bribed it: since I have shown that Oppianicus bribed it, then Cluentius did not. The prosecution evidently had no idea that Cicero was going to deny that Cluentius had corrupted the court, and this came as a surprise to them.[2] *And well it might, since the orator is perpetrating a fallacy of breathtaking brazenness. For, in fact, there was a third possibility about this trial of Oppianicus in 74 B.C.: that both sides had bribed this court. Indeed, it was more than a possibility – it was nearly certain. In one of his speeches against Verres in the intervening period, Cicero himself had declared that at the trial of 74 at least one of the witnesses, Gaius Aelius Staienus, was bribed not only by one side but by both.*[3]

---

1. In this very year, however, he once again pleased knights and annoyed conservatives by supporting the potential war-lord Pompeius in his speech *On the Command of Cnaeus Pompeius (In Support of the Manilian Law)*, *Cicero: Selected Political Speeches*, pp. 33ff. But in the present trial, according to J. Humbert, *Revue des études latines*, XVI, 1938, pp. 288ff., his best hope was to play off the senators and knights among the judges against one another.

2. This is stressed by J. Humbert, *Les Plaidoyers écrits et les plaidoiries réelles de Cicéron*, Paris, 1925, pp. 114ff.; and J. van Ooteghem, *Hommages à Marcel Renard* (Collection Latomus, 102), Brussels, 1969, vol. II, p. 786.

3. Cicero, *Against Verres*, II, ii, 32, 79.

*However, Cicero passes over the logical flaw with a speed and
success which nothing less than his almost supernatural oratorical
talents could have made possible. But later on, it was said, he himself
boasted that he had successfully thrown dust in the eyes of the judges
at this trial (p. 19).*[1] *The launching of this fallacy was one of the
ways in which he did so; others were mentioned earlier. Furthermore,
his long preliminary discussion of the trial of 74, amounting to a huge
proportion of the entire speech, inevitably distracted attention from
the charges on which his present client was currently in the dock eight
years later. Another diversion was the extremely dramatic presentation of the dead Oppianicus and his wife Sassia as a pair of villains
of unspeakable character – the attacks on Oppianicus being open to
grave factual doubts,*[2] *and the onslaught on Sassia recalling standard
moral textbooks of virtue and vice.*[3] *Nor, for that matter, do Cicero's
repeated and lengthy eulogies of the character of his client, however
convincing they might have sounded to the audience, eliminate every
query and reserve from the mind of the more dispassionate reader –
who cannot help wondering whether Cluentius, if he used bribery at
the trial of 74 B.C., might not have committed other crimes as well.*

*So whether Cluentius had really murdered Oppianicus, or
arranged his murder, we cannot tell.*[4] *Nor do we know whether
Cicero believed him to be innocent: not that doubts on this score need
have prevented him from taking on the brief (p. 19). What is
certain, from his gleeful remark about deceiving the judges, is that he
won the case.*[5] *And this is not surprising, for the speech is advocacy*

1. Quintilian, *Institutio Oratoria,* II, 17, 21.

2. Cf. P. Boyancé, op. cit., p. 44, and G. S. Hoeningswald, op. cit.,
p. 113.

3. For example, the allegation that she married the murderer of her
first husband on the condition that he also eliminated his three children
is repeated by Sallust, *Catiline,* 15, 2, against another stock ogress,
Aurelia Orestilla.

4. Hoeningswald, op. cit., p. 123, thinks that he probably had.
J. Humbert, *Revue des études latines,* XVI, 1938, p. 287, also stresses the
weakness of his case.

5. Cf. van Ooteghem, op. cit., p. 787.

as well as oratory, at its highest. It was meant to be heard, not read, and its object was to convince a jury.[1]

The oration is also of the greatest historical value. Not only is it the most singular cause célèbre that has come down to us from antiquity, but it casts a unique ray of light upon the life of a small Italian town in the first century B.C. According to Cicero, it was a life of unceasing financial acquisitiveness resulting in frequent violent crimes and assassinations. No doubt he overpaints the picture, but one does not need to be bemused by his rhetoric to discern that there was something seriously wrong. The elevated, moralizing school of Roman historians, so completely represented in the next generation by Livy,[2] *never missed an opportunity of pointing out that the fine old Roman virtues of honesty, propriety, frugality, austerity, and so on, had departed from Rome, but were still to be found in the simple old-fashioned country towns of the peninsula. There are a number of things mistaken about that view. First, the old, antique Romans had in many ways been nastier than the later ones.*[3] *Secondly, to judge by Cicero – and surely, after taking a pinch of salt, we may – at least one of the country towns of his day possessed leaders whose ethical standards were no better, perhaps worse, than those of most of the contemporary ruling class in the metropolis.*[4] *We had a hint to this effect from another little place, Ameria, fourteen years earlier (p. 28). Perhaps life in the small towns had never been short of its brutish aspects. But now these had been immeasurably accentuated by the horrors of war, devastation, proscription and lawlessness which had blackened the decades responsible for men like Oppianicus and Cluentius.*

1. H. Grose Hodge, op. cit., p. 211.
2. M. Grant, *The Ancient Historians*, Weidenfeld & Nicolson, 1970, p. 233; cf. p. 229.
3. *Gladiators*, Penguin edn, 1971, p. 106.
4. Cf. van Ooteghem, op. cit., pp. 787ff.

CICERO'S SPEECH

1. The Trial and Crimes of Oppianicus

GENTLEMEN:

I noted that the prosecutor divided his speech into two parts. In one of them he was clearly relying with great confidence upon the deeply ingrained popular prejudice against the trial of Oppianicus which was held before Gaius Junius.[1] It was only in the other part of his speech that he dealt with the charge of poisoning which is relevant to the law governing this court,[2] relevant, that is to say, to the present case. And it was evident enough that he was approaching this second matter with marked reluctance and hesitation; he only tackled it at all because custom demanded that he must.

And so I too, as a counsel for the defence, will divide up my speech in the same way as he did. First I will deal with the question of prejudice arising from the trial of Oppianicus, and then I will turn to the actual charges that are before you today. And I will make it abundantly clear to everyone that it is not part of my plan either to evade the facts by suppression or to darken them by misrepresentation. But when I turn my mind to the question of how these two themes can best be developed, it becomes apparent that the second of them – the theme which comes within the scope of this tribunal appointed to try poisoning cases and is therefore the proper object of your investigation – will scarcely demand a great deal of time or oratorical effort. But as regards the other theme, the question of prejudice, the situation is entirely different. That is a matter

1. In 74 B.C., eight years earlier (p. 115).
2. The *quaestio de sicariis et veneficiis* (murder and poisoning court), established by a *Lex Cornelia* with the same designation (p. 13).

which has nothing to do with legal decisions at all. It has much more in common with the seditious agitations of public meetings than with the calm deliberations of the courts. Nevertheless, I can see very clearly indeed that it is going to cause me far the greatest amount of toil and trouble.

Yet confronted though I am with this difficulty, gentlemen, there is one thing which gives me a good deal of comfort. It is this. When a court such as your own is able to concentrate on the actual facts of a charge, you normally expect the defence counsel to provide all the refutation that is necessary. That is to say, you do not consider yourselves obliged to offer any special contribution to the defendant's acquittal over and above whatever arguments his counsel may be able to bring forward to contradict the accusations and prove his own case.

But when, on the other hand, it is a question of prejudice that is involved, you are under an obligation, before deciding between the two sides, to consider not only the pleas which the advocate has actually advanced, but also those which he *ought* to have advanced. Take this case of Aulus Cluentius. In the actual charges against him his own interests are affected, and those of no one else. But seeing that prejudice, too, is so largely involved, the matter becomes more serious, because this means that the common interest, the interest of every one of us, is at stake.

In one part of my speech, therefore, I shall have to employ the language of proof, and in the other the language of entreaty. In one, I shall only need to request your attention: in the other I shall have to appeal for your protection. For against prejudice no man can hope to make any headway at all, unless he feels assured of the sympathetic support of your eminent selves.

I confess I am at a loss how to proceed. Am I to refuse to admit there was a scandal about the bribery of Junius' court? Am I to deny that it was the topic of controversy at public meetings, and argumentation in the lawcourts, and even

comment in the senate? Can I efface from people's minds the
definite opinions they have formed on the subject, opinions
that are deeply rooted and ingrained? It would be beyond my
power. But when this disastrous slander besets my innocent
client like some consuming conflagration, a conflagration
which is perilous to our entire community, it is within *your*
power, gentlemen, to come to his aid.

In other places, all too often, it is truth which proves unable
to mobilize force and conviction. But here, in this court, the
opposite must surely be the case: wrongful prejudice is what
should prove powerless. No doubt it will have its own way at
public meetings, but in courts of law it ought to be completely
impotent. Certainly, prejudice will flourish in the minds and
words of the uninstructed – but it is the duty of trained
intellects to brush it aside. True, its first sudden onslaughts will
inevitably threaten to carry all before them. Yet later, after
time has elapsed and the facts have been duly considered, it is
surely bound to wither away. A definition of a fair trial was
handed down to us by our ancestors, and it is something to
which we should hold fast: in a lawcourt, guilt must be
punished without prejudice, and if there is no guilt, then once
again prejudice must not be allowed to rear its head.

This being so, gentlemen, before I begin to deal with the
charge itself I have certain requests to make of you. First, that
you approach the case without any preconceived opinions –
since nothing else would be fair. For if we, coming to a
tribunal of this kind, insist on basing our judgements upon
conclusions that we have previously formed ready-made in
our homes instead of deciding in accordance with the facts,
our reputations as judges will be gone. Indeed, we shall lose
the right to be called judges at all.[1] However, let us suppose
that you *have* formed a preconceived opinion all the same.
Then, in that case, what I demand is this. If you find that

1. Cicero speaks of himself as a judge because, as praetor, he was
chairman of another court (p. 113).

reasoning uproots that opinion, if rational argument under-
mines it, if truth shatters it, do not, I beg you, offer resistance
to these processes, but dismiss your preconceived opinions
from your minds – if not gladly, at least with all the impartiality at your command. And finally, as I proceed to my
refutation of each successive charge in turn, please do not store
up in your minds, as I go along, mental notes of all the
individual details you feel inclined to query. Instead, wait until
the end. Let me develop my defence in the order I choose. After
I have finished, that will be the time for you to ask yourselves
what, if anything, I may have left out.

I am extremely well aware, gentlemen, that the case I am
undertaking is one which for these eight years, year after year,
you have heard stated from the opposite viewpoint. Indeed,
public opinion has already given its outspoken verdict, and
has left my client condemned. But if the grace of heaven can
win me your favourable attention, I am certain that I shall
be able to convince you that there is nothing more damaging
in the world than this evil phenomenon of prejudice. Indeed,
once hostile prejudice has confronted an innocent man, there
is nothing he longs for more than to be put on trial – a fairly
conducted trial. Because that is the *one* way in which he will
eventually be able to find some means of putting an end to the
groundless slanders, and escaping from their clutches. That is
why, if only I can manage in this speech of mine to deal
comprehensively with all of the points at issue, one after
another, I am full of hope that this court and its judges will
by no means be the source of terror and dread to Aulus
Cluentius that his enemies expected; but will, on the contrary,
prove at long last a haven and a refuge from the storms
which have for all these years assaulted his sorely harassed
fortunes.

Before coming to the facts of the present case against
Cluentius, there are many more things that I could justifiably
say about this matter of prejudice, and how perilous it is for

every one of us. However, I do not want to delay you by dwelling on this point for too long, before I come to the actual charge. Yet at the same time, gentlemen, I must appeal to you, indeed I see I shall have to appeal to you frequently, to give me the hearing I should be entitled to expect if this was the first time the issue was being judged. Elsewhere it has been the subject of so very many 'judgements' already – all quite without validity. But this is the very first occasion when the case has come up for judgement of an authentic kind. Although the charge has been bandied around for ages, it is only today that an opportunity has at last been given to refute it. Until now, the question has always been clouded by misapprehension and bias. And so, while I reply to this accusation of so many years' standing as briefly and clearly as I can, I urge you once again, gentlemen, to give me your most meticulous attention: as I see that you have already begun to do.

Aulus Cluentius is charged with having committed judicial murder[1] – with having bribed the court in order to secure the condemnation of his allegedly innocent enemy, Oppianicus. Now, since it was this believed victimization of the supposedly guiltless Oppianicus which was the principal cause of all this relentless prejudice, I propose to prove, gentlemen, first, that no one was ever placed in the dock on weightier charges or more convincing evidence than Oppianicus was; secondly, that the judges who convicted him had already committed themselves to previous verdicts which, although directed against other defendants, affected his case so adversely that neither the same judges nor any others could possibly have voted for his acquittal. After that, I shall proceed to a further demonstration, which will, I believe, be very much what you are looking for. That is to say, I propose to concede that bribery *was* attempted at Oppianicus' trial before Junius. However, I shall then go on to show that it was employed not on behalf

1. For this concept, see above, p. 117, n. 2.

of Aulus Cluentius, but *against* him. And when I have finished you will be in a position to distinguish between the real facts of the case and the numerous errors that got attached to them, including, especially, all the fictions built up through the influence of prejudice.

The first thing that needs saying is that Aulus Cluentius had every possible reason to feel complete confidence in the case he brought against Oppianicus on that occasion. The charges were absolutely impregnable; and so were the witnesses he brought into court. At this stage, gentlemen, I had better remind you briefly of the precise nature of those charges on which Oppianicus was prosecuted and convicted. And I ask you, Oppianicus Junior who are his son,[1] to believe me when I say that I am entirely reluctant to mention this condemnation of your father, and that I only do so because my obligations and my duty towards my client offer me absolutely no alternative. After all, if I fall short of *your* hopes of me at this moment, I shall still have many future opportunities of making amends; whereas if I fail to give satisfaction to Cluentius here and now, I shall have lost the chance of doing so for ever. Besides, I cannot believe that any pleader would hesitate to defend an innocent man, who is still alive, against a man who was proved guilty and is dead. For the latter does not run the risk of any further disgrace, since he has already been convicted, or of any further sorrow, since he has died; whereas if his innocent opponent, who is still alive, suffers a legal reverse on this issue, he will be overwhelmed by the bitterest suffering and unhappiness, crushed by the gravest personal shame and dishonour.

However, I want you to realize very clearly that what made Cluentius prosecute Oppianicus was not love of litigation, nor desire for publicity, nor passion to make himself known. No, he was compelled to take this action by the abominable

1. The prosecutor in the present case: treated gently by Cicero, p. 117, n. 3.

injuries he had received, by the endless conspiracies to which
he had been subjected day after day, by deadly perils which
manifestly threatened his life. To show what I mean, I have
to start by going rather far back into the past. And when I do
this, gentlemen, I urge you not to be irritated. For after you
have learnt about the earliest stages of the story, you will find
it much easier to understand the situation we have reached at
the present juncture.

Gentlemen: Aulus Cluentius Habitus Senior, the father of
my client, was a man whose personal qualities, reputation and
birth alike combined to make him the most distinguished
person not only in the town of Larinum, to which he belonged,
but in the entire district and neighbourhood. He died during
the consulship of Sulla and Pompeius Rufus,[1] leaving a son aged
fifteen, who is my present client. Cluentius Senior also left a
grown-up marriageable daughter, who shortly after her
father's death wedded her mother's nephew, Aulus Aurius
Melinus,[2] a young man who stood high among his contempor-
aries in character and position.

The marriage was proceeding on a perfectly respectable and
happy course when suddenly there burst onto the scene the
evil passion of a woman devoid of natural human characteristics – and the results were terrible dishonour and crime. The
woman was Sassia, the mother of my client Cluentius here.
Yes, I shall go on describing her as his mother throughout this
speech: his mother she will have to be called, for even
the recital of her appalling misdeeds cannot deprive her of
the name which nature has given her. But the associations of
love and tenderness which the word normally conveys will
not fail to intensify the violent abhorrence you must feel for so
unspeakable a mother who, at this very moment as for many

1. 88 B.C.: the younger Cluentius was therefore aged thirty-seven at
the time of this case.
2. For these and other members of the family, see Genealogical
Tables, II–V.

years past, is set upon nothing less than the murder of her own son.

For what happened was that this woman Sassia, Cluentius' mother, conceived a perverted love for the young Aulus Aurius Melinus, the husband of her daughter Cluentia. At first, as best she could, Sassia somehow managed to suppress her craving, but not for long. For soon she became madly infatuated – consumed and carried away by lecherous transports against which considerations of modesty and decency counted as nothing. Family feeling, duty, public opinion, all failed to exercise the slightest restraint over her; the grief of her son, the misery of her daughter were wholly without effect. The young man was too immature to feel the strengthening influence of wisdom and understanding, and she, therefore, employing all the arts which have the power to ensnare and captivate a youth of that age, went on to complete his seduction.[1] As for her daughter Cluentia, she was not only tormented by the anguish which any woman would feel when her husband had wronged her, but found the spectacle of her own mother as his mistress so completely beyond endurance that even to utter a protest about such a horror seemed to her an unthinkable sin. She decided, therefore, that the disaster which had befallen her must remain her own secret, and so, clasped in the arms of her deeply devoted brother, who is my client, she consumed the best years of her life in tears and lamentations.

But finally, suddenly, she arranged a divorce. Now, at long last, there seemed a good chance that her troubles would come to an end; for she went away and parted from Melinus – neither sorry to do so after everything she had suffered, nor glad, since he had been her husband. But now this marvellous, exemplary mother of hers began to exult openly in her delight and to revel in the victory she had won, a victory in which it

1. This 'seduction' perhaps took place in about 86 or 85 B.C., some two years after his marriage.

was not her lusts that had been vanquished but her daughter. Unwilling, evidently, that the suspicions which were damaging her reputation should remain in any way unconfirmed, she actually gave orders that the identical marriage-bed which she herself had prepared, two years previously, for the wedding of her own daughter should now be got ready and adorned for herself, in the very home from which her daughter had been expelled and hounded out. And so mother-in-law married son-in-law, with no one to declare the omens[1] or give the bride away, amid the gloomiest forebodings from everyone.

What unbelievably atrocious behaviour that woman displayed! Indeed, her conduct must surely be quite unparalleled and unique. Her sexual desires must truly have been insatiable. Even if the might of the gods, the judgement of mankind, did not frighten her, it is strange indeed that she did not feel overawed by the torches, by the threshold of the bridal chamber which contained her own daughter's bridal bed, by the very walls themselves which had gazed upon that other union.[2] In her sensual frenzy there was no obstacle which she forebore to break through and trample down out of her way. Modesty was overcome by passionate lust, caution by unbridled recklessness, reason by mania uncontrollable.

Her son Cluentius took it badly. The disgrace had fearful repercussions upon his family, his kinsmen, and his own good name. And to add to his troubles there were his sister's daily lamentations and unceasing tears. Nevertheless, in spite of his mother's outrageous and inexcusable conduct, he decided that all he would do was to stop treating her as a mother. For if he maintained the filial relationship with his mother – whom

1. In historical Roman times soothsayers (*auspices*) still possessed a formal role in marriage rites, though they no longer played an active part. See also List of Terms (Auspices).

2. After a torch-light procession from her old home, the bride was carried over the threshold of her new one.

he could not even so much as look at any longer without feelings of profound anguish – it would have seemed as if he were not just turning his gaze upon her, but condoning what she had done.

This, then, was how the enmity between my client and his mother originated. You will understand the relevance of these events to the present case when you hear what comes next. One thing, however, I realize very clearly: when a son is on trial, it is not really regarded as correct to mention the depravity of one of his parents – however frightful his mother may happen to be. I should be unfit to conduct any case at all, gentlemen, if I, whose profession it is to defend those imperilled by prosecutions, failed to grasp a principle so deeply ingrained in the common feelings of mankind and indeed implanted in the laws of human nature itself. I entirely appreciate that people are under an obligation to pass over in silence the wrongs they have suffered from their parents, and indeed, even to endure these wrongs with resignation. Yet it still remains true, surely, that endurance and silence can only be expected up to a point: up to the point at which they still remain humanly feasible.

Throughout his entire life all the calamities that Aulus Cluentius has ever had to undergo, all the mortal menaces that have ever threatened him, all the miseries which have ever engulfed him, have been due without exception to the contrivance and instigation of his own mother. And yet, even so, he would not, today, say so much as a single word about any of these misfortunes, he would allow the veil, not perhaps of oblivion, but at least of silence, to cover every single one of them, were it not for the total impossibility, in the position in which he is placed, of maintaining such a silence. For this trial, this peril which it imposes upon him, this accusation, this host of witnesses who are shortly to appear – this whole situation, in every one of its aspects, was created by this mother of his, and is still being organized by his mother today, and promoted by all the resources and riches that she can command.

And indeed she herself has just come hastening from Larinum to Rome, in person, with the express purpose of destroying her own son. Here she is! – violent, wealthy and cruel. It is she who is directing the prosecution; it is herself who marshals the witnesses. Her son's neglected appearance and shabby clothes inspire her to feel not pity, but exultation.[1] She longs for his ruin. She is willing to squander every single drop of her own blood if only she can see his blood shed first.

If I do not succeed in convincing you, during the course of this trial, that every one of these conclusions is correct, then I grant you full liberty to declare that my introduction of this woman into the case is just a gratuitous mistake. But if, on the other hand, her actions shall stand revealed in all their horror, you will be obliged to forgive Cluentius for permitting me to reveal them. Indeed, if I had failed to reveal them, that, surely, would have been something that could never have been forgiven.

I shall now proceed to set forth briefly the charges on which Oppianicus was convicted. This will enable you both to appreciate the high-principled manner in which Cluentius behaved, and to gain insight into the circumstances which shaped his prosecution of Oppianicus. But first of all I want to show you why he brought the accusation, for then you will easily see that he was compelled to do so by sheer necessity.

What induced him to prosecute Oppianicus was the actual discovery of the poison that this man, his own stepfather, had prepared – in order to cause *his* death! This was not merely a question of surmise; there was visible and palpable proof. The resolution and scrupulous care with which Cluentius conducted the prosecution are matters of which I shall speak later on. At the moment what I want you to understand is

1. Defendants appeared in court in dirty tattered clothes in order to excite compassion.

that his one and only reason for bringing the charges against Oppianicus was that this was the only possible way in which he could escape from the mortal perils that encompassed him, and fight off the threats against his life which were maintained unremittingly day after day.

I also want to make you realize that the case against Oppianicus was so strong that the prosecutor had nothing whatever to fear, and the defendant absolutely nothing to hope for. In order to demonstrate that this was so, I will list a few of the charges which Oppianicus had to face. When you have heard them, you will none of you be surprised to learn that he took such a poor view of his chances that he took refuge in Gaius Aelius Staienus – and in bribery.[1]

There was a woman of Larinum called Dinaea. She had three sons, Marcus Aurius, Numerius Aurius and Cnaeus Magius, and she was the mother-in-law of Oppianicus who at one time was married to her daughter Magia.[2] Marcus Aurius, when he was a very young man, had been captured at Asculum during the Social War.[3] He fell into the hands of the senator Quintus Sergius (the man who was convicted in this assassination court),[4] and was cast into the slave-gaol on Sergius' estate. Marcus' brother Numerius Aurius died and left the third brother, Cnaeus Magius, as his heir. After that, Magia, wife of Oppianicus, also died; and so finally did Cnaeus Magius, Dinaea's last surviving son. Cnaeus left his property to Oppianicus Junior here, the son of his sister Magia, directing him to share it with Dinaea.

Meanwhile, however, a reliable and explicit informant came to Dinaea with news that her eldest son, Marcus Aurius, was

1. Staienus was one of the judges at the trial of Oppianicus, and was in fact apparently bribed by both sides, p. 118, n. 3.
2. For these and other names, see Genealogical Table, IV.
3. Otherwise known as the Marsian War (91–87 B.C.), p. 10. Asculum is the modern Ascoli Piceno, where the rebellion began.
4. Otherwise unknown.

still alive and was a slave in the Ager Gallicus.[1] Well, Dinaea had lost all her children: but now she was given the hope of getting one of her sons back after all. So she summoned every one of her relations, and the friends of her son, and begged them with tears to pursue the matter and track the young man down, and restore to her the only one of all her sons whom fortune, in spite of all its blows, had nevertheless consented to spare. However, soon after she had set this quest in motion she fell seriously ill. She drew up a will, in which she made her grandson Oppianicus Junior the principal heir but also left 400,000 sestertii[2] to her missing eldest son Marcus Aurius. A few days later she died. But her relatives, after her death, persevered with the search they had initiated when she was alive, and set out for the Ager Gallicus, accompanied by Dinaea's informant, to look for Marcus Aurius.

Meanwhile Oppianicus (the elder) gave proof of that evil, horrifying criminality of which you will find so many examples in his career. First of all, with the help of a friend in the Ager Gallicus, he conveyed a bribe to the man who had given Dinaea the information. Then, at the cost of a modest sum, he arranged to have Marcus Aurius kidnapped and murdered. Meanwhile the expedition which had set out to locate the murdered man and bring him home wrote back to the Aurii at Larinum, his kinsmen and theirs, stating that their search was encountering difficulties because it had become clear to them that their guide was receiving bribes from Oppianicus.

Now this letter, when it arrived, was read out aloud in the Roman Forum, in front of a large audience including Oppianicus himself. The reader of the letter was a certain Aulus Aurius, a close relation of Marcus[3] and a man of courage and

1. The Adriatic coast between Ariminum (Rimini) and Ancona, where the Senonian Gauls had formerly settled.

2. See List of Terms. The numeral is uncertain.

3. It is not clear what this relationship was. This is not the same man as Aulus Aurius Melinus.

enterprise who occupied a high position in his community. After reading the letter Aulus Aurius added, in a loud voice, that if it should ever come to his ears that Marcus had fallen a victim to murderers he would bring Oppianicus into court. In the meantime the party which had gone to the Ager Gallicus soon returned to Larinum and reported the news of the young Marcus' assassination. On receiving this news, not only the dead man's relatives but the entire population of Larinum were overwhelmed with hatred against Oppianicus and pity for the fate of the young man. Aulus Aurius, too, the man who had already given notice of his intention to prosecute, began to assail Oppianicus with loud threats, and Oppianicus fled from Larinum and took refuge in the camp of the eminent Quintus Caecilius Metellus Pius.[1] This flight was clear evidence of his guilt and guilty conscience: and indeed Oppianicus never again ventured to submit himself to the judgement of the law, or to expose himself unarmed in front of those who viewed him with such detestation.

Instead, profiting by Sulla's triumphant rule of force, he swooped down upon Larinum with an armed band, causing universal panic. Next he proceeded to depose the four prinicipal officials of the town,[2] the men their own townsmen had elected: and he announced that he and three others had been appointed in their place by Sulla himself. Sulla had also, he added, ordered him to arrange the proscription and execution not only of Aulus Aurius (who had declared his intention of bringing a capital charge against Oppianicus), but also of Aulus Aurius Melinus, his son Lucius, and Sextus Vibius (whom Oppianicus was believed to have employed as an intermediary in bribing Dinaea's informant). Thereupon all these men were brutally put to death, and their surviving

1. He had conquered most of north Italy for Sulla from the Marians (83–82 B.C.), and was consul in 80. See Genealogical Table, I.
2. The board of four of an Italian township consisted of the *duoviri iure dicundo* and the aediles.

townsfolk were left in great terror in case they too should be proscribed and executed.

Once these facts had been brought to the attention of the court at Oppianicus' trial, surely it was unimaginable that there could be any chance whatever of his acquittal? And yet these are mere trifles. Listen to the rest, and you will be surprised not that Oppianicus was eventually found guilty, but that he managed to escape this fate for so long.

First of all, consider his sheer audacity. Once he had made the decision to marry Sassia, Cluentius' mother, he had actually planned the murder of her husband Aulus Aurius Melinus as a preliminary step. Whether his effrontery in making the proposal, or her heartlessness in finally accepting it, was the more remarkable, it would be hard to say. Let me just give you an illustration of how noble and high principled the sentiments of this couple were. Oppianicus asked Sassia to marry him, and pressed his suit with great persistence. She saw nothing shocking in this shameless suggestion, and was in no way put off by its impudence; she felt no repulsion at the thought of Oppianicus' home, though it was reeking with her own husband's blood. However, she did reply that she felt reluctant to enter into this new marriage – because the bride-groom already had three sons.

Oppianicus, on the other hand, who was exceedingly eager to get hold of Sassia's money, felt quite prepared to make the necessary domestic arrangements to overcome this obstacle to his wedding. He had his baby boy, Novia's child, with him, but another of his sons, by Papia, was being brought up in his mother's care at Teanum in Apulia, which is eighteen miles from Larinum.[1] Well, at this juncture, without giving a reason, Oppianicus suddenly summoned this boy of Papia's from Teanum, a thing he had only done previously on the

1. Teanum Apulum is near the modern S. Paolo in Civitate. The other of Oppianicus' three sons was Oppianicus Junior. See Genealogical Table, III.

occasion of public games or national holidays. The unfortunate mother, suspecting no evil, sent her son along. Oppianicus left his house, giving out that he was going to Tarentum, but on that very same day the boy, who one hour before sunset had been seen in public enjoying perfect health, was dead before nightfall; and before dawn the next day the body had been cremated. As for his mother, she heard of her shattering bereavement by common gossip, before any member of Oppianicus' household had given her the news. At one and the same time she learnt that her son was dead, and that it was too late for herself to take part in his funeral. Overwhelmed with grief, she hastened to Larinum and performed the boy's rites all over again, although he was already buried.

And then, less than ten days later, Oppianicus' other son, the infant child of Novia, was murdered in his turn. Whereupon he immediately married Sassia,[1] who was in the best possible spirits and felt that all her dreams had come true. No wonder, when she found herself wooed by such an unusual sort of wedding gift, the murder of her bridegroom's own sons. Other men try to get hold of money for their children's sake. Oppianicus, on the other hand, laid hands on Sassia's money at the price of getting rid of his children altogether – which he did gladly.

Gentlemen, I see that my brief recital of these abominable crimes has shocked your humane hearts profoundly. Imagine, then, the feelings of the judges at Oppianicus' trial who had not only to listen to this account, but to pronounce their votes upon it. You, today, are hearing about a person whom you do not have to judge, who does not stand before you, who is beyond the reach of your detestation, who has paid his debts to law and nature alike – the law having punished him with exile, and nature with death. Moreover I myself, who have told you of these happenings, was no personal enemy of his; and you have not had to listen to the accounts of eye-witnesses. Besides,

1. For Sassia's matrimonial affairs, see Genealogical Table, V.

although these are all matters which could be dwelt on at great length, I have only subjected you to a brief and concise version of all that took place.

But the situation of the judges who conducted Oppianicus' trial was entirely different. They were hearing the history of a man upon whom their oaths obliged them to return a verdict, a man whose evil and depraved countenance they saw with their own eyes, a ruffian whose unutterable villainy afflicted them with loathing, a criminal who could never, they felt, be punished severely enough. The story came to them from the mouths of his actual accusers, it came to them from a mass of witnesses, it came to them from the detailed, authoritative and comprehensive speech of that profoundly eloquent orator Publius Cannutius.[1]

Now, who in the entire world, having become acquainted, in this vivid fashion, with the dreadful facts of Oppianicus' career, could conceivably still remain under the impression that his trial was a miscarriage of justice, and he himself an innocent victim?

About what remains to be told, gentlemen, I propose just to give you a summary statement. That is to say, I shall quickly bring my narrative up to the events that have a more direct and immediate bearing on the case which is being tried today. And I ask you to bear in mind that, although it is not my task to accuse Oppianicus, who is dead, nevertheless my determination to persuade you that my client did not bribe the court which condemned Oppianicus makes it absolutely necessary for me to demonstrate, as the very basis and foundation of my defence, that he was a criminal of the most dangerous possible character.

Consider the occasion when Oppianicus, with his own hands, passed a cup to his wife Cluentia, the aunt of my

1. Cicero also refers to this eloquent contemporary in his *Brutus*, 205.

client.[1] As she drank from it, she suddenly cried out that she felt a horrible pain – that she was dying. And indeed, with that cry she perished: as she screamed out those words she breathed her last. Moreover, in addition to the suspicious suddenness of her death, and the significant terms of her dying utterance, all the customary marks and indications of poisoning were detected on her corpse.

And then Oppianicus employed the very same poison to murder his own brother Gaius! Yet even this was not all. The assassination of his brother was surely a deed which might have seemed to exhaust the possibilities of crime. Yet it is also necessary to add that he had paved the way to that monstrous act by others before it. Auria,[2] the wife of his brother Gaius, had been pregnant, and her confinement was believed to be at hand. So Oppianicus administered poison to her as well, in order that the child she was expecting from his brother should die with herself. It was only after this that he turned his attention to his brother Gaius. Gaius drained the fatal draught, and then, as he lamented the destruction that had overwhelmed himself and his wife, he decided to change his will; but in the very act of declaring this intention he fell down dead. The reason why his wife had been murdered by Oppianicus was to prevent her from bearing offspring who would exclude him from his brother's inheritance.

In this way, the murderer robbed Gaius' child of life even before nature had brought it to the light of day. Even the protection of their mother's own body had not availed to rescue Oppianicus' nephews from his murderous designs. He stopped at absolutely nothing. There was nothing in the whole world that he held sacred.   *

1. The first of Oppianicus' wives (not Cluentius' sister of the same name, who was married to Aulus Aurius Melinus). See Genealogical Table, II, III.

2. Not the same as Sassia's daughter Auria who married Oppianicus Junior. See Genealogical Table, III.

I remember a case that came up when I was in Asia. A woman of Miletus was condemned to death because, after accepting a bribe from her late husband's secondary heirs,[1] she had taken drugs to procure an abortion. Her condemnation was entirely justified, because she had deprived the father of his hopes for the future, prevented him from perpetuating his name, dashed away the support on which his family relied, cheated his house of its expected heir, robbed the state of a citizen. Then how much greater was the punishment that Oppianicus deserved, after he committed the same crime! For when the woman of Miletus did violence to her body, it was at least herself that she made suffer, whereas Oppianicus, when he too killed an unborn infant, inflicted pain and death upon another living person. Most men would find it hard enough to murder a number of different people, one after another. Only Oppianicus was capable of committing a multiple murder by the dispatch of one single victim!

However, Cnaeus Magius, the uncle of Oppianicus Junior, had discovered all about this succession of savage murders. When, therefore, he himself fell dangerously ill, and proposed to make his sister's son Oppianicus Junior his heir, he called a meeting of his friends. After they had assembled, in the presence of his mother Dinaea he asked his own wife Papia if she was pregnant.[2] She replied that she was; and on hearing this he requested her, following his death, to live with her mother-in-law Dinaea until such time as the child was born.[3] He also urged her to take every possible precaution to ensure that the baby she had conceived should be brought safely to

1. i.e. those who had been named heirs in the event of her having no surviving children.

2. For these persons see Genealogical Table, III, cf. IV.

3. In the Latin, Dinaea is described as her mother-in-law 'at that time', i.e. while Cnaeus Magius was still alive, since after his death his wife would not, by Roman custom, be looked upon as a member of his family.

birth. Then, with the same purpose in mind, he left her a large sum of money through his son, if a son should be born, but nothing at all if no son were born – in which case a secondary heir would receive the inheritance. Cnaeus Magius' suspicion of Oppianicus emerges very clearly from all this. And it emerges again from his next action. For although he had made Oppianicus' son, Oppianicus Junior, his heir, he pointedly refrained from nominating Oppianicus himself as the young man's guardian.

Now listen to what Oppianicus proceeded to do after that – and you will see that the dying Cnaeus Magius, in spite of all his precautions, had not looked far enough ahead after all. A legacy, as we have seen, was due to Papia through her son, if a son should be born to her. After Cnaeus Magius' death, however, this legacy was paid to her by Oppianicus himself, although she was not yet entitled to it. But payment of a legacy was hardly the right term for this transaction. It would more fittingly be described as the purchase of an abortion. For when she accepted this fee, as well as a considerable number of other gifts which were read out from Oppianicus' accounts at his trial, Papia succumbed to greed and permitted the promise of her womb, which her husband had entrusted to her special care, to go on sale and be sold to the unspeakable Oppianicus. That, you would think, was as bad a crime as anyone could possibly commit. But wait for the sequel. For then this woman, whose absolute duty it was, in accordance with her late husband's solemn plea, to refrain from setting foot inside any house whatever except her mother-in-law's for the whole of the next ten months,[1] proceeded in less than five months after her husband's death to give herself in marriage to Oppianicus.

It should be added, however, that the union did not last long. For its bond was not the sanctity of the matrimonial state, but merely companionship in crime.

1. Ten lunar months was considered the normal period of pregnancy.

Again, take the murder of Asuvius, the rich young man of Larinum. When it took place what a scandal it caused, and how everybody talked about it!

There was a man called Avillius at Larinum, a degraded, destitute scoundrel who possessed a certain talent for pandering to the sexual tastes of adolescents. By his flattering, obsequious attentions, this individual managed to insinuate himself thoroughly into Asuvius' confidence. Oppianicus knew this, and rapidly concluded that he might well be able to make use of Avillius as a siege-engine to overcome the juvenile Asuvius, whose family property he, Oppianicus, would then be in a position to take by storm. The plan was concocted at Larinum, but afterwards it was decided to change the scene to Rome. For whereas solitude had provided the best environment for the hatching of the plot, they felt that the crowded city lent itself better to its execution.

So when Asuvius set out for Rome Avillius accompanied him, and Oppianicus followed close behind them. The life they then proceeded to lead at Rome, with all its parties and debaucheries and grossly extravagant expenditure, with Oppianicus, moreover, not merely aware of what was going on but actively aiding and abetting and personally taking part in their festivities, would take too long to describe, especially as I want to get on to quite other matters.

The young Asuvius had spent the night with some prostitute, and was lingering on at her house upon the following day. At this point Avillius, by prior arrangement with Oppianicus, pretended that he was feeling very unwell, and declared that he wanted to make his will. Oppianicus collected witnesses,[1] choosing men who would not be likely to know either Asuvius or Avillius personally. Then, in front of these

1. There were two forms of a will, 'civil' and 'praetorian'. According to the praetorian form, seven Roman citizens were required to witness the testator's signature, to sign the document themselves, and to affix their seals.

witnesses, he addressed Avillius by Asuvius' name: and it was in Asuvius' name that the will was signed and sealed. After that, the witnesses departed. Avillius, however, promptly recovered from his fictitious illness, and shortly afterwards Asuvius was taken for a walk, ostensibly to the Gardens, but actually to certain sandpits outside the Esquiline Gate. There he was set upon and butchered.

For a couple of days there was a search for him. But he could not be traced in any of the places where his habits led people to think he might be; and meanwhile Oppianicus kept saying in the Forum at Larinum that he himself and some of his friends had recently witnessed the missing man's will. It was widely known, however, that on the day when Asuvius was last seen, Avillius had been in his company; people could vouch for this from their own observation. In consequence, the freedmen of Asuvius and certain of his friends now proceeded to break in upon Avillius, and took him off to the tribunal of Quintus Manilius, who at this time was one of the three commissioners of police.[1] Thereupon, although no one had supplied evidence or information against him, Avillius, terrified by the knowledge of his crime, immediately disclosed the entire story which I have just outlined to you, and confessed he had murdered Asuvius on Oppianicus' instigation.

Oppianicus was lurking in his home, but Manilius dragged him out and had him confronted by Avillius, who had given him away. You will not be surprised, however, to hear what happened next. Most of you know Manilius. Ever since he was a boy, all honourable activities, creditable pursuits, the rewards that come from a good reputation, have had no meaning for him whatsoever. After being nothing better than a wanton and unsavoury buffoon, he had been elevated, in

1. The *tresviri capitales*, who in addition to keeping the peace in the streets assisted the praetors in their judicial functions, e.g. in making preliminary investigations.

time of civil strife,[1] to a seat on the very same tribunal[2] before which he himself had so often been haled as a defendant amid the revilements of the mob. Such was the man who, at this juncture, came to an understanding with Oppianicus, accepted his bribe, and abandoned the case against him – although he had already agreed to handle it, and the facts involved were crystal clear. It was not until Oppianicus' later trial that this charge relating to Asuvius' death was proved, not only by the evidence of Avillius himself, but by a large number of other witnesses as well. This evidence clearly demonstrated that the first and foremost of the guilty parties was Oppianicus – whom the prosecutors in the present case describe as the pathetic, innocent victim of corruption!

And is it not also perfectly obvious, Oppianicus Junior, that your grandmother Dinaea, who made you her heir, was yet another of your father's victims?

He arranged for her to be seen by that doctor of his, that individual whose talents had been so thoroughly well tested on previous occasions and had earned him such numerous successes – by which I mean that Oppianicus had employed him to commit such a large number of murders. Dinaea, however, cried out that she absolutely refused to be looked after by the doctor whose attentions had lost her every one of her children.[3] So instead Oppianicus hastily got in touch with a certain Lucius Clodius, an itinerant quack from Ancona who happened to have come to Larinum at that moment. What they agreed is recorded in Oppianicus' own accounts: he settled with this individual for two thousand sestertii. Lucius

1. This may refer to the disturbances provoked by the consul Marcus Aemilius Lepidus after Sulla's death in 78 B.C.

2. Literally 'column', i.e. the Maenian column in the Forum beside which the *tresviri capitales* had their tribunal.

3. But all that Cicero alleges against Oppianicus in this connexion, up to the date of Dinaea's death, the fact is that Cnaeus Magius regarded him with suspicion at the time when he was making his will; p. 140.

Clodius was pressed for time, since he had numerous other market towns to visit, so he dealt with the job the instant he was brought in. He finished the woman off with his very first dose, and then moved away from Larinum without further delay.

Earlier on, when Dinaea was making her will, Oppianicus, who had formerly been her son-in-law,[1] got hold of the document and rubbed out the legacies with his finger.[2] But feeling it best, once she was dead, to make certain that these rather numerous erasures should not give him away, he had the will copied onto another document, on which he arranged for the seals of the witnesses to be forged.

I am deliberately omitting a mass of details, since I am afraid that even those I have just supplied may already seem all too many. But I do want you to realize that Oppianicus always remained entirely true to his natural character, at other periods of his life as well as those I have been telling you about. For example, the town council at Larinum decided, unanimously, that he had falsified the public records of the local censors.[3] No one would dream of entering into any financial arrangement with him, or indeed would conduct any transaction with him whatsoever.[4] Out of all his numerous kinsmen and connexions, not a single one ever appointed him the guardian of any of their children in their wills. To pay him a visit, or have a chat with him, or meet him on a social occasion, was

1. As husband of Magia, see Genealogical Table, IV.

2. Wills were written with a stilus on waxed tablets. Falsification was punishable under the *Lex Cornelia testamentaria* of 81 B.C.

3. In earlier periods the Roman censors (see List of Terms) had sent deputies to the Italian municipalities to perform censorial duties there. In the course of the first century B.C., however, the municipalities entrusted local censorial duties to their own principal officials, the *duoviri iure dicundo*, every five years, and on these occasions they were known as *quinquennales* (or *censores*).

4. Not, apparently, quite true: see p. 228.

regarded as exceedingly inadvisable. Everybody shrank away from him and detested him, everybody kept clear of his path, just as if he was some nasty and dangerous wild animal, or a contagious disease.

And yet, even so, in spite of all this individual's criminal savagery and general vileness, Cluentius would still never have prosecuted him, gentlemen, if only he had been able to avoid such a step without at the same time sacrificing his own life. Certainly Oppianicus was his enemy. But he was also his stepfather. Certainly Cluentius' mother was a brutal woman who loathed her son. But she was also his mother. Besides, no one could possibly have been more averse from the role of accuser than Cluentius – by nature, by inclination, and by his entire way of life. But when he was faced with the alternatives either of bringing a wholly legitimate charge, which his duty required of him, or of dying a premature and unmerited death, he chose to bring the charge to the best of his ability rather than allow himself to be done away with.

And now I will prove to you that what I have just been saying is the truth. For I am going to tell you about a crime in which Oppianicus was caught manifestly guilty and red-handed. The story cannot fail to convince you that the charge my client brought against him, and the conviction in which it resulted, were both utterly and completely justifiable and right.

At Larinum there are official priests of Mars known as Martiales. They are consecrated to the service of the god by the ancient religious traditions of the local population. These priests are quite numerous, and like the large numbers of Servants of Venus in Sicily[1] they are regarded as belonging to the household of the deity.

In spite of this situation, however, Oppianicus began to maintain that the Martiales were all free men and Roman

1. The Venerei of the Temple of Venus (Aphrodite) at Eryx in north-west Sicily.

citizens. The town council of Larinum and all the people of the town were very upset, and appealed to Cluentius to take the matter up and oppose Oppianicus on behalf of the community. Cluentius had always held aloof from matters of this kind. Nevertheless his position, the antiquity of his family, and his conviction that he had come into the world not merely for his own advantage but also to serve the interests of his fellow-citizens and other friends, combined to make him feel that the unanimous wishes of the people of Larinum must not be disappointed.

And so he accepted the case; and it was duly transferred to Rome. There, day after day, the vigorous dispute between Cluentius and Oppianicus continued, and great determination was displayed on either side.[1] Oppianicus possessed a bitter, brutal nature, and his mad ferocity was further inflamed by the violent hatred which his wife, Sassia, felt towards Cluentius, though he was her own son. She and Oppianicus felt it imperative that he should be prevented from taking up the case of the Martiales. And behind this lay another and more powerful motive, which appealed with particular force to the vigorous acquisitive instincts of Oppianicus. For up to the time of Oppianicus' trial, Cluentius never made a will.[2] To his mother, being such as she was, he had not felt able to bring himself to leave anything at all – and yet he felt equally reluctant to draw up a will from which one of his parents was wholly excluded. He made no secret of this dilemma, so that Oppianicus knew all about it: and Oppianicus also saw clearly that, once Cluentius was dead, all his property, since he was intestate,

1. This is the only evidence Cicero offers for the allegedly long-standing and commonly known enmity between Oppianicus and Cluentius.

2. Intestacy was much more frequent in the Roman world than has been thought: cf. D. Daube, *Roman Law: Linguistic, Social and Philosophical Aspects*, Edinburgh, 1969, pp. 71ff. If Cluentius had died intestate in 75 or 74 B.C. (before the laws of intestacy were modified), his heir would have been his mother.

would pass to his mother.[1] When this had happened, the time would then be ripe for Oppianicus to add her to his list of murders, since by that time her fortune would have become larger than it was now – and the risks would be smaller, since she would no longer have a son to protect her.

So with these motives to urge him on, listen next to how he tried to get rid of Cluentius by poison.

There were twin brothers at Aletrium,[2] Gaius and Lucius Fabricius. They resembled each other closely both in appearance and in character. But they differed markedly from their fellow-townsmen. For the latter, every one of you must be very well aware, are people of the most consistently excellent reputation, who lead thoroughly respectable and orderly lives. The two Fabricii, on the other hand, were at all times intimate friends of Oppianicus. Now I am sure you appreciate the extent to which similarity of personal tastes and personal characteristics cements any friendship. The Fabricii based their lives on the assumption that nothing whatever that brings profit is impermissible. Whatever kind of swindling or trickery cropped up – fraudulence against minors or anything else – it was always they who proved to be behind it. Their viciousness and depravity were common knowledge. That is why Oppianicus had for so many years past been doing everything he could to cultivate their friendship. By this time Lucius Fabricius had died. But Gaius was still alive, and Oppianicus now decided to use him as his instrument in the plot he was concocting against my client.

Cluentius was not well at the time, and his doctor was a certain Cleophantus, a reputable person of good professional status. But Cleophantus had a slave called Diogenes, and it was he whom Fabricius now began to induce, by means of promises and bribes, to administer poison to Cluentius. How-

1. Cf. p. 151.
2. The modern Alatri; a town in the territory of the Hernici, about fifty miles east of Rome.

ever, this slave was by no means a fool, and as it turned out he was a decent and honest person as well. For while he avoided rejecting Fabricius' suggestions openly, he repeated them to his master – who duly informed the intended victim. Cluentius immediately reported the whole matter to a Roman senator who was a close friend of his, Marcus Baebius;[1] and I am sure you remember what an honourable, wise and scrupulous man he was. The advice Baebius gave Cluentius was to buy the slave Diogenes from Cleophantus, since then it would be much easier either to prove the charge against Fabricius on Diogenes' information, or to demonstrate that Diogenes was not telling the truth. And so, to cut a long story short, Diogenes changed hands. A few days later the poison was prepared; and Cluentius made arrangements for a number of reliable men to conceal themselves at an appropriate spot. Then, at the critical moment, out of their hiding place they burst. And they caught a freedman of Fabricius, named Scamander, actually in possession of a sealed package containing the money which was being paid over for the deed.

Now who in heaven's name, after learning of this incident, could still persist in claiming that Oppianicus had been made the innocent victim of a miscarriage of justice? On the contrary, he was quite obviously the most guilty and criminal scoundrel who has ever been put into a dock. Take just this one charge by itself. All the cleverness and eloquence in the world, the most brilliant defence thought up by any advocate you might like to name, would be utterly incapable of refuting it.[2] And this being so, no one on earth, once he had learnt of what happened, once he realized how the crime was detected in the very act, could deny that it confronted Cluentius with

1. Unknown.
2. Cicero is greatly embarrassed in this section because he himself had defended Scamander at his trial, and he wishes it to be understood that even he felt himself unequal to the hopeless task.

simple alternatives: either he must prosecute, *or he would be the next to die.*

Gentlemen, I expect I have said enough to prove that Oppianicus was indicted upon charges on which honest acquittal would have been quite out of the question. But I now want to let you know something else: the developments preceding his indictment were such that he was already, virtually, a condemned man, indeed a man condemned twice over, even before he himself was ever put on trial.[1]

The first person to be prosecuted by Cluentius was Scamander, Fabricius' freedman in whose hands the poison had actually been found.[2] The court that tried Scamander was completely unbiased, and no suspicion of bribery arose. The case the judges were called upon to consider was entirely straightforward, the facts were established, there was one charge and one only. And so at this juncture Fabricius, only too well aware that the conviction of this freedman would involve himself in a precisely similar predicament, recalled that I was a neighbour of the people of Aletrium – indeed most of them are close friends of mine – and so he decided to bring a large deputation from the place to see me in my house. Their opinion of Fabricius, of course, was what it could not fail to be. Nevertheless, because he was their fellow-townsman they felt it was their plain duty to help him by whatever means they could. Consequently they called upon me to come to their rescue and undertake the defence of Scamander, realizing that the result of his trial would decide his patron Fabricius' fate as well. Now, these excellent men were my very good friends, and I did not feel able to refuse any request from

1. i.e. by the condemnation first of Scamander and then of Fabricius. Cicero assumes, without explanation, that their guilt involves the guilt of Oppianicus; cf. below, p. 155.

2. But, just before, Cicero has said that Scamander was caught with the money, not the poison (p. 148). Elsewhere he suggests he was caught with both (p. 152).

such a quarter. I had no clearer idea than they had, when they urged me to take on the case, how damaging and convincing the accusation was. So I promised them everything they wanted.

Then Scamander was cited as defendant, and his trial began. The counsel for the prosecution was that exceptionally able and experienced pleader Publius Cannutius. As far as Scamander was concerned, Cannutius limited his charge to a few words: *the poison was found on his person.*[1] But it was against Oppianicus that he directed all the weapons of his attack, explaining the motives behind his plots, underlining his friendship with the Fabricii, describing his whole career of criminal violence, and finally, after a diversified and formidable survey of every aspect of the charge, reaching his climax with a description of how the poison was actually discovered.

Then I rose to make my reply. I was filled with anxiety, uneasiness, apprehension. I am always very nervous when I begin a speech. Every time I get up to speak I feel as if it is I myself who am on trial, not merely for my competence but for my integrity and conscience as well. I fluctuate between two fears: either I shall be claiming more than I can achieve, which would be impudent, or I shall not be making the best of my case, which would be a blameworthy act of negligence, a failure to meet my obligations. And so it was on this occasion, too. I felt desperately agitated, overcome by every sort of terror. If I said nothing, I was afraid I should be judged the feeblest kind of speaker. But if I said a lot – my case being as weak as it was – I would be regarded as altogether exceeding the bounds of decency.

Finally I pulled myself together. I must take a determined line, I decided; for I realized that if a young pleader, as I was at that time, did not altogether fail one of his clients who was in the dock even though the client's case was not a strong one, he was generally regarded as not having done too badly. And

1. Literally, 'the poison was detected.'

so I did my best. I fought with every weapon that came to hand, and exploited all the legal devices and evasions I could possibly think of. The result was, though I say so with due modesty, that no one could possibly have complained that I was letting my client down.

And yet, every time I seemed to have got a grip on some argument, the prosecutor managed to wrench it out of my hand! If I challenged him to point to any unfriendliness between Scamander and Cluentius, he was perfectly prepared to admit that there was no such thing – but he immediately went on to say that Oppianicus, for whom Scamander was working, had been and still was Cluentius' bitterest enemy. Or if I argued that Scamander did not stand to gain anything from Cluentius' death, the prosecutor freely admitted that this was so – but pointed out that when Cluentius died all his property would go to his mother Sassia, the wife of Oppianicus, a wife-murderer of no mean experience. And when I next put forward the argument, which has always been considered perfectly respectable when one is defending a freedman, that Scamander was well thought of by his former slave-master, the prosecutor again conceded that this was perfectly true – but he would like to ask, he added, whether anyone thought at all highly of the patron. And finally, when I turned to the trap which Diogenes had enabled us to set for Scamander, and when I made an effort to explain that what Diogenes was going to hand over to the freedman was not poison at all, but medicine – bought in some entirely irrelevant and ordinary connexion – he asked why, in that case, Scamander chose such a deserted spot to come to, and why he came there all by himself, and why his sealed package contained money!

Moreover, at this juncture the wreckage of my case was completed, because of testimonies provided by witnesses of unimpeachable integrity. First Marcus Baebius gave evidence that it was he who had suggested that Cluentius should purchase Diogenes, and that he had been present in person when

Scamander was caught with the poison and the money. Then Publius Quinctilius Varus,[1] a much respected man of the highest principles, likewise testified to the plot that had been formed against Cluentius, and announced that Cleophantus had told him about the attempt to bribe Diogenes, immediately after this had occurred.

Yet although this was a trial in which the man who was being prosecuted, and whom I was defending, was ostensibly Scamander, there is no doubt that he was the defendant in name only. The real defendant, the man whom Scamander's trial, at every stage, really threatened with condemnation, was Oppianicus. Indeed, he himself made not the slightest secret of this, and was entirely unable to conceal it. He was constantly in court, soliciting support the whole time, and throwing all the energy and influence he could muster into the struggle. Indeed, in the end he actually came and sat down on these very benches reserved for the defence, as if it were he himself who was being tried – a performance which did Scamander's cause no good whatever. It was towards Oppianicus, not Scamander, that the eyes of all the judges were constantly turned. And even if his guilt may have been only a matter of suspicion until this moment, the terror and agitation he now proceeded to display, the nervous and anxious expression on his face, his frequent changes of colour, replaced suspicion by impregnable certainty.

When the time came for the judges to consider their verdict on Scamander,[2] the president of the court, Gaius Junius, in accordance with the appropriate Cornelian Law which was then in force, asked the defendant whether he wished them

1. Possibly the same as the Publius Quinctilius who had been assessor to the judge in the trial of Publius Quinctius, defended by Cicero in 81 B.C.

2. Cf. above, p. 16. It is not known whether the judges retired before registering their verdicts. It is possible that they voted forthwith.

to give their votes secretly or in public.[1] On the advice of
Oppianicus, who pointed out that Junius was a friend of
Cluentius, Scamander decided in favour of a secret ballot.
Then the judges proceeded to register their verdicts. By every
vote except one – which Gaius Aelius Staienus later acknowledged to be his – Scamander was pronounced guilty, without
the necessity for a second hearing.[2]

Every single person who was in court at the time realized
that this conviction of Scamander implied a judgement against
Oppianicus also. The whole point of Scamander's condemnation was that the poison which had been procured was
intended for Cluentius: and no suspicion that Scamander
wanted to murder Cluentius purely on his own account ever
occurred to anyone, or could possibly have done so. This
being the situation, the result of the trial left Oppianicus
virtually condemned in everyone's eyes, though the official,
legal pronouncement of his guilt still remained for the future.
Yet, even so, Cluentius did not have him put on trial at once.
For first he wanted to find something out. What he wanted to
test was whether judges were accustomed to reserve their
severity for the actual persons whom they knew to have been
caught with poison in their possession, or whether they
considered that the planners and accessaries of crimes of this
kind were equally deserving of punishment. With this in mind,
he lost no time in bringing a charge against Gaius Fabricius,
since Fabricius was a friend of Oppianicus and could therefore
be assumed to be his accessary. And, in view of the obvious
relevance of Fabricius' case to the recent trial of Scamander,

1. A *Lex Cassia* of 137 B.C. had made the secret ballot obligatory in
criminal trials, but evidently a *Lex Cornelia* of Sulla had made this
optional. The secret ballot became obligatory again shortly before the
trial of Cluentius.

2. In criminal courts (other than the extortion court), a second hearing
was provided when a majority of judges at the first hearing voted 'not
proven'.

Cluentius succeeded in getting it placed at the very top of the list.

On this occasion Fabricius did not, as before, bring his neighbours and friends from Aletrium to visit me. Indeed, he found himself unable to secure their services any longer, as witnesses either to his innocence or his character. On the occasion of Scamander's trial, at a time when nobody yet knew how the matter was going to turn out, it had been their opinion – which I shared – that considerations of humanity required us to support the cause, even when somewhat suspect, of a man with whom we possessed a connexion. But once the verdict on Scamander had been reached we felt it would be highly improper to aim at a reversal. Consequently Fabricius, in distress and desperation – his case being what it was – felt compelled instead to resort to the brothers Caepasius,[1] industrious advocates who regarded any available chance of pleading in court as a compliment and an asset. It does seem very unfair that, when a man is physically sick, a really serious illness is thought to require a proportionately excellent and eminent doctor, whereas when someone is in court on a capital charge, a thoroughly bad case can only attract an advocate who is proportionately bad and obscure! But perhaps the reason may be this: a doctor only provides his skill, but counsel has to stake his reputation as well.

Anyway, Fabricius was taken to court and the proceedings began. Cannutius led for the prosecution with only a short speech, because he considered the case already prejudged by the trial of Scamander. Then the elder Caepasius began to speak. He opened with a long and far-fetched introduction, which at first seemed to be receiving an attentive hearing. Oppianicus started to feel less dejected and depressed. Fabricius, too, began to cheer up. He failed, however, to realize that what was absorbing the attention of the judges was not the eloquence of the speaker but the outrageous brazenness of his

1. Gaius and Lucius Caepasius.

plea. And when Caepasius moved on to deal with the facts of the case, he gratuitously added fresh weaknesses to those that were already there. Obviously, he was doing his best. All the same, it really appeared at times as if, far from conducting Fabricius' defence, he was acting in collusion with the prosecution.

For example, priding himself on a very clever turn of phrase, he drew deep from the inmost storehouse of his craft, and the following weighty words emerged: 'Look, gentlemen, upon the fate of mortal men! Look upon their dubious and diverse destinies! Look upon the advancing years of Gaius Fabricius.'[1] And after he had finished embellishing his speech with all these 'looks', he took a look himself. But what he saw, when he looked, was that Fabricius' seat was empty; he had left his place with hanging head, and had gone away. Whereupon the judges burst into laughter. The advocate lost his temper, furious because he could not finish his series of 'looks', so that his speech was ruined. Indeed, he actually seemed on the point of going in pursuit of Fabricius and bringing him back to his seat by the scruff of his neck, so that he could carry on with his peroration according to plan.

Well, Fabricius was found guilty: first, as I have just suggested, by the telling verdict of his own conscience, and then subsequently by the weight of the law and the votes of the judges. After that, what more needs to be said about the character of Oppianicus, or his trial? For the next thing that happened was that he himself was arraigned before the very same board of judges, after their two previous verdicts had virtually pronounced him guilty already. And these judges, whose condemnation of Fabricius and his henchman, Scamander, had made it so inevitable what their decision about Oppianicus had to be, placed his case at the head of the list.

1. The Latin word *respice*, 'look back', also means 'have some regard for', 'take into account'.

The offences he was charged with were a formidable array. They included not only those crimes that I have briefly indicated already, but a great many others as well, which I propose to pass over in silence. Since the very same members of the court had already convicted his agent Scamander and his accessary Fabricius, one is really inclined to ask whether it was more to be wondered at that Oppianicus was convicted or that he had ventured, in the first place, to contest the case at all. Surely the judges were absolutely compelled to convict him. Even if, for a moment, we wanted to imagine that they had been quite wrong to condemn Fabricius and Scamander, consistency would still have made it inevitable that they must stand by their previous decisions when they came to Oppianicus. Other judges, when they reach a verdict, take meticulous care to ensure that it does not clash even with the decisions already given by quite different courts. So the judges called upon to try Oppianicus could scarcely be expected to reverse verdicts which *they themselves* had pronounced! And once they had convicted both Fabricius' freedman, because he had been the agent who carried out the crime, and Fabricius himself because he had acted as an accessary, it was manifestly out of the question to acquit the man who had been the leader and architect of the whole abominable enterprise. Such an acquittal would have meant that the courts of that day, composed as they were of judges selected wholly from among the members of the senate,[1] could no longer be described as merely the targets of misplaced criticisms, but would have been branded with real and total disgrace, overwhelmed with such infamy and scandal that it would be out of the question for anyone to speak in their favour.

For what could the judges have replied, if someone had asked them: 'You found Scamander guilty: on what charge?' 'The charge,' they would have answered, 'was intending to

1. At the time of Oppianicus' trial the judges had all been senators, as ordained by Sulla; see above, p. 14.

kill Cluentius by poison, administered through the doctor's
slave.' 'What was Scamander proposing to gain by Cluentius'
death?' 'Nothing, but he was the tool of Oppianicus.' 'And
you also condemned Gaius Fabricius: what was the charge in
this case?' 'Since Fabricius was a very close friend of Oppianicus, and since Fabricius' own freedman was caught in the act
of committing the crime, it would have been the reverse of
plausibility to suppose that he himself was not a party to it.'
Quite so. And in consequence, if they had then gone on to
acquit Oppianicus and had thus flown in the face of what were,
in effect, his twofold previous convictions – consisting of
verdicts that *they themselves* had given – then indeed no one in
the whole world would have failed to denounce the utter
degradation of the courts, the complete inconsistency of the
successive decisions and the lamentable capriciousness of the
judges.

If you now see what my whole speech has aimed at establishing,
that Oppianicus could not conceivably have been found anything other than guilty at his trial, especially as he was tried
by the very same judges whose two previous verdicts had
already thoroughly committed them to convicting him, then
you must also, surely, appreciate a further point: that Oppianicus' prosecutor on that occasion, my present client Cluentius,
could not have had any possible motive for bribing the court.

For I want to ask you certain questions, Titus Attius. Setting
aside all other considerations for the moment, I demand that
you should tell me whether you really believe that Fabricius
and Scamander were wrongfully convicted, and whether you
maintain that at their trials, too, the judges were bribed.
Before you answer, remind yourself that Scamander found
no one to vote for his acquittal except Staienus alone: and that
Fabricius virtually condemned himself by his own withdrawal
from the court. And if, therefore, you reply that their
convictions were justifiable, then I want you to indicate the

offences for which they were found guilty. The only allegation against them, surely, was that they had procured poison to assassinate Cluentius. The only matters under discussion at both of their trials were these plots made against Cluentius by Oppianicus with the help of Fabricius. You will find that there was no other issue involved, judges, absolutely none whatever. We have our memories to rely upon; and there are the public records too.[1] If I am mistaken, contradict me: read out the evidence of the witnesses. Inform the court, if you can, what charges, or even what aspersions, the defendants at these two trials were called upon to face over and above this single issue: Oppianicus' attempt to commit murder by poison. And I could go on at length listing all the reasons why these verdicts against Fabricius and Scamander were wholly inevitable.

However, I know there is one thing you are expecting me to speak about, gentlemen, and I will meet your impatience halfway. No one has ever received a more courteous and attentive hearing than you have been giving me today; and that is something which I deeply appreciate. Nevertheless, although you have not said so, I am aware that all this time you have been waiting for me to deal with quite another aspect, and it is an aspect which, at first sight, seems to present an obstacle to my case. 'Yes, this is all very well,' you are complaining, 'but do you really propose to deny that the court which tried Oppianicus was bribed?' No, gentlemen, I do not. *But I deny that the man who bribed it was Cluentius.*

Who did bribe it, then, you naturally ask. And here I have three points to make. First, even if the result of that particular trial had not been a certainty already, it would still be more reasonable, on general grounds, to suppose that the bribery was undertaken by the defendant, who had every reason to fear conviction, rather than by the prosecutor, who had nothing in the world, apart from his adversary's acquittal, to

1. This indicates that the official records (*tabulae publicae*) included summaries of criminal trials.

feel afraid about. Secondly, since there was, in fact, no doubt what the verdict upon Oppianicus was going to be, the bribery was far more likely to be undertaken by the party who had good cause to be anxious about the outcome than by his opponent who had no cause whatever to feel any such alarm. And thirdly, it was far more probable that a bribe would be offered by the individual who had twice received setbacks from these very same judges in the trials of Scamander and Fabricius than by the man who had won both these cases before them.

Now, there is one point at least which I am quite sure that no one will fail to concede to me, however hostile to Cluentius he may be. It is this. If there is agreement that the judges at the trial of Oppianicus were bribed, then they were bribed either by Cluentius or by Oppianicus.[1] If I can show you, therefore, that they were not bribed by Cluentius, then I have proved that the bribery was done by Oppianicus. And if I prove that it was done by Oppianicus, I have demonstrated that Cluentius was not responsible. Now, I have already given you adequate proof that my client had no motive for bribing the court. It therefore follows that it was Oppianicus who supplied the bribes.

But please continue listening while I now give you an additional justification for my belief that this was precisely what happened. Before I do so, however, let me just mention the existence of certain other arguments that point strongly in this same direction, though I will forbear to go into them at length. For example, the more likely of the two contestants to have recourse to bribery was the man who was not only, as I said, in danger of conviction, and mortally afraid, and without any other hope whatsoever of salvation, but who throughout his whole life had always been boundlessly dishonest in all his actions. And there are many other argu-

1. Cicero does not mention the third and greater probability: that the bribery was undertaken by both parties. See above, p. 118.

ments of the same kind. But since I am speaking of an issue which does not admit the slightest doubt but is entirely clear and evident, the rehearsal of a whole series of such arguments ceases to be necessary: and I will concentrate on just one point. Well, what I am claiming is that Oppianicus gave a large sum of money to one of his judges, Gaius Aelius Staienus, in order to bribe the court. Does anyone deny this? You, Oppianicus Junior, and you too, Attius, both of whom lament Oppianicus' condemnation – one with mute filial devotion and the other with articulate eloquence – I challenge each of you to protest that what I am saying is untrue. Deny, if you have the nerve to do so, that Oppianicus gave money to Staienus. Though it is my turn to speak, I grant you full permission to get up and deny it here and now!

But I have to conclude, apparently, that you are both equally speechless. And indeed, seeing that you brought an action to recover the money and then proceeded to recover it, you openly admitted the existence of the sum: so that denial is out of the question. I cannot see how either of you, Oppianicus Junior or Attius, can have the face to speak of bribery at the trial of Oppianicus, when you have openly acknowledged that your side gave money to one of the judges before the trial, and snatched it away from him after the proceedings were over.

You may well ask how all this came about. So allow me, gentlemen, to carry my narrative a little farther back. For upon all the happenings that have up to now, for so long, been lurking in deep obscurity I propose to throw such a glaring light that you will imagine you are witnessing them with your own eyes. So please continue to give me the same careful hearing that you have been good enough to afford me hitherto. You can rest assured that I shall say nothing that could be considered beneath the notice of this hushed gathering, or beneath your own sympathetic consideration.

As soon as the Scamander case began to show Oppianicus

the fate that was evidently in store for himself as well, he immediately set out to win the friendship of Staienus: an individual who was both needy and unprincipled, who knew from personal experience everything that there was to be known about how to bribe judges – and who was himself one of the judges in all these actual trials. Oppianicus had set things in motion at the proceedings against Scamander, where the successful deployment of his presents and subsidies had already enabled him to think of Staienus as a partisan rather than an objective judge.

Later on, however, after not a single one of the judges – with the sole exception of Staienus – had voted for Scamander's acquittal, and after Scamander's former master Fabricius had virtually voted against acquitting himself, it became amply clear to Oppianicus that more drastic measures were needed to get himself out of trouble. And so, in an attempt to rescue his imperilled status and fortunes, he turned once again to Staienus. For Oppianicus saw this individual as a highly inventive schemer, a person of unlimited audacity, an extremely efficient man of action. And so he was, up to a point, though by no means to the same brilliant extent as he pretended.

Now you will be aware, gentlemen, that even wild animals, under the stimulus of hunger, generally come back to the places where they have found food earlier. Two years before the occasion we are speaking about, Staienus, when he undertook the case relating to Safinius' estate at Atella,[1] had taken it upon himself to bribe the court with a sum of 600,000 sestertii. But once he had received the sum from Safinius, who was a minor and a ward, he kept it in his own possession instead, and after the case was over he returned it neither to

1. Safinius was a minor who apparently brought an action against his guardians for the fraudulent sale of his property. It is uncertain whether he lost or won his case. Atella, near the modern Orta di Atella, was in Campania.

Safinius nor to the people who had purchased the property. Afterwards, when Staienus had squandered the money so that there was nothing left even for his daily needs (much less for his pleasures), he decided to go back to the same methods of judicial swindling which had provided him with plunder before. And so, seeing Oppianicus in a thoroughly bad way, with the verdicts against Scamander and Fabricius threatening to cut his throat, Staienus tried to reassure him, and told him he must not give way to despair. And it was at this stage that Oppianicus started imploring Staienus to find him some means of bribing the court.

Thereupon Staienus – and here I am quoting the version which Oppianicus later recounted himself – agreed that he was the only man in the country who could do what was being asked of him. At first, it is true, he feigned reluctance, pointing out that he was standing for the aedileship[1] against persons of very distinguished antecedents, and did not therefore want to incur popular displeasure. Subsequently, however, after renewed entreaties, he gave way. At first, the amount of money he demanded was an enormous one. But finally he came down to a sum which it was within the bounds of possibility to raise: Oppianicus was told to bring 640,000 sestertii to his house.

But as soon as the money was brought to Staienus, this unsavoury creature began to ponder; and he came to the conclusion that it would really suit him best after all if Oppianicus could be convicted. For if he was acquitted, it would be impossible to avoid either distributing the money to his fellow-judges or, alternatively, returning it to Oppianicus himself. But if he was convicted, nobody would be in a position to ask for the money back. With these reflections in mind, Staienus concocted a very remarkable scheme.

The story I am telling you is a true one, gentlemen, but you will find it easier to believe if you will be good enough,

1. See List of Terms.

although so much time has passed since then, to recall Staienus' career and character to your minds. For if we are to form a just assessment of the actions a man has performed, or failed to perform, an estimate of his personality is a great help.

Well, he was penurious, extravagant, brazen, cunning and fraudulent. And the sight of such a large amount of cash deposited in his own home – which was a wretched hovel, quite devoid of any possessions of his own – caused him to turn his thoughts towards treachery of a peculiarly unscrupulous kind. 'Why on earth should I give the money to my fellow-judges?' he reasoned to himself. 'What do I stand to gain from doing so, except danger and disgrace? Can't I think of some way of making sure that Oppianicus gets condemned? Because just imagine if, by some accident or other, he managed to escape his fate – after all, anything can happen. In that case wouldn't I have to hand the money back? Well, he's on the edge of the precipice. Let's give him a push. He's done for, and only needs finishing off.'

And so Staienus formed the following scheme. He would promise money to some of the less scrupulous judges, but would not, in fact, hand it over to them. Then, when the time came for voting, the honest members of the bench would no doubt produce a severe verdict quite spontaneously, while he would meanwhile have ensured that their less honest colleagues were infuriated with Oppianicus for having deceived them. So, with his usual wrongheadedness and perversity, Staienus made a start with his fellow-judge Marcus Atilius Bulbus.[1] He found this individual yawning in deep gloom, since no pickings had come his way for a long time; and now Staienus applied a gentle stimulus. 'Well, Bulbus,' he said, 'how about giving me a bit of help, so that all this service we are giving to the state makes us a bit of profit?' As soon as

---

1. 'Perversity' because *bulbus* means a vegetable such as an onion, which the Romans ate not at the beginning of their meals, but at the end, as a savoury. This whole passage is full of puns of the same kind.

Bulbus heard the word 'profit', he replied: 'All right, you lead, and I'll follow. But what's the plan?' Whereupon Staienus proceeded to offer him forty thousand sestertii for Oppianicus' acquittal, and asked him to approach his cronies in the same sense, while he himself, as the cooker-up of the whole scheme,[1] had a word with his colleague Tiberius Gutta, thus sprinkling a drop of oil [gutta] over the onion [bulbus]. And Bulbus too, by what he had to say, provided a number of people with a very savoury titbit.

However, a couple of days passed, and the prospects still looked extremely uncertain. There were no signs yet of anyone to deposit the money with, or to go security for the sum. At this point Bulbus accosted Staienus and said in the most winning manner he could muster, 'Well, Paetus' (for Staienus had taken over the noble surname of Paetus from the pedigree of the Aelii, preferring to avoid the family's other surname 'Ligur' in case people would mistake him for a savage Ligurian):[2] 'Well, Paetus, about that matter you mentioned to me – they are asking me where the money is.' Then Staienus, loathsome trickster that he was, waxing fat on judicial fraud and happily conscious of all this money stacked away, wrinkled his brow – you remember the bogus, hypocritical look he used to put on – and said something fully worthy of all the skill and application with which he had seasoned his already naturally dishonest and lying character. For he roundly declared that Oppianicus had let him down. And, in consequence, he added, since all the judges were going to pronounce their verdicts openly, he for his part proposed to cast his vote in favour of conviction.

Meanwhile a rumour that there had been talk about bribing the judges leaked out. True, the whole business was by no

1. *Conditor* with a long 'i' means 'seasoner' and with a short 'i' means 'founder'.

2. A people of uncertain origin in N.E. Italy; they had once occupied the coast all the way from the Rhône to the Arno.

means as completely out in the open as the public interest demanded; but it was also not so secret as those directly concerned would have preferred it to be. In this atmosphere of general uncertainty and suspicion the prosecutor Cannutius, who was an experienced man, got wind of the idea that Staienus had accepted a bribe. Whereupon, guessing that the plot had not yet actually been put into effect, he suddenly arranged for it to be announced that the hearing was terminated. At this stage Oppianicus did not feel particularly worried, because he was under the impression that Staienus had already completed his arrangements. The judges who had to pronounce their verdicts were thirty-two in number; sixteen votes were needed to secure acquittal.[1] To secure that number, forty thousand sestertii were available for each judge, and it seemed reasonable to suppose that Staienus would put the finishing touch by adding his own vote to make seventeen – in the hope that by this means an even larger reward would come his way.

However, Cannutius' action was so sudden that, when it occurred, Staienus himself was absent from the court, defending some case or other before an arbitrator. Cluentius was quite content that he should be absent, and so was Cannutius. But Oppianicus felt very differently, and so did his counsel Lucius Quinctius who, being a tribune of the people at the time,[2] complained in the most abusive terms to the president of the court, Gaius Junius, that it would be entirely wrong for the judges to register their verdicts without Staienus. Convinced that Staienus' failure to turn up was due to an intentional lapse on the part of the attendants, Quinctius left

1. If the votes were equal in number, the defendant was given the benefit of the doubt.

2 In respect of the criminal courts the tribunes (see List of Terms) exercised a right of intervention known as *prohibitio*. When Cicero returned from Sicily, where he had been quaestor from 75–74 B.C., he found that Lucius Quinctius, who was evidently a powerful speaker, was leading the agitation to rescind the measures of Sulla (d. 78) which had restricted the powers of the tribunes.

the tribunal, proceeded to the private court in which Staienus was pleading, and by virtue of his official position ordered it to adjourn. Then he conducted Staienus back to the trial of Oppianicus.

And now the judges rose to pronounce their verdicts. Oppianicus had indicated his wish, as he was entitled to at that time, that they should vote openly and in public,[1] so that Staienus would be able to see whom he had to pay. The judges varied in character. The corruptible ones, comparatively few in number, were the most adamant against the defendant. It was like the annual elections of offices of state, in which those of the voters who have got used to taking bribes exceed everyone else in hostility to the candidates whose money, as they are unpleasantly aware, has failed to come their way. For in this trial, too, the judges who had been disappointed of their bribes proceeded to vote in a spirit of extreme malevolence towards the defendant. And as for their colleagues who were honest, they knew very well that Oppianicus was as guilty as he could be, but all the same they waited to learn the verdicts of the others – the ones they suspected of corruption – since then they would be able to discover, from the way the voting went, who had been responsible for handing over the bribes.

As it happened, the draw of the lot decided that the first judges called upon to pronounce their verdicts included Bulbus, Staienus and Gutta. There was intense curiosity on all sides to see which way these three worthless and mercenary judges would vote. In the event, every one of them unhesitatingly declared the defendant guilty. This made people puzzled and uncertain about what could have happened. The next to vote were men of sagacity, trained in the school of the older courts. These were the sort of judges who were equally incapable either of acquitting a person whose guilt was unmistakable or of convicting, at the first hearing and without further examination, someone who was suspected of being the

1. See above, pp. 153, 164.

victim of bribery. In consequence, they voted *not proven*. But some further judges, likewise men of strict principles, evidently took the view that what needs investigating is the motive behind any action. And so, with this consideration in mind, they concluded that although the first group had only pronounced Oppianicus guilty because they had been bribed to do so, nevertheless this was the correct decision, and they themselves ought to act consistently with the verdicts they had given in the previous cases: in consequence, they too voted guilty. Only five of the judges pronounced your poor innocent Oppianicus not guilty. Either they were stupid, or they felt sorry for him, or they hoped it would somehow turn out to their advantage.

And so he was convicted. But Lucius Quinctius, who was extremely keen to win popular favour, had his ears cocked to catch every breath of opinion emanating from private rumours and public discussions alike. And now, immediately after his client had been condemned, he saw an excellent opportunity to advance his own interests by exploiting the unpopularity of the senate: for it was amply clear to him that the lawcourts, with their membership of senators, were now regarded as utterly disreputable. So Quinctius delivered a couple of ferocious and impressive speeches. In his capacity as tribune of the people he cried out that the judges had been bribed to convict an innocent man. The welfare of the entire community was at stake, he declared, and the courts were quite worthless, and no man who possessed a wealthy enemy could any longer regard himself as secure. So it began to seem to people who knew nothing about the case, and had never set eyes on Oppianicus, that an admirable and entirely respectable individual had been victimized by bribery. Filled with profound suspicions of this kind, they began to demand that the whole case should be brought up again and handed over to themselves in the Assembly for reconsideration.

This was the state of affairs when, at Oppianicus' invitation, Staienus came by night to the house of Titus Annius,[1] a man of complete integrity who is my own personal friend. What took place there has now become common knowledge. Oppianicus raised the question of the money with Staienus, and Staienus promised he would give it back. Their conversation was overheard by reliable witnesses who had lodged themselves in adjacent hiding places for the purpose. And so the entire plot was detected and taken to court; and Staienus was compelled to disgorge the entire sum.

The sort of part he had been playing was now abundantly clear to one and all, and indeed his character readily lent itself to the gravest possible suspicions. All the same, people who heard about the case at public meetings still did not realize that he had first promised to employ the money in the defendant's interests and had then kept it back, because no one told them that this was what had happened. What they knew very well, however, was that bribery had been mentioned in connexion with the case. They were assured that an innocent man had been convicted. They saw that Staienus had voted for his conviction. And so, realizing what sort of a man he was, they concluded he did not do so for nothing. And similar suspicions were attached to Bulbus, Gutta and a number of others.

I am perfectly ready, therefore, to admit – and I feel entirely free to do so, especially before this court – that the trial of Oppianicus aroused a very considerable amount of criticism and resentment. This was partly because nothing had hitherto been known about the defendant's way of life – even his name had never been heard before – so that when people were told that an innocent man had fallen a victim to bribery, they felt duly shocked. And this suspicion that bribes had changed hands was intensified by their knowledge that Staienus was an evil character, and by the bad reputations of a number of his

1. Unknown.

fellow-judges of a similar type. Moreover, popular feeling was successfully whipped up by Lucius Quinctius, who not only enjoyed the authority of his office of tribune but also knew all about how to excite the emotions of a crowd. And so Gaius Junius, the chairman at Oppianicus' trial, was sacrificed to the flames which had now begun to rage. I remember the whole affair very well. He had already served as an aedile, and public opinion pointed to him as a coming praetor.[1] But now the Oppianicus trial cost him his practice at the bar, and destroyed his entire position in public life. And yet there was never, at any time, a formal proposal to censure him. It was all done by popular clamour.

I must say I am glad to be defending Cluentius now rather than then. It is true that his actual case is exactly the same as it was, because nothing can change the facts. But those days of prejudice and unfairness are gone for good. The result is that the disadvantages of the earlier epoch no longer stand in my way, whereas the full strength of Cluentius' case can be given adequate expression. In this happy situation, I am pleasantly conscious of the close attention I am receiving. And those who are listening to me so carefully are not only the judges, the men who will actually be called upon to pronounce their verdicts, but also everyone else who is capable of forming an opinion about the issue. Whereas if I had been obliged to make the same speech at that previous period, no one would have listened to me at all. It was not that the case was different then. Indeed, as I have said, it was precisely the same. But the times were entirely different.

Let me give you an illustration of the contrast. In those days nobody could have even ventured to suggest that Oppianicus' conviction had been justified. Now, on the other hand, nobody could deny it. In those days it would have been impossible for anyone to convince an audience that the person who bribed

1. Such chairmen of tribunals as were not already praetors were ex-aediles; cf. above, p. 14, and List of Terms.

the court was Oppianicus. Now, it would be impossible to convince them to the contrary. In those days no one felt at liberty to point out that Oppianicus was only put on trial after the two recent verdicts against Scamander and Fabricius had, in effect, already condemned him in advance. Now, no one would dream of disputing that this was so. At long last, we have succeeded in getting all that prejudice eliminated. The passage of the years has worn it away. The arguments I have offered you have made it obsolete. Now that the facts have been objectively discussed, your own good faith and sense of justice, gentlemen, have finally committed it to oblivion. And, this being so, there is really no case left for me to answer.

That bribery was employed in Oppianicus' trial is generally agreed. The only question is whether it came from the side of the prosecutor or of the defendant. Let me tell you how Cluentius, who was the prosecutor, sees the matter. 'In the first place,' he says, 'the charges I was bringing were so convincing that no bribery was needed. Secondly, the man I was prosecuting had virtually been condemned already in advance, so that bribery would have been pointless (and, incidentally, his own bribery didn't even manage to save him). Thirdly, even if the defendant had been acquitted, it would not really have done me a great deal of harm, since my own resources would still have remained intact.' Whereas all that Oppianicus could have managed to say would have been this. 'First, I was terrified by the number of charges against me, and by their gravity. Secondly, I was all too well aware that the convictions of Fabricius and Scamander, as accessaries to my criminal acts, meant that my own conviction, too, was inevitable. Thirdly, I had reached a situation in which my entire future depended on the result of this one single trial.'

It must be concluded, then, that Oppianicus had numerous weighty motives for bribing the judges, and that Cluentius had none. Next we come to the question of the actual origins of the money that was expended. Now, Cluentius has kept his accounts with meticulous care. This is important, because it means that no addition or subtraction whatever relating to his family assets could possibly have passed unrecorded. Eight whole years have gone by, Attius, since you first began thinking over this case, hunting up and turning over and analysing every single item in the accounts of Cluentius or anyone else that could possibly be relevant. Throughout this entire period, you have not been able to find a single trace of the sort of outlay by Cluentius that you are looking for. That being so, is it really necessary for us to go on following up the scent of the bribes which, in fact, obviously came from Oppianicus? Why can't the prosecution admit this, and without any further trouble lead us straight to his lair?

For consider the circumstances. 640,000 sestertii are found at a certain specific spot. They are found in the hands of a thoroughly criminal individual – who also happens to be one of the judges. I ask you, what further evidence do you need? The other side argues that the man who had instigated Staienus to bribe the court was not Oppianicus but Cluentius. In that case, how do you explain the fact that Cluentius and Cannutius were perfectly willing to let Staienus be absent from the court at the time when the judges rose to consider their verdicts? If it was Cluentius and Cannutius who had given him the money, why did they not insist on his being present when they chose to bring the proceedings to a close? No, the people who insisted on his presence were Oppianicus and Quinctius – and it was Quinctius himself who employed his powers as a tribune to prevent the votes from being taken before Staienus arrived. Your answer, I know, is that Staienus then proceeded to vote against Oppianicus, and not for him. Certainly. But that was purely and simply because he had to demonstrate to Bulbus and the rest that Oppianicus had tricked him.

So the situation is this. Your side had a motive for bribing the court. Your side got the money. Your side had Staienus.

Your side disposed of every conceivable kind of dishonesty and trickery. We on our side, on the other hand, can point to impeccable honesty and integrity, without a trace of bribery, indeed without the slightest motive for bribery at all. And so the truth stands revealed, and there are no possible grounds for misapprehension. I therefore demand you to concede that the infamy of this criminal act be transferred where it belongs – to the individual who has been responsible for so many other evil deeds as well. Suffer my client, at long last, to be liberated from the slur! For by now there can surely be no doubt in your minds that he was completely and totally blameless.

However, it appears, Attius, that you still have another argument to put forward. While not disputing that Oppianicus gave the money to Staienus, you explain that he did so not in order to bribe the court but to bring about a reconciliation with Cluentius. Really, it is hard to see how a man of your knowledge, practice and experience can hazard a theory of so wild a kind. There is a saying that the wisest individual of all is he who thinks of the right idea for himself, and next comes the man who adopts someone else's good ideas.[1] To stupidity the opposite applies. For a person who has no ideas of his own at all is less stupid than somebody who accepts stupid ideas from another.

Anyway, it was not you who thought up that reconciliation story. It was Staienus. He concocted it when he was hard pressed by his own critical situation, and when events had got him by the throat. Or possibly *he* picked up the whole fairy tale, with its explanation about the making up of the quarrel, from a suggestion made to him by Publius Cornelius Cethegus. At least, that was the gossip at the time; you will remember that such a rumour did exist. It was said that Cethegus detested Staienus, felt determined to get his deplorable activities removed from public life, and believed that Staienus, by actually admitting that he, himself a judge, had secretly and

1. Cf. Hesiod, *Works and Days*, 293f.

irregularly accepted a bribe from Oppianicus, had finished himself off completely: so Cethegus quite deliberately gave him this misleading advice. My own view is that, if Cethegus really acted in this unscrupulous fashion, he did so because he hoped to eliminate Staienus' rivalry in the elections.[1]

All the same, if Staienus was not in a position to deny his acceptance of the money, then it certainly would have been both disgraceful and perilous to have admitted the real purpose for which he had taken it; and, this being so, Cethegus' advice was sensible enough.

But in any case, Attius, whatever explanations Staienus may have offered, they have no bearing on your present case, because they related entirely to his own situation at the time. Anything in the world that he could have said, in his critical position, would have been less disreputable than a confession of what he had actually done. But I must say I am surprised that this ancient farce, which was hissed and hooted off the stage at that time, should have seemed to you suitable for revival here and now. For surely a reconciliation either between Cluentius and Oppianicus, or between Cluentius and his mother Sassia, was completely out of the question. Oppianicus' trial was already in hand, with himself and Cluentius inscribed in the public records as defendant and prosecutor respectively. Moreover, Fabricius and Scamander had been found guilty. Whoever his prosecutor might have been, it would still have been wholly impossible for Oppianicus to get off. And if Cluentius had abandoned the task, he would undoubtedly have come under the gravest suspicion of having launched the prosecution in the first place without legitimate grounds.[2]

1. Publius Cornelius Cethegus was a former Marian who made his peace with Sulla. Probably he and Staienus were rival candidates for the aedileship.

2. In certain circumstances this exposed the would-be prosecutor to legal proceedings (p. 76).

Or was Oppianicus' bribe intended to secure the collusion of Cluentius?[1] That, too, would have constituted judicial corruption. But if such was his intention he would surely not have needed to seek the services of one of the judges as his intermediary. And least of all would it have been necessary to conduct the whole business through Staienus, a degraded criminal who had no direct contact with either party! It would surely have been far better to use the services of some honest man who was a friend and connexion of both sides.

But I really don't have to go on labouring the point, as though it was something worth arguing about. For, after all, the actual quantity of the money handed over to Staienus reveals very much more than just a figure: it reveals the whole purpose of the transaction as well. If Oppianicus was to be acquitted, as I have said, sixteen judges had to be bribed. Now, the amount paid to Staienus was 640,000 sestertii. If, as you maintain, the payment was made with a view to effecting a reconciliation, what was the point of the additional forty thousand? But if, as I suggest instead, the idea was to give each of the sixteen judges the round total of forty thousand, Archimedes himself could not have worked out the division sum better.[2]

2. Previous Verdicts Quoted Against Cluentius

You claim that the attribution of the bribery at Oppianicus trial to Cluentius is corroborated by a lot of judicial decisions, penalizing quite other persons, that have been taken between then and now. But this is quite untrue. Until today, such

1. This term, *praevaricatio*, is used of prosecutors who dishonestly conduct their case in the interests of the other side.
2. Archimedes of Syracuse, the mathematician and inventor (c. 287–212 B.C.).

an assertion has never once been directly tested by a court of law. Certainly, the case has evoked a vast amount of discussion and canvassing. But up to now it has never actually been argued out in court. It is only today, for the first time, that truth, lent courage by the judges who constitute this tribunal, has been able to raise its voice and shout unfair prejudice down.

Besides, what do those alleged judicial decisions amount to? I have got a convincing reply about every single issue they raised; and I shall be only too glad to consider, one after the other, each and all of the proceedings which followed upon Oppianicus' trial and were said to invalidate its result. Some of them, as I shall show you, bore a closer resemblance to convulsions of nature, or hurricanes, than to processes at law. Others, so far from operating against Cluentius, actually prove of assistance to his cause; while others again were not really ever regarded or described as legal actions at all. I will now deal with these cases one by one. And, gentlemen, I must ask you once again to note everything that I shall say with extreme care – though my request is a purely conventional one, because I am perfectly sure that you will be careful listeners without any special appeal from myself.

One of the cases resulted in the condemnation of Gaius Junius, who had been the chairman of the court which tried Oppianicus. He was actually condemned before his tenure of that chairmanship had ended. The tribune Quinctius showed himself singularly unindulgent to Junius' need to prepare his case.[1] Moreover, he displayed equal impatience with the requirements of the law.[2] For although it was illegal for Junius, as chairman of his court, to leave that court in order to take

1. A defendant was usually allowed ten days for the preparation of his case.

2. It was forbidden for an officer of state (and therefore, Cicero maintains, for the president of a criminal court) to be brought to trial during his year of office.

up any other public duty, he was actually wrenched away from it to be haled, as defendant, into another court altogether. And what court was that, I ask you, gentlemen? This was a question I had thought I might have to pass over in silence. But the expressions I see on your faces encourage me to believe that I can speak freely about the matter after all.

Well, how should this so-called tribunal that tried Junius really be defined? Ought it to be described as a court at all, or could we call it a judicial investigation, or a public tribunal, or what? I suppose we could just manage to call it by one or another of those various names. However, the crowd attending the proceedings was violently excited – in those days such mobs had to be humoured – and I should like to ask anyone who happened to be present at the time just to tell me, if he can, *on exactly what charge* Junius had been arraigned. Ask any of the spectators you care to choose, and this is the answer you will get: 'on the charge of accepting a bribe and ruining the innocent Oppianicus'. Yes, that is what people believe. But if this had been the real charge against Junius, he surely ought to have been charged according to the law under which Cluentius is being charged now.[1] But that was impossible, since the chairman of the court which was responsible for the administration of that particular law was still Junius himself! One might think that Lucius Quinctius could have waited another few days. But he was in a great hurry to conduct the prosecution before his own tenure of the tribunate came to an end – and, let me add, before popular prejudice was allowed time to subside. From this you can see that he did not propose to let his prosecution rely on its intrinsic merits at all. On the contrary, his intention was to take advantage of the tense atmosphere of the time – and to exploit the privileges of his tribune's office.

Quinctius demanded that Junius should pay a fine. Do not ask me what law this demand was based on. But it had to be

1. The *Lex Cornelia de sicariis et veneficiis*; see above, p. 17.

done, if you please, because Junius had somehow omitted to take the customary oath that he would administer his court according to the regulations in force – though such an omission had never been held against anyone as a criminal offence before. Quinctius also produced a second reason for demanding this penalty. It was concerned with the city praetor Gaius Verres – and everyone knows, or don't they, what a model of respectability and conscientiousness he is![1] Well, the records of Verres (containing a good many suspicious erasures) were produced at the trial, and apparently, according to Quinctius, they contained no note of Junius having taken any steps to fill a vacancy which had occurred among the judges on his bench, as he ought to have done.[2] Those, gentlemen, were the charges on which Junius was found guilty. They were excessively slender, indeed trivial in the extreme, and they never ought to have been brought into court. In other words, Junius' conviction was not due to the facts of his case at all. It was entirely due to the high emotions surrounding the whole business at the time.

Now consider whether that trial of Junius ought to be regarded as reflecting adversely on the present case against Cluentius. Why ever should it? All right, let us suppose that Junius did perhaps violate the statute relating to appointments to vacancies. Let us suppose that on some occasion or other he had failed to take some oath he ought to have taken. But surely his conviction for these technical offences did not imply, even in the smallest degree whatsoever, that *Cluentius* had done anything wrong. I really do not see how anyone could possibly take the opposite view.

And indeed, to go back to Junius, Quinctius' only conceivable way of justifying his attack on the man would have been to suggest that Junius was found guilty of these particular

---

1. Prosecuted successfully by Cicero for extortion in 70 B.C.; cf. *Cicero: Selected Works*, pp. 35ff.
2. For the procedure, see above, p. 14.

offences because he was, in fact, guilty, even if guilty of another misdeed altogether. But in that case it surely cannot be pretended that Junius' trial deserved the name of a trial at all! 'Yes,' we shall be reminded, 'but one must not forget the situation: people in Rome did feel great hostility towards Gaius Junius, because they believed that the bribery of his court at the trial of Oppianicus was his fault.'

Now, since that time, the Oppianicus case itself – for this at least will have to be agreed – cannot surely be regarded as having become something other than it was. The facts involved, the reasons why the trial was held, the character of the entire proceedings, cannot in the nature of things have undergone any sort of a retrospective transformation. I put it to you that not one single fact of this case, belonging to the past, can have altered in the slightest degree. Well, that being so, one has to ask why the speech I am making now, in defence of Cluentius, is being listened to in the most attentive silence, whereas on that occasion Junius was not even given an opportunity to utter a single word in his own defence. The reason is this. Junius' case, at the time when the trial was held, was entirely at the mercy of prejudices, misconceptions, suspicions, and violent popular agitations, stirred up at a continual series of public meetings day after day. The prosecutor Lucius Quinctius was an office-holder, a tribune of the people, and he continued to behave like a tribune of the people not only at his own mass-meetings but also in our courts of law. Indeed, he used to come straight to the court from his own mass-meetings – and he brought his audiences with him. Those Aurelian Steps over there (they were new then)[1] provided a convenient theatrical auditorium for the trial. When a prosecutor filled them with an excited crowd, it was quite out

1. These steps, to the south-east of the Forum, led up to one of the places where tribunals were held. They were perhaps built by, and named after, Marcus Aurelius Cotta, consul 74 B.C.; cf. M. Grant, *The Roman Forum*, Weidenfeld & Nicolson, 1970, p. 218.

of the question for the defendant to get so much as a chance to speak. Indeed, it was beyond his powers even to rise from his place, in the hope of getting a word in.

Not so very long ago, the judges belonging to the court presided over by Gaius Orchivius, my present colleague in the praetorship,[1] refused to reserve a place on their programme of trials for an action by a tribune of the people against Faustus Cornelius Sulla,[2] who was accused of the unlawful retention of public funds. Now this was not because they deemed him above the law; nor was it because they considered an issue relating to public funds too trivial to be worthy of their notice. But the court in question took the view that, if a tribune of the people intended to conduct the prosecution, it was impossible for the two sides to confront one another on equal terms.

In the present case, the same argument not only applies once again, but applies a good deal more strongly. This is because of certain significant differences between Faustus Sulla and Junius, between the tribune who sought to prosecute Faustus and the tribune Quinctius who prosecuted Junius, between the one occasion and the other. Faustus was a man of enormous resources, possessing numerous relatives, extensive marriage connexions, a host of friends and dependants. Junius, on the other hand, was equipped with these advantages only to a small and insignificant extent, and in so far as he possessed them at all they had been acquired by his own efforts. And then again the tribune who wanted to attack Faustus was a moderate and self-respecting man, by no means seditious himself and strongly opposed to such tendencies in others, while Quinctius is a harsh, contentious and turbulent demagogue. Moreover, when the attempt was made to charge Faustus the situation was perfectly calm and peaceful, whereas Junius' trial occurred at a time when the most violent tempests

1. Orchivius was president of the court relating to peculation.
2. The son of the dictator Sulla.

of prejudice were raging. Yet in spite of the much less unfavourable circumstances surrounding the case of Faustus, the
judges considering the application against him decided that
such a hearing could not be conducted in fair conditions, since
his opponent would be able to supplement his legal rights as
a prosecutor by all the weight of his authority as tribune.

Gentlemen, your wisdom and humanity require you to
consider this point very carefully. It is your duty to appreciate
fully all the harm, all the peril, to which every one of us is
liable to be exposed by the powers of the tribunes, above all
when prejudice has been aroused and a public meeting is
excited to violence. Why, even in the good old times, when
a man's idea of protecting himself was not to perform antics
in the hope of ingratiating himself with the public but to lead
an upright and honourable life, men as eminent as Publius
Popilius Laenas and Quintus Caecilius Metellus Numidicus
found it beyond their powers to stand up to the opposition
of a tribune.[1]

How much less, therefore, could we feel ourselves secure at
this present epoch, when society and officialdom are in the
state we see them in today, unless we felt confident of the
protection afforded by the courts, and the wisdom with which
you yourselves are conducting them.

Gentlemen, the proceedings against Junius really bore not
the slightest resemblance to a trial, no resemblance whatsoever.
They were entirely unrestrained. They allowed customary
procedures to go by the board. They permitted the defence
no sort of hearing. They were just plain violence – a sort or

1. Publius Popilius Laenas, consul in 132 B.C., prosecuted the followers
of the tribune Tiberius Sempronius Gracchus, and in 123 was compelled
by his brother, the tribune Gaius Gracchus, to go into exile. Quintus
Caecilius Metellus Numidicus (see Genealogical Table, I) went into
exile in 100 rather than take the oath by which the tribune Saturninus
(p. 257) forced senators to abide by his agrarian law.

natural convulsion, as I said before, or a tornado; certainly the very opposite to anything like a trial or an investigation or a legal case of any kind.

Nevertheless, let us still imagine the existence of someone who might take the opposite view and argue that the action against Junius was an authentic trial, resulting in a verdict by which we are under some obligation to abide. And yet even he, if he exists, ought to make a distinction between that case and the present one. In regard to Junius, we are told that the proposal was to fine him, either for the omission to take his oath or for failure to fill a vacancy on his bench. But in any case these charges, and the laws under which they were brought, are totally irrelevant to Cluentius.

However, you go on to point out that Junius was not the only judge in Oppianicus' trial to be convicted, since Marcus Atilius Bulbus was found guilty as well. Yes: but you must admit that what Bulbus was condemned for was *treason*[1] – which makes it perfectly clear that his trial, once again, does not possess the slightest relevance to the action we are engaged upon now. You will no doubt wish to remind me that Bulbus was also charged with bribery in the trial of Oppianicus. Yes, I realize this. But it was also made very clear by letters from Gaius Cosconius,[2] and by the evidence of numerous witnesses, that what Bulbus had really done was something quite different: he had tried to incite a legion in Illyricum to mutiny. *That* was the charge relevant to the court which tried him, and applicable to the law of treason which provided its terms of reference. 'All right,' you say, 'but it was the other matter, the bribery, which particularly told against him.' Ah, there you are just guessing. And if we are going to be allowed to guess, you will I think have to agree that a guess I am now going to offer is

1. *Maiestas*; see below, p. 258, n. 4.
2. Gaius Cosconius, governor of Illyricum (Yugoslavia) *c.* 78–76 B.C., conquered most of Dalmatia and took Salonae (Split).

a good deal closer to the mark. In my opinion, the reason why Bulbus got himself so promptly convicted was because he was an infamous, depraved rogue, already tainted by an extensive criminal record long before he ever came into that particular court. What you are doing is to select from the whole, voluminous dossier of Bulbus just the one single point that suits your argument, so that you can go on to pretend that *this* was the point which impelled the judges to give their verdict against him.

In actual fact, however, Bulbus' trial should no more be regarded as prejudicial to my present defence of Cluentius than were the trials of Publius Popilius[1] and Tiberius Gutta. True, the prosecution describes these, also, as indicative of Cluentius' guilt. But what Popilius and Gutta were actually tried for was something quite different, namely corrupt practice at the annual elections of officers of state – their prosecutors being men who had been found guilty on similar charges.[2] And the reason, surely, why these actions earned the prosecutors the restoration of their own lost rights could not possibly have owed anything to the suggestion that Popilius and Gutta had taken bribes in the Oppianicus case, but was entirely because the prosecutors had succeeded in proving to the court that these defendants had committed the same electoral offences as they themselves had been convicted for: a demonstration which according to the law entitled them to this reward. For this reason I regard it as indisputable that the condemnation of Popilius and Gutta for corrupt electoral practices can by no

1. Not the same as Publius Popilius Laenas (p. 180).

2. The laws and lawcourt relating to *ambitus* (corrupt electioneering practices) provided for the complete rehabilitation of any person who, having been convicted of this offence, secured the conviction of another for the same offence. For a discussion of the legal problems involved here, see W. Peterson (ed.), *Cicero: Pro Cluentio*, pp. 181ff. Bribery in a criminal case such as the trial of Oppianicus (including 'judicial murder') came under a different law altogether, the *Lex Cornelia de sicariis et veneficiis* (p. 17).

manner of possibility be regarded as having the slightest connexion with the present case of Cluentius, or with the jurisdiction of your court.

Then we come to the fact that another man found guilty was Staienus. I will forbear to stress the point – though it is once again surely far from irrelevant – that he, too, was convicted not for bribery but for treason. For the evidence (though again I will not dwell on it here) provided against him by highly reliable witnesses who served under the eminent Mamercus Aemilius Lepidus Livianus[1] as generals, prefects and military tribunes[2] indicated that it was Staienus, as quaestor, who was principally responsible for stirring up a military mutiny. I will also say nothing more about the 600,000 sestertii which he accepted for services he was going to render in the action brought by Safinius[3] – except to add that in the end he quietly kept it for himself, just as he subsequently kept the money paid him at the trial of Oppianicus.

These considerations, then, and a great deal of other evidence against Staienus that came up at his trial, I pass over in silence. But what I do want to emphasize is that those honourable and eloquent knights who were his prosecutors, Publius and Lucius Cominius,[4] maintained the same contention against Staienus then as I am maintaining against Attius now. For the Cominii argued, as I argue, that Staienus received the money from Oppianicus in order to bribe the court – in direct contradiction of Staienus' claim that he only took it in order to effect a reconciliation between Oppianicus and Cluentius. The court trying Staienus just laughed at all this talk about a

1. Consul 77 B.C., the year in which an uprising of Marcus Aemilius Lepidus (consul, 78 B.C.) was put down.

2. See List of Terms.

3. See above, p. 161. For the mutiny, p. 181 and n. 2.

4. Publius Cominius was the prosecutor, and his brother Lucius his assistant (*subscriptor*).

reconciliation; indeed they found Staienus' whole assumption of the role of a decent man thoroughly comic. This was the sort of masquerade he had already attempted to perform when he set up gilded statues of the kings of Rome in the temple of Juturna, with inscriptions on their bases declaring that by erecting these statues it was he who had brought the ancient monarchs back into favour at Rome.[1] All Staienus' frauds and sharp practices were brought out into the open, and a whole lifetime devoted to such crimes was laid bare. His hand-to-mouth existence was described, and reference was made to his methods of extracting an income from the courts. His pose, on the other hand, as the paid agent of general peace and harmony failed to carry the slightest weight. The result therefore was that Staienus, after taking the same line as Attius is trying to take now, was found guilty; and the Cominii, after taking the line that I myself have taken throughout the present action, were duly victorious.

Now, this condemnation of Staienus was tantamount to a decision that Oppianicus had tried to bribe the court at his trial, handing over a sum of money to one of the judges for the purchase of votes. For it is agreed that bribes were given *either* by Cluentius *or* by Oppianicus: and whereas there is no trace whatever of Cluentius transferring any sum to any of the judges, money recovered from one of their number, Staienus, after the trial had demonstrably come from Oppianicus. It is therefore beyond all possible doubt that the condemnation of Staienus, so far from telling against Cluentius, very greatly strengthens my case for his defence.

To sum up these various cases, then, the proceedings against Junius can only be described as an outbreak of revolution, a demonstration of popular turbulence, an insurrectionary act

1. The temple of Juturna, goddess of springs and fountains, was erected in the Field of Mars in 241 B.C. For the fluctuating reputations of the quasi-mythical kings, see M. Grant, *Roman Myths*, pp. 112ff., 151f.

by a tribune. But a trial they cannot be called. And furthermore, even if you *could* contrive to find some individual who
is still disposed to define what happened as an authentic trial,
even he will have to admit that the fine which was demanded
from Junius could not be regarded as carrying the faintest slur
against Cluentius. However, as I say, the whole action against
Junius must be regarded as nothing better than a manifestation
of violence. And as for Bulbus, Popilius and Gutta, the
convictions against them, too, provide not the slightest scrap
of evidence against Cluentius: whereas the condemnation of
Staienus actually assists his cause.

And now let me tell you about another case which likewise
tells in his favour. One of the judges who voted for Oppianicus' guilt was Gaius Fidiculanius Falcula. Because he had done
so, a charge was subsequently brought against him as against
the others, although the trial of Oppianicus took place only
a few days after Fidiculanius had for the very first time taken
his seat on the bench, to which he had been nominated by the
chairman in order to fill a vacancy. This position as a nominated
substitute stood against him very seriously when his own turn
came to be tried.[1] Indeed, such was the violence of the prejudice
which Lucius Quinctius had worked up against him, at the
lawless and turbulent public meetings he continued to hold
day after day, that Fidiculanius was actually taken to court not
just once but twice. At the first of these trials an endeavour
was made to get him fined (the penalty inflicted upon Junius)
on the technical grounds that he had taken his seat on the
bench when it was not the turn of his panel to provide the new
judge.[2] Consequently, the actual charge that was brought
against him, and the law under which it was brought, were

1. i.e. it was felt that he was just a puppet of the chairman, Gaius
Junius.
2. For the legal position, see W. Peterson, op. cit., pp. 185ff. But the
details remain obscure.

much the same as those which had been employed against Junius. By the time of Fidiculanius' trial, however, the atmosphere had become much calmer: the proceedings were not marred by any agitation, or violence, or lawlessness. In consequence, he was easily acquitted, at the very first hearing.

However, I do not propose to make much of this acquittal,[1] because, even if Fidiculanius did not commit the actual offence for which the fine was proposed, it still remains possible that he *did* receive a bribe (from Oppianicus) while serving as a judge in that man's trial – just as Staienus was guilty, though he too was never brought to court on that particular charge.[2] And indeed, at his second trial Fidiculanius was specifically prosecuted for bribery on the occasion in question – the accusation being that he had accepted 50,000 sestertii *from Cluentius*.[3] Being a member of the senate, the defendant was tried under the law which is customarily employed when senators have to answer charges of this kind, the law of extortion.[4] But he was acquitted of this particular charge without a stain on his name. For the trial was conducted in the good old traditional manner, without a trace of violence or intimidation or danger to life and limb. Every point in turn was duly set forth and expounded and proved, and then the court came to its decision. It was persuaded to conclude that even if a judge

1. Cicero was uncomfortably aware that in his speech *In Defence of Caecina* (69 B.C.), 29, he had shown little confidence in the innocence of Fidiculanius – whose provincial-sounding names he ridiculed.

2. He was convicted in the treason court, not this court dealing with bribery in criminal cases, cf. below, p. 258. But the reading is very uncertain.

3. The figure is uncertain: 50,000 is a conjecture based on a passage in Cicero, *In Defence of Caecina*, 28 (but there too the figure is not certain).

4. The *Lex Cornelia de repetundis*; like the *Lex Cornelia de sicariis et veneficiis* (p. 17) it contained a clause penalizing judicial murder, operative only against senators. This passage may suggest that cases of such a kind were more frequently tried under the former than under the latter law.

happened not to have attended for the entire duration of a trial, his vote in favour of conviction *may* have been perfectly honest all the same. The court also decided that although Fidiculanius' knowledge of the case of Oppianicus had been limited to the previous trials (involving other persons) which had a bearing on the charges against that defendant, nevertheless it would have been wrong to consider that he was under an obligation to hear any additional evidence when the action against Oppianicus was being heard.

By this time even those five judges whose eagerness to angle for the cheap applause of ignorant audiences had inspired them to vote for Oppianicus' acquittal were becoming exceedingly reluctant to accept congratulations on the mercy they had shown him. For if someone had inquired from them whether they had already served as judges in the trial of Gaius Fabricius, they could obviously not have denied such a suggestion. And, if asked whether it was not true that Fabricius had been charged with one crime and one only, the attempted poisoning of Cluentius, they would again have been obliged to reply that this was so. Had they been questioned regarding the verdicts they had given in the case of Fabricius, they would further have been compelled to admit that they pronounced him guilty – because, after all, not one single vote had been cast in favour of his innocence. Moreover, if the same questions had been put to them about the trial of Scamander, they would unmistakably have had to give the same answers. It is true that one vote, one single vote, favoured his acquittal. But at this later stage none of these five judges was willing to identify that vote as his own.

In consequence of all this, one may well ask which group of persons should feel clearer consciences about their votes in the Oppianicus case, those who could proclaim that they had remained true to themselves and their previous verdicts, or those who would have been forced to reply that, after displaying conspicuous harshness to mere accomplices and accessaries, they had shown clemency to the principal criminal. To express a view about the way these five judges voted at the trial of Oppianicus is not part of my job. But what happened, one may surmise, was that these worthy gentlemen suddenly became suspicious that something had gone wrong, and that was why they went back on their previous opinions. However, their leniency in voting for Oppianicus' acquittal can be passed over, as far as I am concerned, without critical comment.

But at the same time I do want to commend the consistency of their colleagues who, immune from the trickery of Staienus, spontaneously voted in accordance with the verdicts they had already given earlier in the Fabricius case. And I applaud the good sense of those other judges who voted 'not proven'. They were perfectly well aware that the defendant was thoroughly guilty. After all, they had virtually convicted him twice already, so it was out of the question for them to acquit him now. But in view of the scandalous aura surrounding the whole case, and the deplorable goings-on that were strongly suspected, they felt it best to postpone their condemnation for a short time until all the relevant facts had been brought to light.

The verdicts that they registered are already proof enough of their wisdom. But I should also like you to consider the personalities of these particular judges, since you will then be able to feel quite certain that everything they did must have been honourably and wisely done.[1] Take Publius Octavius Balbus, for example. It would be impossible to find a more highly intelligent person, a greater expert in the law, a man more scrupulously determined to live up to all the demands of good faith, and conscience, and duty. Well, he did not vote for Oppianicus' acquittal. And then there was Quintus Considius, whose experience as a trial judge was only equalled

1. The nine persons whose names follow are all unknown. Probably all of them voted 'not proven', though it is conceivable that Cicero also included one or two names of those who voted 'guilty'.

by his acute consciousness of the grave responsibility that such a task involved. He did not vote for acquittal either.

But it would take too long to recount the virtues and the careers of all these judges in turn. Besides, they are known to us all; they stand in no need of any verbal embellishment. Think of Marcus Juventius Peto, a judge of the fine old school. Think of Lucius Caulius Mergus, Marcus Basilus, Gaius Caudinus; they are men whose great days at the public courts coincided with the great days of our nation. And with them should be named Lucius Cassius and Cnaeus Heius, their peers in character and sagacity alike. Not one of these men voted that Oppianicus should be acquitted. Nor did Publius Satureius, who was the youngest of them all in years, but equalled any of those I have already mentioned in intellectual strength, industriousness, and high principle.

Oppianicus' innocence must have been of a very peculiar variety, when we reflect that the judges who wanted to acquit him were suspected of corruption, those in favour of postponing judgement were given credit for prudence, and those who voted for condemnation were held to deserve the biggest prize of all – because they were the ones who had been truly consistent!

At the time, however, nothing was said about all this, either at public meetings or in court. This silence was due to Lucius Quinctius. For he himself forbade all mention of such matters; and the emotions he had whipped up among the crowd made it impossible for any other speaker to get a hearing. And so, by his doing, the ruin of Gaius Junius, the chairman at the trial of Oppianicus, was completed. After that, Quinctius dropped the whole matter. For one thing, it was only a few days later that he went out of office. Besides, he realized that the popular excitement had cooled down. But if, during those same days when he was accusing Junius, he had also decided to bring an action against Fidiculanius, his victim would not have had the slightest chance of standing up for himself. Indeed, Quinctius had already made a beginning: because he issued a general threat against every one of the judges who had voted that Oppianicus was guilty.

You had good reason to know what an utterly shameless individual Quinctius was. You were aware of his conceit, and all the bombast we got from him as a tribune. Heavens, what a presumptuous creature he was, and how dreadfully pleased with himself! What airs he used to put on! How grossly he overestimated his own virtues! His whole display of arrogance was truly monstrous and unendurable. Indeed, all his criticisms of the trial of Oppianicus really stemmed from one grievance and one only – his feeling that the court should have acquitted the defendant, in deference to himself as counsel for the defence: and yet they failed in this manifest duty. Whereas, in reality, the very fact that Oppianicus had ever turned to this type of advocate at all ought to have been proof enough that everyone else had abandoned him. For Rome was filled with eloquent and reputable barristers, and surely it would have been possible to find just one who was prepared to defend a Roman knight enjoying a high position in his own community – if only such a barrister could have convinced himself that the case would not be a thoroughly dishonourable one to take on.

But what pleading had Quinctius ever done before, in all his fifty years?[1] Nobody had ever seen him appear in court, even as a character witness or legal adviser, much less as an actual pleader. However, the rostrum had long stood vacant, and no tribune had uttered a sound from it ever since the arrival of Sulla.[2] So Quinctius himself seized possession of the

1. But, between that date and this, Quinctius had been the prosecutor when Cicero delivered his speech *In Defence of Marcus Tullius* (71 B.C.).

2. The dictator Sulla had placed serious restrictions upon the activities of the tribunes, and these restrictions were not completely removed until 70 B.C. (p. 116).

platform. The population of Rome was long since un-
accustomed to public meetings, but Quinctius revived them to
some sort of semblance of the ancient practice. This meant that
for a short time he gained popularity with people of a certain
type. Yet how everyone came to hate him later on! And this
included his own followers, too, upon whose backs he had
climbed on his way up in the world. Their hatred was under-
standable enough, if you will cast your mind back to the
pompous manner in which he carried on, and if you will
recall the expression he wore on his face, and the sort of
clothes he used to affect – especially his purple robe which
trailed right down to his feet.[1] Such was the man who found
it quite intolerable that he had been defeated in court; and
in consequence he transferred the case from the tribunal to
the public platform.

After we have witnessed all this, it is really no longer easy
to complain that our state does not offer sufficient rewards to
the self-made man.[2] Surely the prizes it offers are the greatest
you could find anywhere in the world. For if a Roman, however humble his origins, lives in such a way that his character
seems capable of sustaining the dignity of high rank, he will
be able to advance every bit as far as his own hard work and
decent behaviour warrant. Indeed, a man whose *only* notable
quality is his humble birth frequently reaches loftier heights
than he would have attained had he been a high aristocrat
with the same failings. Take Quinctius as an example. If he
had been of noble stock, no one would ever have put up with
his insufferable pride and insolence. But his origins being
what they were, people tolerated him to the extent of convincing themselves that any good features nature may have
bestowed upon him ought to be counted to his credit.

1. A tribune had no right to the purple-fringed toga worn by high
officials.

2. i.e. *novus homo* (like Cicero), whose forebears had never reached
the consulship (p. 258 n. 1).

And as for his haughtiness and arrogance, in a man of his modest birth these seemed ludicrous rather than dangerous qualities.

But to continue. You are fond of quoting previous legal decisions, Attius. So what do you suppose the acquittal of Fidiculanius proved? Obviously, it proved that in Oppianicus' trial his verdict had not been secured by a bribe. Certainly, he had voted in favour of the man's conviction, because he decided that this was the right thing to do; and he evidently did not have to sit through the entire trial before coming to this decision. Moreover, he voted as he did in spite of the many violent attacks Quinctius had directed against him at public meetings. That is to say, the whole story of Fidiculanius' acquittal is a further proof that all the prosecutions that had been previously launched by Quinctius[1] were nothing better than sheer injustice, fraudulence, violence, demagogy and subversiveness.

Well, then, you cannot contradict my assertion that Fidiculanius received no bribe from Cluentius. That being so, we have to assume that at least one of the men who voted for Oppianicus' condemnation did so without being bribed. And we must also, therefore, conclude that the chairman at the trial, Junius, can be cleared of the allegation that he deliberately filled vacancies on the bench with men who would accept a bribe to vote against Oppianicus.[2] For it is quite evident that one judge, at least, voted against him in perfect good faith – and did so even without having attended the whole hearing.

But if Fidiculanius is innocent of taking bribes when he voted that Oppianicus was guilty, then I ask you which of his fellow-judges in the case can be regarded as having done so. If he did not accept a bribe before giving his adverse vote, who did? I must emphasize that Quinctius, in attacking the other

1. Against Junius, Bulbus, Popilius, Gutta and Staienus.
2. See above, p. 116.

judges, did not bring one single accusation which was not brought against Fidiculanius as well. Their cases, each one of them, were the same as his in every detail. Now, Attius, in launching your charges today, it has been clear how greatly you have relied on the decisions in these previous trials. So what I have just been saying confronts you with a plain alternative. Either you have to protest that the acquittal of Fidiculanius was mistaken, or if you concede that it was right then you are obliged to make the further admission that Oppianicus' conviction was not brought about by bribery after all.

The correctness of my argument is surely proved by what followed after the acquittal of Fidiculanius: for none of the other judges who had acted in Oppianicus' trial were taken to court. To quote the convictions some of them may have received for *giving* bribes (in the annual elections of state officials), a matter which involves quite a different law,[1] is entirely irrelevant, however specific the charges may have been and however numerous the witnesses. As far as the proceedings against Oppianicus were concerned, the issue was whether they had committed the crime of *taking* bribes, not giving them; and if you are going to say that the taking of bribes told against them even when they were being tried under the law for giving bribes, it would obviously have counted against them a great deal more if their trials had been held under the law which is concerned with the taking of bribes.[2] And, secondly, if your allegation that they had taken bribes at the Oppianicus trial was so convincing that, quite regardless of the specific law (against giving bribes) under which they were being prosecuted, the taking of bribes still

1. The *Lex Acilia Calpurnia de ambitu* (67 B.C.).
2. i.e. the relevant clause of the *Lex Cornelia de sicariis et veneficiis*, under which the present case was being held. The 'extortion' law (*Lex Cornelia de repetundis*) was likewise directed against the taking of bribes (p. 186).

remained the charge which proved responsible for their ruin, then why on earth were Fidiculanius' colleagues not likewise put on trial for the same offence? After all, there was no lack of possible accusers, or for that matter of inducements either.

It is pointed out, in an effort to refute me, that Publius Septimius Scaevola, when his penalty was being assessed after conviction on another totally unrelated charge,[1] received a severer assessment on the grounds that he had received a bribe while serving as a judge at the trial of Oppianicus. However, an assessment of penalty is not, strictly speaking, a judicial action. In view of your own great experience, gentlemen, I do not need to explain the nature of this procedure in detail. But I would like to remind you that, in these final stages of a case after the verdict has already been pronounced, judges do not by any means always display the same amount of care that they have devoted to the previous phases of the trial.

When they are assessing penalties, for example, they are inclined to adopt one or two courses. If there has been a demand that the convicted man's assessment should take the form of a capital penalty,[2] they may well turn it down, because they are conscious that they have already made a personal enemy of the defendant just by finding him guilty, and they do not, therefore, want to pursue the matter any further. Or alternatively, under the impression that they have completed their duty by pronouncing the verdict, they do not bother to pay much attention to the aftermath. One thing which sometimes happens is that a man gets acquitted on a treason charge but subsequently convicted on a charge of bribery, and then, when

1. The assessment of penalty (*litis aestimatio*) followed after the verdict. It could include evidence of offences committed by the defendant under laws relating to courts other than the court in which he had just been tried.

2. See above, p. 17.

his penalty is assessed for the bribery conviction, the judges make it stiffer because they are still bearing the treason accusation in mind. And there is another phenomenon, too, which we see every day when a panel of judges is assessing a penalty: they incriminate someone for receiving bribes, but subsequently, when the incriminated person is brought to trial, they themselves decide to pronounce him not guilty. When they do this, they are not reversing a judicial decision, for they are admitting, in effect, that an assessment of penalty is not a judicial proceeding at all.

Scaevola was found guilty of charges quite unrelated to the trial of Oppianicus, on the evidence of a large number of witnesses from Apulia. But his penalty was assessed as if he had been found guilty in connexion with Oppianicus' trial, and, once again as if that had been so, powerful efforts were made to induce the judges to assess his penalty as a capital one. If, however, the assessment had rated as a judicial process, surely his enemies – either these same enemies or others – would have made sure that he was subsequently brought to trial under this very same law under which we are operating today. But that did not happen.

Next we come to the question of the black marks imposed on certain of Oppianicus' judges by the authority of the censors.[1] Once again, the prosecution declares that these marks possess the force of a judicial decision. But that is not how our ancestors ever described them; and they never accorded them the respect that such a judicial ruling would warrant.

Before I begin to discuss this particular question, I want to interpose a word or two about my own conception of the task

1. The judges were Manius Aquilius and Tiberius Gutta: see below, p. 202. For the Roman censors, see List of Terms. As guardians of public morals, they placed a mark (what we might call a 'black mark') against the names of senators or knights whom they regarded as meriting degradation.

I am undertaking today. While I have made the greatest effort to do everything in my power to protect my client in his present ordeal, I would like you to appreciate that I have also, at the same time, been trying my hardest to meet the claims of other responsibilities and friendships. Now, both these admirable citizens who were our last pair of censors are my friends,[1] and with one of them, as most of you are aware, I enjoy a particularly intimate friendship based on a variety of mutual services. In consequence, whatever criticisms I may have to offer about the black marks for which these two censors have been responsible, I hope you will realize that my words imply no sort of reflection on anything that they personally have done, but represent a critical comment on the duties of censors in general.

As for one of this recent pair, my friend Cnaeus Cornelius Lentulus, I want to take this opportunity of expressing my particular admiration of his noble character and the magnificent career which the Roman people has seen fit to grant him. And I know I can feel entirely confident that he will not object to my doing everything in my power to defend the interests of my imperilled client, just as he himself has always been ready to help his friends in need with every kind of loyal, unremitting, forceful and outspoken support. Nevertheless, as is only proper, I intend to discuss this question with caution and restraint. True, the last thing I want is to be found deficient in my duty to my client. But I am also most anxious not to give the impression of disrespect towards anyone's position, and not to let myself seem guilty of a breach of friendship.

Well, I observe that these two censors imposed black marks on certain of the judges of Junius' court which tried Oppianicus, alleging the very reasons upon which you insist. But I must remind you once again that our state has never assigned as

1. These censors (of 70 B.C.) were Cnaeus Cornelius Lentulus Clodianus and Lucius Gellius Publicola, the first men to hold this office since its revival by Sulla.

much weight to a censorial black mark as to a judicial decision. This is a known fact, and I shall not waste time over it. But perhaps I may just give one example all the same. Gaius Hosidius Geta was expelled from the senate by the censors Lucius Caecilius Metellus Delmaticus and Cnaeus Domitius Ahenobarbus.[1] And yet afterwards Hosidius actually became a censor himself. Here, then, was a man whose conduct had been stigmatized by the censors, and yet who was subsequently appointed to supervise the conduct of the entire Roman people, including the very men who had constituted themselves his own critics!

Surely, if a censorial black mark was regarded as a judicial decision, no one who had once suffered its stigma could possibly expect to resume his official career or ever be allowed back in the senate. For if the black mark had carried as much force as all that, his situation would be the same as that of a person who had been convicted by a judicial decision involving formal degradation: which would mean that he was debarred from every office and deprived of all standing for the rest of his life. As it is, however, there is a difference. Once a man is convicted in court, on a charge of theft for example, then, even if his accuser is only a humble freedman – a freedman, let us say, of Cnaeus Lentulus or Lucius Gellius Publicola – he will lose every civil privilege he ever had and will never again be rehabilitated to the slightest degree; whereas when our wise and eminent censors themselves, Lucius Gellius and Cnaeus Lentulus, placed black marks against people's names for stealing or taking bribes, men they had reprimanded in this way not only found their way back to the senate but actually won acquittal by the lawcourts concerned with those very offences.

Our forefathers ruled that no one should act as a judge in a question affecting a man's reputation, or even affecting the

1. In 115 B.C.; Geta had been consul in the previous year. For Delmaticus, see Genealogical Table I.

most trivial of his financial interests, unless both the parties concerned agreed to accept him. In consequence, all the laws defining the various disqualifications which prevent a person from holding offices of state, or serving as a judge, or acting as a prosecutor, make no mention whatever of this censorial stigma. That is because earlier generations were content with empowering the censors to inspire fear, and had no intention whatever of letting them inflict punishments for life. For this reason, as I propose to show, the black marks assigned by censors have often been subsequently annulled. They have been annulled by the Roman electorate, and they have been annulled by the decisions of judges – men, I would remind you, who are obliged under oath to display particularly scrupulous vigilance in arriving at their verdicts. When, for example, the senators and knights of Rome serving as judges have been called upon they have very frequently preferred to be directed by the prompting of their own consciences rather than by the guidance thus provided by the censors.

A second example is supplied by the city praetors.[1] They are obliged, again on oath, to fill their roster of judges with the best men they can find.[2] But they have never taken the view that a censorial black mark ought to exercise an adverse influence on a candidate. What is more, the censors themselves have very frequently reversed the verdicts of their own predecessors (if 'verdicts' is really the right word): and indeed they attach so little significance to each other's rulings that on certain occasions a censor has not merely criticized, but actually cancelled, a decision taken by his own colleague in office. For example, you will find one censor proposing to expel a man from the senate, and the other intending to keep him there, and maintaining that he is entirely worthy of that elevated rank. Or you will get one of the pair determined to

1. See List of Terms (Praetor).
2. This implies the existence of a general list of those eligible for judgeships; cf. above, p. 14.

disfranchise a man[1] or remove him from his tribe,[2] while his fellow-censor then proceeds to veto this intended action.

So it is clear enough that such acts by the censors are subject to reversal by the Roman people and subject also to contradiction at the hands of judges, bound by solemn oaths; state officials are quite capable of ignoring them; subsequent censors are apt to cancel those which their own predecessors have affixed; and even a single pair of censors is not always by any means of the same mind. When you attempt, therefore, to equate their pronouncements with judicial decisions, you are making a serious mistake.

In the light of these general conclusions, let us just try to form an estimate of the verdict the censors are supposed to have passed upon the bribery at the trial of Oppianicus.

What we have to decide first of all is whether they assigned black marks because these were deserved – or whether they only seemed to be deserved *afterwards*, because the censors had assigned them. If the latter was the case, gentlemen, you will have to be very careful indeed, or you will find yourselves presenting future censors with a tyrannical power over our entire community. For if this is how things are to be, a black mark from the censors will become as perilous a scourge to the citizens of Rome as those horrible proscriptions;[3] and we shall find the censor's pen-point, which our ancestors took so many precautions to blunt, as terrifying as the point of the dictator's sword.

I imagine you will reply, however, that these particular black

1. Literally, 'relegate to the *aerarii*', a class of citizens who were originally excluded from the tribes (see List of Terms). From the later fourth century B.C. onwards, however, they were admitted to the rustic tribes (which later included freedmen also).

2. i.e. moved from a superior (country) tribe into an urban tribe, of which the members constituted a lower class: see W. Peterson (ed.), *Cicero: Pro Cluentio*, p. 204.

3. i.e. of Sulla.

marks we are speaking of, those placed against the names of the judges who tried Oppianicus, ought to be given great weight all the same, for the simple reason that they were fully justified. Well, then, our first task must obviously be to inquire: *were* they justified – or were they not?

To answer that question, you must first dismiss every irrelevance from the issue. And then you must specify the actual bribe that Cluentius allegedly gave, you must say where he got it from, you must explain how he handed it over. In fact it is up to you to convince us that there really is the slightest trace whatever of any bribery on Cluentius' part. Finally, after you have done that, you must demonstrate equally convincingly that Oppianicus was a completely honest and reputable man, that nobody ever regarded him as anything else, and that his case had not been already damned by any previous trials. Then, and only then, will you be entitled to quote the pronouncements of the censors, and maintain that they have any bearing on the question we are considering.

Until you have succeeded in doing all that, the established facts continue to present a singularly different appearance. They place it on record, for example, that Oppianicus was the individual who made fraudulent erasures in order to alter a will, and subsequently arranged for bogus witnesses to sign and seal it. Then he proceeded to assassinate the person in whose name these frauds had been perpetrated. He struck down the son of his own uncle – after the man had been taken prisoner and enslaved. He had his own townsmen proscribed and put to death. He paid out money to procure an abortion. He murdered his mother-in-law. He murdered his wives. At one fell swoop he murdered his brother's wife and the children she had in her womb, and his own brother. Finally, he murdered his own children. Next, planning to give poison to his stepson, he was caught in the act. His accomplices and accessaries were duly convicted, and then he himself was put

on trial – whereupon he tried to bribe one of his judges to buy
the votes of the others.

So long, I repeat, as these charges are brought home against
Oppianicus, whereas the allegation of bribery against Cluentius totally lacks even one single piece of supporting evidence,
I submit that this suggestion or whim of the censors, whichever one may prefer to call it, entirely fails to make the
slightest contribution to your argument, or to the destruction
of my innocent client.

Why, then, did the censors behave as they did? Surely they
themselves will admit that their action was based on nothing
more than mere gossip and rumour – to put the matter at its
very strongest. Even they, surely, will not pretend that they
got any information from witnesses, or from documents, or
from any other valid source – or that they made the slightest
serious attempt to undertake a study of the problem before
acting in this way.

But in any case, even if none of these things were true, it
would still be wrong to consider their conclusion so irrevoc-
able that it cannot be reversed. As I said, there are numerous
occasions on which such reversals have taken place. I do not
propose to quote them at length; nor do I propose to drag up
instances from the remote past – or cite instances in which
powerful or influential individuals were involved. But I
should just like to speak of one humble aedile's clerk, of the
name of Decimus Matrinius. I was recently defending him
before the praetors Marcus Junius and Quintius Publicius, and
the curule aediles Marcus Plaetorius and Gaius Flaminius:[1]
and I succeeded in persuading them, on the strength of the
oaths they had taken upon assuming office, to appoint him to
his clerkship in spite of the fact that those censors of yours had
confirmed his degradation to a lower class.[2] For since the
judges considering his record could find nothing wrong with

1. See List of Terms (Praetors, Aediles). This case was in 69 B.C.
2. See above, p. 199 nn. 1, 2.

him, they felt determined to treat him on his own merits, rather than on the basis of anything the censors had said.

But to return to Oppianicus' trial: when the censors spoke of the 'corrupt judgement' with which it concluded, is there any real reason to suppose that their own judgement on the matter was founded on any proved facts or careful research? I see that the recipients of the black marks in this connexion were Manius Aquilius and Tiberius Gutta. What are we to deduce from that? Well, if the censors are proposing to say that only two of the judges at Oppianicus' trial were bribed, it must be inferred that all the others who declared him guilty were innocent of taking bribes. If that was so, Oppianicus was in no sense the victim of intrigue or corruption, and Quinctius was quite mistaken, at those mass meetings of his, to maintain that everyone who voted his client guilty must be regarded as culpable or suspect. For, as I say, the censorial pronouncement did not attempt to associate more than two of the judges with the scandal. Yet, if the verdict against Oppianicus was to be stigmatized as corrupt, the censors were surely under an obligation to prove that the criminal act which they alleged against two of the judges was shared by the others who had likewise voted in favour of the defendant's conviction.

The institution of the censor's black mark is defended as a product of military tradition. But this is an entirely untenable view. True, our ancestors decided that if a large group of soldiers had committed a serious military offence the penalty should be inflicted upon a small proportion of them, chosen by lot.[1] The intention evidently was that, although only a few of the delinquents actually suffered punishment, none of them should be allowed to escape the fear that they *might* be punished. But it does not in any way follow from this that the censors, too, when they are called upon to decide who should

1. The traditional punishment of decimation – the execution of one man in ten, clubbed to death by his fellow-soldiers; cf. A. W. Lintott, *Violence in Republican Rome*, pp. 41ff.

be permitted to sit on the senate, or when they have to pass judgement on other Roman citizens and reprimand their moral shortcomings, should proceed in the same fashion. For, after all, a soldier, even if he has on one occasion deserted his post, or displayed cowardice in the face of a ferocious enemy attack, may nevertheless, at some future time, prove himself a better soldier, and a good man, and a useful citizen. That is why our forefathers felt that this was the right way to treat soldiers who had failed in their duty in the field. The fear of punishment and death must be instilled into every one of them; yet in order that executions should not take the toll of too many lives it was decided that lots should be drawn.

But if you were a censor and were drawing up a list of the senate, I cannot believe that you would choose to proceed in the same manner. If a number of people have taken bribes in order to get an innocent man convicted, surely you would not propose, instead of punishing them all, to select just a few of them for degradation, on some entirely arbitrary basis. Would it not be the very height of impropriety for the senate to keep one single senator in its ranks, for our public tribunals to keep one single judge, for our nation to keep one single citizen, if he is a man who, to your certain knowledge and before your own eyes, has sold his honour and his character in order to ruin an innocent individual? If you do not agree, you are openly admitting that if a man has robbed an innocent citizen of his country, his possessions and his own children, it is perfectly all right, as far as you are concerned, that he should evade the black mark of censorial displeasure. But how, if you were a censor, could you still declare yourself to be the inspector of morality, the instructor in the stern school of ancient virtue, if you deliberately retain as a senator an individual tainted with such an appalling crime, without any regard for the principle that people who have committed identical crimes ought to receive identical penalties?

To suggest that a type of punishment devised by our

ancestors to combat cowardice in time of war should be applied
to dishonest senators in time of peace is by no means a sensible
proposition. However, let us assume for a moment that this
was what really had to be done, that this military custom
really had to be regarded as the precedent for censorial black
marks: then, even so, surely, lots should have been drawn, as
in the army. It might well be argued, I admit, that censors
would be wrong to distribute their punishments according to
the hazards of the lot, since this would subject their treatment
of criminals to the caprices of fortune. But, granted you may
not want to follow that particular method, it still remains
wholly improper, when many are guilty, to *select* a small
number of them as recipients of the shameful mark.

However, we all realize perfectly well that what the censors
were really trying to do was to catch the breeze of popular
favour. The question of Oppianicus' trial had been taken up at
mass-meetings at the instance of a tribune of revolutionary
inclinations, and, although there had never been the slightest
investigation of the facts, the crowd applauded his attitude.
No one was given an opportunity to speak against the view
he was putting forward: indeed, no one so much as tried to
argue the opposite case at all. Besides, the lawcourts at that
time had become highly unpopular – and only a few months
after the trial they once again became seriously discredited
when it was discovered that certain voting tablets bore private
markings.[1] There was a general feeling that the censors simply
had to take some note of such deplorable judicial scandals.
Here were these judges, who seemed to have behaved very
badly and were already in deep disgrace, and the censors
considered it only proper to deepen this disgrace still further
by the imposition of the black mark. They were also influenced

1. This was at the trial for extortion of Marcus Terentius Varro
Lucullus (see Genealogical Table, I), whose counsel and relative Quintus
Hortensius Hortalus had the voting-tablets privately marked so that he
could see which way the judges bribed by himself had voted.

by another consideration as well. For it was in this very year, during their own tenure of the censorship, that knights had been admitted to join the senators on the judicial panels.[1] This made the censors particularly anxious to indicate, by inflicting degradation upon suitably chosen individuals, that they were expressing their disapproval of the courts as these had formerly been constituted, with a membership of senators only.

Yet if only I, or someone else, had been given the chance to contest those black marks before the censors in question, men of their lofty intellectual qualifications could not have failed to see that my objections were thoroughly justified. For the whole story makes it quite clear that they had no reliable sources of information of their own to depend upon. Their only purpose in affixing the black marks was to get themselves talked about and win popular applause. The censor Lucius Gellius Publicola for example, when he was stigmatizing Publius Popilius, one of the judges who had voted for Oppianicus' condemnation, stated explicitly that the reason why he was taking this action was because Popilius had accepted a bribe to condemn an innocent man. Well, gentlemen, Gellius must have had powers of second sight if he could be so certain of the innocence of Oppianicus, whom he may well never have set eyes upon, when a number of exceedingly shrewd judges, after hearing all the facts of the case, had preferred to give a verdict of 'not proven' – not to speak of those who voted for conviction.

However, let that be. Gellius declared that Popilius had acted wrongly, concluding that he accepted a bribe from Cluentius. But the other censor, Lentulus, did not share this opinion at all. Certainly, Lentulus agreed that Popilius should not be a member of the senate, but that was for another reason altogether – because he was the son of a freedman.[2] And in

1. The *Lex Aurelia* of Lucius Aurelius Cotta (70 B.C.); see above, p. 116.
2. See List of Terms. In 312 B.C. the censor Appius Claudius Caecus had made the sons of freedmen ineligible for the senate.

spite of holding this view, Lentulus still permitted Popilius to retain a senator's seat at the Games, without making the slightest attempt to discredit him. In other words, he was virtually pronouncing that when Popilius had voted for Oppianicus' condemnation he had done so without having taken a bribe. Moreover, at a subsequent bribery trial at which Popilius was called upon to give evidence, Lentulus actually complimented him, in no uncertain terms, on his reliability as a witness.

So Lentulus took a different attitude from Gellius: and Gellius criticized the opinion of Lentulus. Since, therefore, even the two fellow-censors themselves felt unable to abide by one another's decisions, I quite fail to see how anyone could argue that censorial black marks should be regarded as unalterable and binding for evermore!

The prosecution goes on to say that the same censors also stigmatized Cluentius himself. Yes, they did: but not because he had done anything disgraceful. Indeed, in all his life he had never performed a wicked action, and never even a mistaken one. A man of higher principles or more honourable conduct, a man more meticulously scrupulous in carrying out all his obligations, would be impossible to find.

Now, the censors do not deny this at all. All that they were doing by their action towards Cluentius was to proceed in accordance with the longstanding rumour that the court trying Oppianicus had been bribed. With regard to my client's fine character, integrity, and blameless life, their opinion was no different from what I should have wished it to be myself. But what they felt was that having penalized the judges they could not very well leave the prosecutor untouched.

Many precedents from our past history have a bearing on this point; but I will quote only one of them, and then I will say no more. The incident I want to mention concerns that very great and famous man, the younger Scipio Africanus.

During his term of office as censor[1] he was conducting the periodical review of the knights[2] when Gaius Licinius Sacerdos appeared in the parade. Whereupon Scipio, in a loud voice which was audible to everyone present, asserted that, to his certain knowledge, Licinius had committed deliberate perjury. Scipio added that if anyone wished to bring a formal action against the man, he himself would give evidence in support of the charge. But no one came forward as prosecutor. So then Scipio bade Licinius carry on, and told him he could lead his horse past. The censor, Scipio, was a personage whose judgement had always been quite good enough for the people of Rome – indeed good enough for all the nations of the world. Yet when it came to inflicting disgrace upon another man, he was not prepared to regard his own personal knowledge as enough.

Had Cluentius received as fair treatment as that, he would have had not the slightest difficulty in overcoming all those groundless suspicions, and all the prejudices stirred up by mob oratory – even if the censors themselves had been his judges.

However, there is also another argument you have put forward against me: and this, I must admit, presents a dilemma, upon which I do not find it easy to pronounce. I refer to the passage you read out from the will of the elder Cnaeus Egnatius, in which he announced that he was disinheriting his son on the grounds that the latter, as a judge in the trial of Oppianicus, had accepted a bribe to secure the defendant's conviction.

But does the testator seem to you a wise and honourable

1. Publius Cornelius Scipio Africanus the younger (Aemilianus) was censor in 142 B.C. with Lucius Memmius.

2. The knights, in Republican times, paraded before the censors in the Forum (in imperial times the review became annual). This was an archaic survival of their original role as a cavalry force. Censors could take the opportunity to 'deprive unworthy persons of their horse', i.e. strike them off the list. Those to whom they found no objection were bidden to 'lead their horse past'.

man? I can assure you he is not. On the contrary, it would be difficult to find anyone more completely frivolous and inconsistent. I do not propose to enlarge on this point, but do please just take another look at the will itself, his document you were reading out. For there you will see that Egnatius, in the process of disinheriting the son for whom he had formed such a dislike, contrives in the most unpredictable fashion to leave his inheritance not only to his other son, whom he liked, but also to a set of people who were total strangers and had not the slightest connexion with either himself or his appointed heir.

But this brings us to a question, Attius, which I advise you to study with extremely anxious care. Tell me: do you propose to attach weight to the conclusions of the censors, or to those of the elder Egnatius? If it is Egnatius whom you are going to support, then you have no alternative but to ignore the black marks that the censors allotted to Oppianicus' judges: because this very same Egnatius, whose authority you find so significant, was himself one of those who were expelled from the senate! If, on the other hand, you prefer to side with the censors, then I have to ask you to bear in mind something else: the younger Egnatius, whose father disinherited him in such a truly censorial style, was actually allowed to remain a member of the senate by the very same censors who expelled his own father.

Another point emphasized by the other side is that the allegation of bribery at the trial of Oppianicus was confirmed by a unanimous decision of the Roman senate.

What action, in fact, did the senate take? Well, it went into the matter, and passed a resolution.[1] Of course, once a question of this kind had been officially brought to its attention it could

1. The senate passed a resolution referring in general terms to the circumstances of the trial of Oppianicus, and requesting the consuls to investigate any alleged cases of bribery at criminal trials.

not possibly refuse to take cognizance of the matter. Once a tribune of the people had stirred up the crowd practically to the point of physical violence, once the cry had gone forth that a good man, an innocent citizen, had been the victim of bribery, once the senate itself (which was still responsible for the lawcourts at the time) had become bitterly unpopular because of suspicions that this was what had happened, it became imperative that they should pass a resolution. To have left all that popular outcry completely unnoticed would have involved grave danger for the state. But please consider the actual *terms* of the decree that the senate passed. It was framed with complete impartiality, consummate intelligence and meticulous care. *If there are any*, the decree began, *who have been responsible for the corruption of a public court of law.* That is to say, the resolution makes no attempt to assert that corruption has taken place. Had Aulus Cluentius himself been asked for his opinion about the trial of Oppianicus, he would have expressed himself in precisely the same terms as these senators – the very men whom you suppose to have censured him!

And then we come to the question whether the senate's resolution actually led to the passage of any legislation through the Assembly. That is to say, did the consul at the time, the very learned Lucius Lucullus,[1] in fact propose any law on the subject? He did not. Or did the consuls of the following year, Marcus Terentius Varro Lucullus and Gaius Cassius Longinus? For it was upon them, as consuls designate at the time of the decree, that the senate relied for the execution of its wishes. No, they too did not pass any such law. And this total absence of legislation on the subject, which you once again attribute, without any shred of supporting suspicion, to bribery on the part of Cluentius, must, instead, primarily be credited to the fairness and wisdom which these two successive pairs of consuls displayed. For confronted by a senatorial decree which

1. See Genealogical Table I. Lucius Lucullus' colleague in that year (74 B.C.) was Marcus Aurelius Cotta.

had only been passed, after all, in order to calm down a temporary outburst of popular feeling, they decided that they were under no obligation to bring it before the Assembly as a legislative measure.

And then the very same Roman public, which Lucius Quinctius' lying protests had goaded into clamouring for a bill of precisely such a kind, subsequently got into such an emotional state when they saw the tears of the little son of Gaius Junius, the chairman at Oppianicus' trial, that they proceeded to flock to an uproarious meeting with the specific purpose of disowning the proposed law setting up the inquiry!

This was an excellent illustration of a frequently noted phenomenon. The sea is habitually calm; but under the impact of strong winds it becomes rough and stormy. The people of Rome are just the same. When left to themselves, they are peaceful. But the speech of a demagogue like Quinctius can whip them up with the effect of a furious hurricane.

There is also another expression of opinion which I have to contend with. And I can hardly deny that it carries great weight, because this time I am supposed to have uttered the words myself. Attius quoted from some oration or other, which he maintained I had delivered,[1] a passage exhorting the judges in that particular case to give their verdicts honestly. In the course of this passage I mentioned a number of legal actions that had not been satisfactory, and among them was this trial of Oppianicus.

However, you must admit that at the very beginning of the speech I am delivering now I freely admitted that the case had

1. Probably Cicero's first speech against Verres, in which there is a critical reference to Marcus Atilius Bulbus and others unnamed, who are probably Gaius Fidiculanius Falcula and Gaius Aelius Staienus; *Cicero: Selected Works*, pp. 51ff. Cicero's deliberately vague reference to 'some speech or other' was probably intended to raise a laugh, since his Verrine orations were famous.

aroused a great deal of criticism. And when I was delivering
that other speech to which Attius refers, how on earth, since
my specific subject at the time was the scandalous situation in
the courts, could I possibly have failed to mention something
of the sort? But I was neither speaking of a matter of personal
knowledge, nor submitting sworn evidence. The terms of my
address were prompted by the demands of the moment rather
than by any authoritative conclusions I might have formed
about the specific question of Oppianicus' trial. As counsel for
the prosecution I had to make it my first objective to work
upon the emotions of the public and the judges. So I was
determined to draw upon every available rumour which
could supply me with criticisms of the courts; this did not
necessarily mean that those rumours represented opinions of
my own. In such a situation it was quite obviously out of the
question to maintain complete silence about the trial of
Oppianicus, which was the subject of such acute popular
excitement at the time.

For it is a serious mistake to imagine that the speeches we
pleaders make in the lawcourts represent an authentic record
of our personal attitudes. All orations of this type reflect the
requirements of some particular case and circumstance, not
the private opinions of the advocates themselves. If a case
could speak for itself, no one would bother to employ an
advocate at all. But since a spokesman has to be found, we
are called in, and it is our job to express not our own
individual points of view, but whatever conclusions the facts
of the case seem to warrant. There is a story about something
that very talented man Marcus Antonius used to say.[1] He
had never written any of his speeches down, and the reason
for this, he remarked, was because, if one of them happened
to include some statement he might later prefer to have

1. For the two great orators of the previous generation, Marcus
Antonius and Lucius Licinius Crassus, see *Cicero on the Good Life*,
Penguin, pp. 230ff.

left unsaid, he would then be at liberty to deny he had ever said it. Though, in fact, a lot of things that we say, and actions that we perform, get remembered very well, even if we have never committed them to writing.

On this sort of point one of the models I myself prefer to follow is that paragon of eloquence and learning Lucius Licinius Crassus. On one occasion he was defending Cnaeus Plancus against Marcus Junius Brutus the Prosecutor, an orator of great forcefulness and skill.[1] Brutus brought two readers into court and got them to read out, one after another, two passages from different speeches by Crassus which directly contradicted each other. In one of them, while opposing a bill intended to disband the settlement of Roman citizens at Narbo,[2] Crassus had done everything possible to bring the senate into disrepute. In the other speech, however, which was in support of the law of Quintus Servilius Caepio,[3] he praised the senate most warmly. And then Brutus arranged for a further passage to be read out, from the same speech. This consisted of violent and repeated attacks upon the Roman knights – Brutus' intention being to discredit Crassus with the judges, who were knights and not senators at that time.

That embarrassed Crassus considerably. When he got up to reply, he started by explaining that his speeches that had been quoted were the products of two quite different sets of circumstances, for which it had been necessary to adapt two correspondingly different tones.

Next, in order to show Brutus the sort of person he had

1. Marcus Junius Brutus was known critically as the Prosecutor, because 'he made a regular profession of prosecution'; Cicero, *Brutus*, xxxiv, 130. Plancus' family name was Munatius or Plancius.

2. The modern Narbonne, in southern France. The 'colony' was probably founded in 118 B.C., but the present passage refers to a subsequent attempt to abolish it; cf. B. M. Levick, *Classical Review*, 1970, p. 376.

3. See above, p. 14 n. 2.

been trying to provoke – for Crassus was a man of great wit and humour, as well as remarkable eloquence – he in his turn produced readers, and this time no less than three of them: they appeared carrying in their hands the legal treatises, a different one in each case, left by Marcus Junius Brutus, the father of Brutus the Prosecutor. In due course the readers got up, one after another, and proceeded to read out in turn the opening sentences of these three essays. I expect you remember how they go. One of them starts: 'I happened to be at my country house at Privernum.' When this had been read out, Crassus intervened and asked what had become of this Privernum estate. The second opened with the words: 'I was at Alba with my son Brutus' – on hearing which Crassus inquired about the Alba property, too. And the third treatise had a different beginning: 'I happened to be sitting with my son Brutus at my estate at Tibur' – whereupon Crassus expressed a desire to know about that estate as well.[1] He also added two comments. The elder Brutus, he said, being a prudent man and well aware of his son's exceptional extravagance, evidently wanted to leave behind this written record of the various properties he was going to bequeath to him! And indeed, if the father had been able to add that he had been in the young man's company in his baths as well – as considerations of propriety prevented him from doing, in view of his son's extreme youth[2] – he would no doubt have taken the opportunity to include a mention of that building too: as it happens, however, the elder Brutus' baths are not mentioned in his literary works, though they figure very prominently in his accounts, and in the censors' register as well.[3]

1. The towns mentioned are the modern Priverno, Castel Gandolfo and Tivoli respectively.

2. 'According to our custom, grown sons do not bathe with their fathers, nor sons-in-law with their fathers-in-law.' Cicero, On Duties, I, xxxv, 129.

3. The elder Brutus had built these public baths as a speculation.

So that was how Crassus got his own back on Brutus, and made him regret that he had had the excerpts from Crassus' two speeches read aloud. For the speeches in question had been concerned with affairs of national importance, in which consistency is perhaps more to be expected, and Crassus was probably annoyed at being caught out.

Your own recitation of the passages from my speeches, on the other hand, does not cause me the slightest annoyance. My remarks in them were perfectly well adapted to the times when the speeches were delivered, and to the lawsuits with which they were concerned. Moreover, in making the remarks you quoted I did not commit myself to anything which hinders me from defending the present action with absolute honesty and unrestricted freedom.

And if I should go on to admit that, although I now know all there is to be known about Cluentius' case, at that earlier time I was not altogether immune from the popular prejudice of the epoch, who, I ask you, could find fault with me for that? Be fair, gentlemen, and grant me the request which I put forward at the outset, and which I repeat at this juncture: if you entered this court feeling inclined to criticize the verdict against Oppianicus, you should wholly abandon that view now that you have seen what the case was really all about, and have learnt where the true facts lie.

3. The Innocence of Cluentius

Well, Attius, I have answered every one of the points you raised about the trial and conviction of Oppianicus. And I think you will have to admit that you made a very serious mistake. You imagined I was going to base my defence of Cluentius not on the merits of his case at all but on legal technicalities. That was why you kept on repeating how you had heard that my defence was proposing to rely heavily upon the letter of the law governing this court. Am I not right?

Did your possession of this advance knowledge mean that some of my friends are traitors without my knowing it? Am I to assume that one of these so-called friends is the kind of man who is prepared to communicate my plans to my opponents? How happy I should be to identify the scoundrel who gave you this information! Or did I, perhaps, tell someone myself? But, actually, I do not believe anyone in particular is to blame. I suspect that what suggested the idea to you was the phrasing of the law itself.

Surely, however, it must have dawned on you, before long, that in the course of this speech I have not even made one single reference to loopholes in the law: I have conducted my whole defence on the assumption that Cluentius enjoys no legal exemption whatsoever. You may well be surprised that I have chosen to adopt this approach, since after all, so far as any fallible human being is entitled to say, I have taken care not to neglect the smallest point that might help me to refute this unjust allegation against my client. In view, therefore, of my refusal to invoke legal technicalities, it may well occur to someone to ask whether, in answering a capital charge, I think it wrong to take refuge in a point of law. No, gentlemen, that is not my opinion. But I am doing what I always do. When I act as counsel for the defence of a man of honour and intelligence, I never allow myself to be guided by my own ideas alone: I also make a particular point of deferring to the views and wishes of my client. And that is what I did on this occasion as well.

Now it is my business, clearly, to have some knowledge of the laws under which we advocates have to operate and proceed. Consequently, when the brief was first brought to me, I immediately informed Cluentius that the clause beginning *Whosoever shall have conspired to secure a man's condemnation* did not apply to himself as a knight, though it applies to my own senatorial order.[1] However, Cluentius at once began to implore me, in the most urgent terms, not to base his defence upon the letter of the law. I told him I did not agree with this attitude: but he finally converted me to this own view. For he protested, with tears in his eyes, that even his Roman citizenship itself[2] did not mean more to him than his good name. And so I gave way to his wishes. It is true that clients ought not always to be humoured, but the reason why I did so on this occasion was because I saw that the case could be defended more than adequately upon its own merits, without having recourse to the technicalities of the law at all. I also realized that, although the line of defence to which Cluentius objected would have been a good deal less arduous, the approach that I have instead adopted is the more honourable of the two. If all I had been concerned about was to secure a favourable verdict, I should merely have read the law out aloud and then sat down.

All the same, I cannot say I am impressed by Attius' argument that the framing of the law, which imposes sanctions against a senator who corrupts a court, but not against a Roman knight who does the same, is deplorably wrong. I will consider this question in due course. But meanwhile, even if I were prepared, for purposes of argument, to concede that it might be wrong, you for your part would have to concede to me that it is a great deal more wrong still, in a country which depends upon its laws, to refuse to obey them. For law is the bond which assures to each of us his honourable life within our commonwealth. It is the foundation of liberty, the fountain-head of justice. It is what keeps the heart and mind and initiative and feeling of our nation alive. The state without

1. Cicero refers to the clause of this law (the *Lex Cornelia de sicariis et veneficiis*) relating to judicial murder, which was operative only against senators (p. 117 n. 2). This whole issue was a delicate one for Cicero, who wished to offend neither the senators nor the knights on the bench (pp. 116 ff.).

2. Which he stood to lose if he lost this case; p. 17.

law would be like a body without brain; it could make no use of its sinews, its blood or its limbs. The magistrates who administer the law, the judges who act as its spokesmen, all the rest of us who live as its servants, grant it our allegiance as a guarantee of our freedom.

Tell me, Quintus Voconius Naso, what gives you the right to sit in that seat?[1] What is the power that has elevated you to preside over your distinguished fellow-judges? And you, gentlemen, please indicate why you rather than anyone else, a small body of men out of the large community of Roman citizens, have been called upon to pronounce verdicts affecting the entire fortunes of other human beings? Tell me by what right Attius has been given the opportunity to say all that he pleased, and by what right I myself, too, have been permitted to address you at such length. Tell me the purpose of these scribes and attendants, and all the other functionaries whom I see engaged in the work of this court. It is at the bidding of the law that every one of these things is done. The law, I repeat, is the controlling mind which rules and governs every activity of this court.

And just the same is true of every other criminal court that we possess. It is true, for example, of the second and third sections of this murder court, under Marcus Plaetorius and Gaius Flaminius respectively. It is true of the embezzlement court of Gaius Orchivius. It is true of the bribery court of which I myself am chairman. It is true of the court of Gaius Aquilius, which is at this very moment conducting a trial for bribery in elections. And the same applies to all the other courts as well.[2] And if you then look round at all the various departments of our government, you will once again find that every one of them, without exception, is under the direction and control of the law.

1. He was chairman of the court.
2. For these *quaestiones*, cf. above, pp. 13, 179. Cicero's court was the *quaestio de repetundis*, Aquilius' the *quaestio de ambitu* (p. 193).

Imagine, Titus Attius, that someone was proposing to prosecute you in my court. Being a knight, you would loudly declare that the law does not apply to you. And if you made a declaration of this kind, one would by no means be entitled to interpret it as an admission that you had taken a bribe. For you would merely be refusing, quite legitimately, to undergo a lot of risk and trouble which you are not obliged to undergo, since you are exempted from it by law.

Now let us consider how this point affects our present case, so that we can see the implications of the legal principles you are trying to establish. The law which governs this court instructs its chairman, that is to say Quintus Voconius Naso, together with yourselves, gentlemen, who are the judges appointed to work with him, to investigate cases of poisoning. To investigate whom exactly? No limitation is proposed: *whosoever shall have made the poison, sold it, bought it, possessed it, or administered it.* But then read what the law goes on to say next: *the court shall try him on a capital charge.* What does 'him' mean? Who is to be tried? Any man who has conspired or joined a plot for this purpose? Not at all. For next follows this definite restriction. *Whatsoever military tribune of the four first legions, whatsoever quaestor, whatsoever tribune of the people*[1] – and then come the designations of all the officers of state, one after another – *or whosoever has given, or shall have given, his vote in the senate.* And then: *whosoever of them has, or shall have, conspired or joined a plot to secure a conviction by a lawcourt of the state.*[2] Note 'whosoever *of them*'. Whosoever of whom? Of those, surely, who have just been mentioned in the preceding

1. For military tribunes, quaestors, and tribunes of the people, see List of Terms. There were four first legions, five second, and four third. The four first were the original legions which had been assigned in early times to the consuls: their twenty-four military tribunes ranked among the officers of state (*magistratus*), since they were appointed not by nomination of the consuls but by popular elections from the senators or knights.

2. This is the 'judicial murder' clause (p. 17).

list. There is a deliberate distinction being drawn here, and the wording makes it perfectly clear: because where, on the other hand, the law is intended to have universal application, it states as much explicitly. For example, it says: *whosoever has, or shall have, made a poison.* This makes every single individual, man and woman, free and slave, liable to trial on this particular charge. If, therefore, the intention had been the same with regard to conspiracy, the law would have included the additional phrase *or whosoever shall have conspired.* But, instead, it goes on to ordain that the court *shall try on a capital charge him who shall have held office as an officer of state or shall have given his vote in the senate: whosoever of these has, or shall have, conspired,* and so on.

Does Cluentius come under this definition? No, obviously he does not. What heading does he come under, then? Not that it really matters, since in any case he has refused to allow his defence to be based on a point of law, and, that being so, I cannot insist on the legal point; I am letting my client have his way. Yet all the same, Attius, I do want to offer a brief refutation of your assertions, and to develop certain arguments of my own, quite regardless of my defence of Cluentius. For, granted that there is an aspect of the case in which he feels that his own personal view ought to prevail, there is also an aspect in which I, too, have special interests at stake. He believes it is best for himself that his innocence should be demonstrated on its merits and on the facts, and not on legal technicalities. Whereas I, on the other hand, cannot help feeling it essential from my own personal standpoint to prevent anyone from concluding that I have been worsted by Attius upon any of the issues that we have been disputing.

For this is not the only action I am called upon to plead. I place my efforts at the disposal of anyone and everyone who may feel willing to rely on my abilities as an advocate. And, in consequence, I should be deeply reluctant for anybody who is present in court today to interpret my silence as indicating that I agree with the assertions which Attius has made about the law. Certainly, I will fall in with your wishes, Cluentius, to the extent of not reading this law out aloud. However, just at this moment, I repeat, I am not speaking as your advocate at all; I am speaking on my own behalf. And I propose, therefore, to develop arguments which I know are expected of me.

You maintain it to be unjust, Attius, that all men are not bound equally by the same laws. Well, let us suppose, for a moment, that I would be prepared to admit that you are right. If so, however, what requires to be done is that the laws should be changed – not that we should fail to obey them in their existing forms. And there is another aspect of the matter as well. The members of our senate are men who have been elevated by the favour of the Roman people to a higher rank than other Roman citizens; and this being the case they have always felt it right, also, to regard themselves as bound by correspondingly more stringent legal restraints. For there are numerous advantages in life which we senators just have to forgo. There are a great many inconveniences and difficulties that we are compelled to accept. Nevertheless, we believe we are compensated by the honour and glory of our position.

But you try applying the same conditions to the knights and the other orders of the state. They would simply refuse to put up with them. For since they have been unable to reach the highest eminences of the Roman official career – or perhaps they have not even made the attempt – they maintain that they should also be less exposed than our state officials, drawn from the senate, to all the entanglements created by statutory and judicial restrictions. There are, in consequence, certain laws which are binding upon us senators but not any other class.

I need only mention a single one of these laws here: and that is the statute under which Cluentius is being tried today. It was proposed by Gaius Sempronius Gracchus to deal with false witness to compass a man's death – and his motive was to help the people, not to oppose them. Later on came Lucius

Cornelius Sulla, who was anything but the people's friend. Yet even he, when he established a court to deal with this sort of charge – the present court, created by the law under which you are operating today[1] – even he did not venture to impose this unfamiliar type of tribunal upon the Roman populace in general, which had always hitherto been free from any such sanctions. And yet if he had believed it within his power, nothing would have given him greater pleasure, in view of his notorious hatred of the knightly order, than to make this court into the principal instrument of the venomous proscriptions he was directing against the knights who had served as judges under the previous regime.

But now, gentlemen, I have to ask you to give special heed to what I am going to say next, and take every possible precaution against a very grave danger. The danger is this: the entire purpose of Attius' manoeuvre is to widen the scope of this law so as to extend its penalties to the order of knights as well. Not every senator shares this aim; but there are certainly a few who do. The opposite view, however, is taken by all those members of the senate whose high principles and integrity give them the strength to stand firm; and I can confidently assume that this applies to every one of yourselves. Every such senator, indeed any senator whatsoever who is capable of rising above the biases of party politics, desires that the knights should occupy a position second only to his own order, and united with it by the most harmonious relations. But there are certain other individuals who want to see all power concentrated in their own hands, without anyone else, or any other order, being allowed a share of it at all.

What these people hope is that the mere threat that knights who have served as judges may be subjected to prosecutions like the present one will make it possible to bring the entire body of knights under their own control. For they see that

1. i.e. the clause was perpetuated as the judicial murder clause of Sulla's *Lex Cornelia de sicariis et veneficiis*.

this element in the community is getting stronger and stronger. They see, also, that the part it now plays in providing judges for the courts[1] is winning popular favour. And what they are really after – and now I am addressing you members of the knightly order – is that by exposing you to this menace they will be able to remove the sting from the strictness that you display in court. For it is hardly to be expected that any judge will venture to pass sentence on a man whose position in the community is even slightly more powerful than his own, when he sees that he is likely to make himself liable to trial on charges of conspiracy and combination.

Now, when Marcus Livius Drusus was tribune of the people,[2] the one purpose of that eminent and formidable man was precisely to hale knights, who had served as judges, before the appropriate courts. The entire nobility of the time supported his efforts – and the Roman knights who tried to resist him displayed an impressive amount of courage. Gaius Flavius Pusio, Cnaeus Titinius, Gaius Maecenas[3] – knights who were the backbone of the Roman people – and all the other members of their order were very far from sharing Cluentius' present fears that there is something shameful about resisting such attempts. On the contrary, they opposed Drusus right out in the open. With bitter protests, they intrepidly and honestly pointed out, for all the world to hear, that had they wished to devote their efforts to the pursuit of a public career, the Roman people might well have appointed them to the loftiest positions in the state.

'We are well aware,' they went on to say, 'of the splendour,

1. i.e. since the *Lex Aurelia* of 70 B.C.; see above, p. 116 and n. 2.

2. Marcus Livius Drusus, tribune 91 B.C., was the son of an opponent of Gaius Gracchus. His measures to check the corruption of the courts were strongly opposed by the knights, and were cancelled after his assassination.

3. A member of the Etruscan family, from Arretium, which was to produce Augustus' adviser of the same name.

privilege and grandeur of a senator's life. We have never despised these things. Yet we felt satisfied with our own rank, which was the rank our fathers held before us. That is the peaceful and tranquil life we have preferred to follow, a life sheltered from tempestuous public animosities – sheltered, for example, from this kind of trial. Either you must give us back the years of our prime so that we can embark on official careers after all, or, since that is impossible, you must leave us to lead our own sort of lives, in favour of which we sacrificed all such electoral ambitions. We chose to forgo the prizes of office, because we wanted to avoid the dangers that accompanied them: and since, in view of this, we have renounced all public recognition, it would be unjust if we were made liable to unprecedented forms of judicial proceedings. Now a senator, we maintain, would have no right whatsoever to make the same sort of protest as we are making now. For it was in full knowledge of this liability that he embarked upon his career. Besides, he has very many advantages to counterbalance its drawbacks: rank, prestige, a magnificent life in Rome, fame and influence in foreign states, the purple-bordered robe,[1] the insignia of office, the official attendants' rods,[2] armies, commands, provincial governorships. In bestowing all these things upon members of the senate, our ancestors intended to ensure that they should be resplendently rewarded for their noble deeds. But at the same time they made sure that, if a senator did wrong, his penalty should be correspondingly heavy.'

It should be added that the knights who raised protests of this kind certainly did not envisage that they might be brought within the law under which Cluentius is being prosecuted today – at that time it was the Sempronian and now it is the Cornelian Law – since they appreciated that this was framed

1. The *toga praetexta* of the higher state officials.
2. The *fasces* carried by the lictors who walked in front of the leading Roman officials.

in such a way that it could not be made to apply to knights at all. But what they were anxious to avoid was liability to some entirely fresh legislation.

As for Cluentius, he had never objected to rendering an account of his life even under a statute which does not, in fact, concern him. If you think it is right and proper that he should render such an account, then surely the correct course would be to bestir ourselves to get the jurisdiction of this court extended at the earliest possible moment to cover every order of society, as it does not at present. But in the meantime, for heaven's sake, let us abide by the laws *in their existing form*. For it is our possession of these statutes that safeguards everything in the world that we hold of value – our rights, our freedom, and our security alike. And just think of the gross unfairness of stepping right outside the law of the land. Here is something the Roman people are not on their guard about at all: why should they be? They have entrusted their country and their fortunes to your safe keeping. They are not worrying. It does not enter their minds to suspect that a small group of judges is going to force them into a subjection to an enactment they have never passed, and to a court from which they believed themselves to be completely free and exempt.

Attius on the other hand, and he is an honourable and eloquent young man, was attempting to maintain that *every* law is binding upon *every* Roman citizen. You listened to him in attentive silence, as you should. All the same, the plain fact remains that Aulus Cluentius, who is a knight, is being tried under a law which does not apply to knights at all, since it is only applicable to members of the senate and former officers of state. Yet Cluentius will not allow me to protest against this; he firmly refuses to let me shelter within the citadel of the law, and employ it as the bulwark of my case on his behalf. If, therefore, he emerges victorious, as my confidence in your fair-mindedness assures me that he will, then everyone will believe, and will rightly believe, that he triumphed purely

and simply because he was not guilty – since that is the line
I am adopting in his defence; and it will be abundantly clear
that technical points of law made no contribution to his
success, since he is refusing to rely upon them in any way.

Nevertheless, the legal aspect, as I mentioned before, is of
concern to me personally, and I cannot therefore let it pass
without mention. It is relevant to a debt I owe the Roman
people. For the life I lead is one which requires me to dedicate
all my care, all my endeavours, to the defence of men subjected
to the perils of the law. And what is evident to me now is the
formidable, menacing, unlimited powers of this novel sort of
court which the prosecution, by taking a law which was
applied only to us senators and by seeking to extend it to the
entire Roman people, is evidently determined to establish. The
existing law runs: *whosoever shall have conspired* (you see how
wide a range that covers) *and plotted* (which is equally vague
and undefined) *and combined* (which is not only undefined but
obscure, and might mean anything at all). And then follow the
words *shall have given false evidence*. Well, Attius' proposal to
apply these provisions to the entire community would mean
that every Roman commoner who had ever given evidence in
his life would henceforward have the menace of prosecution
perpetually hanging over his head. And as for the future, I can
tell you one thing for certain, and it is this: if the citizens of
Rome are going to be made liable to legal proceedings of this
kind, not one of them is going to be prepared to give evidence
again for the rest of his life.

Meanwhile, I offer this promise to anyone who is interested.
If ever it should happen that a person who is outside the scope
of the law in question were brought before you as if he were
subject to its provisions, and if he should want me to defend
him, I will gladly do so: and I will base my arguments on the
specific safeguards the law supplies. In such an event, whether
the case in question were to be heard before the judges who
are trying today's case, or before any other board of judges

whatever, I anticipate not the slightest difficulty in convincing them of my point of view. But I shall certainly insist on mobilizing the full legal protection which, in unavoidable deference to the wishes of my client, I am not permitted to call upon today. So let us suppose, gentlemen, that this is what occurs, and that you find yourselves confronted with an action of this kind, in which the defendant belongs to a category exempted from the law. Well, if this were the situation, even if he was the manifest object of the most widespread hostility and detestation, even if you yourselves hated him and would be deeply reluctant to vote for his acquittal, I am perfectly confident that you would acquit him all the same: since you would feel obliged to subordinate your hatred to your conscience.

For a thoughtful judge cannot avoid reflecting that the Roman people has assigned and entrusted to him a certain range of duties – and that the commission he has received from them extends to that point and not one single step farther. He must bear in mind not only the powers he has been granted, but the trust that has been placed in him as well. He must have the courage to acquit a man he dislikes, and to condemn a man he does not dislike at all. He must unceasingly keep before his eyes not merely his own inclinations, but the duty he owes to the law – and to his own idea of what is right. He must also note with the most meticulous care the legal provisions under which the charge is being brought, the sort of person that the defendant is, and the facts that have been brought to the attention of the court.

These are all matters a judge must never lose sight of. But if he is really good and wise, he will also feel, when he takes his voting-tablet to record his verdict, that it is his duty to remember something else as well. He does not stand alone. He is not at liberty to follow his own whims. For there are other matters he has got to take into consideration. They include the law, and his knowledge of what is right and fair, and the demands of honour. Feelings such as caprice, malice, prejudice, fear, personal passions of every kind, he must just dismiss from his heart. He must place the promptings of his own conscience above everything else. We were given our consciences by the immortal gods, and nothing can take them away from us. If *they* remain satisfied with everything we do and plan throughout our entire lives, then other people will approve of us, too, and we shall be able to live out our whole existence without ever being frightened of anything at all.

If Titus Attius had understood any of these things, indeed if he had so much as thought about the matter at all, surely he would never even have started upon the argument which he has developed at such length: that a judge is entitled to decide as he thinks best without feeling in any way hampered by the letter of the law.[1]

I am well aware, I repeat, that the remarks I have made on this subject go beyond what my client Cluentius would have wished – though they still fall short of the deep significance of the theme. But I believe, gentlemen, knowing your wisdom, that they will be sufficient to convince you that I am right.

The prosecution's other points that remain to be discussed are extremely few; and the only reason why they ever saw fit to invent them for production here was because they had to make it appear that they had something more than plain prejudice to offer. Because if prejudice was all they brought into court, they would appear in a singularly contemptible light.

For what I am now about to say, I request your particularly close attention, because the brevity of my comments will show you, by way of contrast, that I only spoke at greater length about earlier matters because I had no alternative. Now,

1. The unfairness of the exemption of non-senators from the judicial murder clause had evidently caused Attius to stress the clash between the letter and the spirit of the law – as Cicero himself did in his speech *In Defence of Caecina*, 54ff.

on the other hand, I shall prove to you quite clearly that whenever I have a chance to prove a point in the smallest possible number of words, this is precisely what I do.

One of your allegations was that Cnaeus Decidius the Samnite, the man who was condemned in Sulla's proscriptions,[1] received insulting treatment, in his misfortune, from the slaves of my client. On the contrary: no one could possibly have treated Decidius more generously than Cluentius did. Indeed, it was Cluentius' money which saved him when he was destitute, as Decidius and all his friends and relations are extremely well aware.

You also alleged that my client's bailiff delivered a physical attack upon the shepherds of Ancharius and Pacenus. But what really happened was that one of the usual disputes between shepherds arose in the mountain pastures, and Cluentius' bailiffs were obliged to defend their master's interests, and his rights of ownership.

Another of your assertions is that Publius Aelius, in his will, disinherited his own relatives, and decided instead that Cluentius should be his heir, although the testator did not know him at all. But Aelius did this because he had to, in order to discharge an obligation. Besides, my client played no part in the drawing up of the will. Indeed, it was signed and sealed by his enemy Oppianicus. You likewise accuse Cluentius of refusing to pay over a legacy which Aelius had left to Florus. In fact, exactly the opposite is the truth. Even though the testator's will specified the sum of 30,000 sestertii (not 300,000 as Florus said), so that his claim to the larger sum was in Cluentius' view unconvincing,[2] Cluentius nevertheless wanted

1. The Samnites of central Italy had resisted Sulla on his return from the east and had been crushed by him outside the Colline Gate of Rome in 82 B.C. Cnaeus Decidius may have been defended by Caesar in court; Tacitus, *Dialogue on Orators*, 21, 6 ('Decius'); cf. R. Syme, *The Roman Revolution*, O.U.P., 1939, p. 80.

2. The exact meaning of the Latin phrase is uncertain.

Florus to have the balance so that he should feel he had been generously treated. So although it is true that Cluentius at first denied the obligation, he subsequently paid over the whole sum without the slightest complaint.

You have also asserted that after the Social War[1] a certain Ceius, another Samnite, brought an action against Cluentius for the recovery of his wife. Actually, however, although my client had purchased this woman as a slave from the property broker,[2] as soon as he discovered that she was not a slave but a free woman he returned her to Ceius without the matter ever having to come to court.

The next charge is that Cluentius keeps possession of certain goods which really belong to a man called Ennius. In fact, this Ennius is an impoverished individual in Oppianicus' pay, who specializes in bringing fake prosecutions. For many years nothing had been heard of him. But then he brought an action against Cluentius' slaves for theft; and he has recently started trying to reclaim the alleged losses from their master. In the civil action that is being brought on this issue[3] you can take it from me that, even if he employs you yourself as his counsel, he is not going to escape the consequences of having brought a fraudulent accusation.[4]

I have also received another report. This is to the effect that you are suborning a certain Aulus Bivius, who runs an extensively patronized inn on the Via Latina,[5] to declare that he was assaulted on his own premises by Cluentius and his slaves. About this Bivius there is no need for me to say anything at the present moment. But if he honours us with his usual invitation, we shall subject him, I can assure you, to such

1. The Italian revolt of 91–87 B.C., also known as the Marsian War.
2. For these, see above, p. 71.
3. In Roman law *furtum* (theft) was treated as a private wrong rather than a crime; the remedy was a civil suit for damages.
4. See above, p. 76.
5. An ancient road running south-east from Rome to Campania.

warm treatment that he will regret ever having deviated from his ordinary line of business into these criminal paths.[1]

And that, gentlemen, is the sum total of the aspersions on Cluentius' character which the prosecution has succeeded in raking together – though they have been engaged in the search for no less than eight years, and it has ranged over his entire career. Well, how utterly trivial these accusations are! They are also grossly untruthful – as it is perfectly simple to demonstrate.

Now I have to ask you to turn your attention to the specific matters which relate to your oath and jurisdiction, and are your responsibility under the law at whose bidding you are assembled here today, the law concerned with charges of poisoning. It will then become abundantly clear to everyone that I could, in fact, have dealt with this case very briefly indeed. The only reason why I was obliged to extend my speech was because I had to include certain material at the request of my client, though it was irrelevant to the terms of reference of your court.[2]

One of the charges, then, against Cluentius is that he poisoned Gaius Vibius Capax. Fortunately we have in court today the senator Lucius Plaetorius, a man of irreproachable trustworthiness and impeccable character, who was Vibius' host and close friend.[3] It was at Plaetorius' house in Rome that Vibius was living, it was in his house that he lay sick, it was in his house that he died. Yes, they say, and look what happened – the heir to his estate turned out to be Cluentius. But that, in fact, is untrue. I am able to assure you that Vibius died without leaving any will at all. After his death, in accordance with the praetor's code, his property was handed over to Vibius'

1. There is a pun on the word *via* – he left the Via Latina to come to Rome, and used to go 'out of his way' to invite travellers to his inn.

2. Cf. above, p. 215.

3. The phrase suggests that Plaetorius was not a formal witness (p. 114).

sister's son, Numerius Cluentius.[1] You can see him here in court today. He is a perfectly respectable and honourable young man, and a Roman knight.

A second charge against Cluentius under the same heading claims that he attempted to poison Oppianicus Junior. The supposed occasion was a dinner-party to which that young man had invited a large number of guests on the occasion of his wedding,[2] according to the custom of Larinum. The allegation is that the poison had been prepared for Oppianicus Junior in a cup of honey-wine, but that a certain Balbutius, a friend of his, intercepted the cup instead, and drank it, and instantly died.

Were I treating this accusation as though it really deserved disproval, I should go into the matter at greater length. As it is, however, I propose to dismiss it quite briefly. Cluentius has never in all his life done anything to suggest that he would not find such a crime utterly repugnant. Furthermore, he had not the slightest reason to feel the acute fear of Oppianicus Junior that alone could have motivated such an action, since the man he was supposedly planning to kill has not so much as opened his mouth during the whole of this trial. And in any case, even if Oppianicus Junior had been removed, this would by no means indicate Cluentius had disembarrassed himself of all his accusers, so long as his mother Sassia remains alive – as I shall demonstrate to you shortly. After all, Cluentius could hardly have been eager to add yet another to the still undiminished list of charges with which he was faced. Nor, incidentally, did a social occasion of that kind, when so many people were present, offer the slightest opportunity of administering a dose

1. It is uncertain whether Numerius Cluentius' father was Aulus Cluentius, or another Cluentius, or Aulus Aurius Melinus (allegedly killed by Oppianicus in 82 B.C.); cf. next note.

2. To Auria, a daughter of Aulus Aurius Melinus by Sassia. See Genealogical Tables II, III, V. For the alleged attempt to poison Oppianicus Junior, see p. 114 n. 2.

of poison. And one wants to know the answers to so many questions. Whom, for example, did he choose as his accomplice to the deed? Where did he get the poison? How are we to explain the alleged interception by Balbutius? Why was the attempt not repeated? The possible replies to all these questions are very numerous. But I do not want to give the impression that I have hinted at more than I am prepared to state, so let me add that the solution is provided clearly enough by what happened next. You declare that the young Balbutius died immediately after he drank from the cup. I say that he did not die on the same day at all, and that your suggestion is a monstrous and shameless lie. For I can tell you what actually happened. The youth was already suffering from indigestion when he arrived at the party. While he was there he over-indulged himself, as persons of that age are inclined to do, and in consequence he fell ill. His illness went on for several days, and then he died.

From whom has this information reached me? It comes from the man who is in the best position to bear witness to his own sorrow, the bereaved father himself, the father of the young Balbutius who died. If even a shadow of suspicion against Cluentius had crossed his grief-stricken mind, he would have been only too ready to take his place over there and testify against my client. But instead he gives evidence on his behalf. Please read it out.

[The evidence of Balbutius senior is read out]

And you, yourself, Balbutius, if it is not asking too much of you, would you please stand up for a moment and nerve yourself for the distressing experience of this recital?[1] Thank you; now I shall obviously not need to dwell on this charge any longer, seeing that you yourself have so nobly decided to

1. It seems difficult to understand why, since the elder Balbutius was present, he did not give his testimony in person. Possibly he had sent his evidence in writing, and had then decided to attend after all.

intervene, refusing to let your bereavement allow an innocent man to be brought into ruin by a lying accusation.

Gentlemen, there is still one outstanding accusation of the same kind. Its nature will help you to understand what I emphasized at the outset of my speech: whatever pains Aulus Cluentius has suffered throughout all these years, whatever troubles and anxieties he is experiencing now, every one of them has been the creation of his own mother. I am referring, specifically, to your allegation that Cluentius instigated the death of Oppianicus, and that this was brought about by the administration of poison in a piece of bread by Cluentius' friend Marcus Asellius.

My first question is this. What motive could Cluentius have had for murdering Oppianicus? I admit that they did not get on well with one another. But if a man hopes for the death of his enemy, it is because he either fears him or hates him.[1] Now, as to the former, it is quite impossible to point to any fear which could conceivably have induced Cluentius to undertake the responsibility of so appalling a crime. Indeed, there was no longer any reason for anyone to be afraid of Oppianicus at all, now that he had paid the penalty for his misdeeds – expulsion from the community.[2] For what was there, in fact, to be frightened about? An attack from a ruined man, an accusation from a convicted criminal, the evidence of an outlaw? these presented no perils whatsoever. Or alternatively, seeing that the two men were enemies, let us imagine for a moment that Cluentius was so blinded by hatred that he could not bear Oppianicus to stay alive. But surely he cannot have been stupid enough not to realize that the life which Oppianicus was living at that time could scarcely be described as a life at all. For his existence was that of a condemned man, an outcast,

1. See above, p. 115.
2. i.e. when his conviction in his trial of 74 B.C. resulted in his legal outlawry.

an individual whom everyone had abandoned; a scoundrel so repulsive that no one would accept him under his roof, or go near him, or even speak to him; no one would so much as give him a single glance.

Cluentius was not going to grudge a man like that his life. On the contrary, if he really hated Oppianicus as ferociously and intensely as all that, he ought to have been eager that the man should go on living for as long as possible. For Oppianicus' lot was so wretched that death would have been a happy release from his miseries. Why on earth, therefore, should one of his enemies volunteer to gain him this release in advance? Indeed, if Oppianicus had been strong and courageous enough, he would have done like many a brave man before him when afflicted by grievous misfortune, and would have committed suicide. In other words, there was no imaginable reason why Oppianicus' enemy should be anxious to grant him what he had every possible reason to desire for himself.

He is dead now, and what harm can his death be said to have brought him? Unless we believe the stupid tales which would have us suppose that he is enduring the tortures of the damned in the underworld; that he has encountered even more of his enemies down there than he left behind him on earth; that the avenging furies of his mother-in-law, his wives, his brother and his children have driven him headlong into the regions reserved for the habitation of the damned. But if these stories are untrue (as everyone knows that they are), then it is clear enough that death has deprived him of nothing whatever – except the capacity to feel pain and to suffer.

Well, who actually administered the poison, according to your version? Marcus Asellius, you say. But the fact is that he had no connexion with Cluentius at all. Indeed, if they had any relationship whatever, it was probably hostile, because Asellius was a close friend of Oppianicus. It is surely the height of improbability to suppose that Cluentius would have employed as his instrument, in a criminal plot against Oppianicus, a man who, as he well knew, was not too well disposed towards himself but was intimate with the proposed victim! Besides, if Cluentius did employ this Asellius for such a purpose, it is necessary to ask Oppianicus Junior, whose filial loyalty impelled him to bring the present prosecution, why he has allowed Asellius to remain unpunished for so long. One wonders why Oppianicus Junior did not act like Cluentius,[1] and secure a prior verdict against Asellius for administering the poison – hoping that this would prove prejudicial to my client.

In any case, this alleged use of bread for purposes of poisoning is exceedingly unusual, and strange, and unlikely. Surely the application of poison in this fashion, hidden away in some corner of a piece of bread, would mean that the fatal dose was unlikely to permeate the victim's veins and frame nearly as quickly as if it were mixed with some liquid that could be drunk instead of eaten. Furthermore, once suspicion was aroused, it would have been considerably easier to detect the presence of poison in the bread than if it were dissolved in a liquid, in which case its detection might well be impossible.

You make the point that Oppianicus died very suddenly. Well, suppose he did. And so do many other people too: but that does not necessarily mean that they have been poisoned! Besides, even if he did die suddenly, even if the suddenness aroused some suspicion, it would be directed against others before it ever fell upon Cluentius. But actually this story of his sudden death is a bare-faced fabrication. To prove that this is so, let me tell you the true facts about Oppianicus' death – and let me tell you also how, after he was dead, Cluentius' mother made every effort to pin the responsibility falsely upon her own son.

When Oppianicus had been banished and was leading the

1. Who had prosecuted Fabricius and Scamander before prosecuting Oppianicus.

life of a vagabond, nobody wanted to have anything to do with him. However, he found his way to the house of Gaius Quinctius,¹ in the Falernian district.² And there he fell ill, and his illness was serious and prolonged. Sassia was with him. But she spent most of her time with a beefy farmer called Statius Abbius,³ on terms of very much greater intimacy than even the most dissipated of husbands could have tolerated if he had not come so far down in the world. For Sassia took the view that her lawful bonds of matrimonial fidelity were virtually abolished by her husband's conviction. Apparently, however, or so it is said, Oppianicus was kept thoroughly well informed by a favourite slave called Nicostratus, a faithful individual who was highly inquisitive and not inclined to tell lies. After a time Oppianicus started to get better – and began to find the misbehaviour of the Falernian farmer intolerable. So he moved off in this direction, and came to a place in the neighbourhood of the city where he rented some sort of an apartment outside the gates.⁴ But then we learnt that he had a fall from his horse. He was still in poor health when the accident occurred, and the fall seriously bruised his side. He was brought as far as the city, suffering from a high temperature, and died a few days later. The circumstances of his death, gentlemen, were not such as to arouse suspicion.⁵ But even if there had been grounds for suspicion, then it would have to be directed towards the

1. Unknown; but the alternative reading 'Lucius Quinctius' (the name of the tribune who had taken revenge on the judges who convicted Oppianicus in 74) does not appear to be correct.

2. On the borders of Latium and Campania: famous wine-growing country.

3. These were also the first names of the two Oppianici – reading 'Abbius' instead of 'Albius'; cf. above, p. 113 n. 4. Evidently he was a relative of theirs.

4. Being an outlaw he could not enter Rome.

5. Cicero does not attempt to present witnesses as he did (after a fashion) for the alleged poisonings of Gaius Vibius Capax and Oppianicus Junior.

persons within his own four walls; no one outside his own household could possibly be regarded as a suspect.

After Oppianicus' death, the abominable Sassia immediately began to plot the downfall of her own son, Cluentius. To begin with, she decided to institute an inquiry into the causes of her husband's death. Oppianicus' doctor had been a certain Aulus Rupilius, and Sassia bought from him a slave called Strato, ostensibly with the same motive as had inspired Cluentius' purchase of Diogenes.[1] For she announced that she was going to subject this Strato to an examination, as well as a slave of her own called Ascla. She also demanded that her stepson Oppianicus Junior here should make his young slave Nicostratus available for a similar examination, because she suspected Nicostratus both of talking too freely and of being too loyal to his own master.[2] Oppianicus Junior was only a boy at the time, and since the investigation was supposed to be about the death of his father he did not dare refuse her anything,[3] although he was in fact confident that the slave had been just as devoted to his father Oppianicus as he was to himself.

When Sassia held her inquiry, many of his father's and mother's friends, and people they had exchanged hospitality with, were requested to attend – all respectable, reputable figures. The proceedings included a rigorous examination of the slaves, in which various forms of torture was applied.[4] Although every pressure, in the form of promises and threats

1. He had bought Diogenes in order to facilitate his examination; cf. above, p. 148.

2. This seems to imply that Oppianicus Junior was really opposed to the attempt to blame Cluentius for the death of Oppianicus (cf. p. 117); Cicero wants to treat him leniently.

3. It was a son's filial duty to attack the prosecutors of his father. Oppianicus Junior was perhaps about eighteen at the time.

4. Slaves were normally tortured before giving evidence, since it was not believed that they would tell the truth otherwise.

alike, was brought to bear on them in the hope that they would give something away, they were so greatly overawed – by the authority of the gathering, I suppose – that they persisted in telling the truth and refused to admit that they knew anything whatever about any plot to murder Oppianicus. Finally, at the suggestion of the assembled friends of the family, the inquiry was called off for that day. But after a considerable interval they were invited to attend once again, and the examination was repeated.

Tortures of the most unpleasant nature were employed. Finally, when the witnesses felt unable to endure the spectacle any longer, they protested. In the heart of the savage, unnatural Sassia the only feeling was rage, because her scheme had totally miscarried. However, at long last, when the torturer and even his instruments of torture were worn out, and still she showed not the slightest intention of calling a halt, one of the men who had been summoned as witnesses, a person of high position and unimpeachable character, declared he had come to the conclusion that the purpose of her inquiry was not to find the truth at all: it was to force the slaves to say something untrue. There was a general agreement with this, and it was unanimously resolved that the investigation must go no further.

Nicostratus was returned to Oppianicus Junior, and Sassia and her people went back to Larinum. She was utterly dismayed to think that her son Cluentius would now apparently remain unharmed. For no authentic charge could touch him, and his innocence was even proof against trumped-up suspicions. The open attacks of his enemies had failed to bring him down; and even the secret intrigues of his own mother had fared no better. So she returned to Larinum.[1] When she got there, incidentally, she presented her slave Strato with a surgery, furniture and equipment, so that he could set up as a doctor in the town. And yet he was the man whom

1. The examinations had taken place at Rome.

she had pretended to accuse of giving poison to her husband!

A year passed by, and then a second, and a third. During all this time Sassia made no further move. It was beginning to look as though she had given up planning and plotting the downfall of her son Cluentius, and was now content just to hope, fervently, that it would somehow come about. But then came the year when Quintus Hortensius Hortalus and Quintus Caecilius Metellus Creticus were consuls.[1] At this point Sassia arranged that Oppianicus Junior should get married to her own daughter Auria, whose father was Sassia's former son-in-law Aulus Aurius Melinus.[2] The new bridegroom was by no means enthusiastic, since he had been occupied with quite other matters and nothing was farther from his thoughts than becoming the husband of this girl. But Sassia hoped that the marriage-link, supplemented by the hold she maintained over Oppianicus Junior because of his expectations from her will, would bring him completely into her power.

At about the same time Strato, the slave who had been set up as a doctor, committed both theft and murder in her home. It happened like this. The house contained a safe, and inside it, as Strato knew, there was a quantity of money and gold. So one night, as a preparatory step, he murdered two of his fellow-slaves as they lay asleep, and threw their bodies into the fish-pond. Then, with the help of another of the slaves, who was quite a young boy, he cut the bottom out of the safe, and removed a large amount of cash[3] and five pounds weight of gold.

The next day the theft was discovered; but all the suspicion fell on the two slaves who had disappeared. It was noticed that the bottom of the safe had been cut out, and there was a good deal of speculation about how this could have been done. But then one of Sassia's friends recalled having lately been at some

1. 69 B.C.   2. See Genealogical Tables, II, III, V.
3. The figure is missing from the manuscripts.

auction where he had seen a small circular saw with an indented handle and teeth all round the edge. It seemed possible that this might have been the instrument which had cut round the base of the safe. And so, to make a long story short, inquiries were made from the men who are employed to collect the money from purchasers at auctions, and it was found that the saw had been bought by Strato. This naturally brought him under the gravest suspicion. When he was taxed with the crime, his youthful accomplice got into a panic and disclosed the whole story to their mistress, Sassia. The corpses were found in the fish-pond, Strato was put in chains, and the money, though not by any means all of it, was found in his surgery.

An inquiry was now held. Obviously its purpose was to investigate Strato's theft – not the death of Oppianicus or anything else. For what had been discovered was the theft, and certainly not some piece of new evidence relating to Oppianicus' alleged murder. After the plain facts of the burglary of the safe, the removal and partial recovery of the money, and the murder of the two slaves, you cannot really hope to argue, Attius, that this renewed investigation by Sassia had any business to concern itself with the issue of Oppianicus' death. Nobody, surely, could maintain any such thing, since it would be a wholly implausible suggestion. Nor, apart from everything else, was it reasonable that an inquiry should be investigating Oppianicus' death three whole years after it had happened.

Yet Sassia seized the opportunity of Strato's crime to re-establish the inquiry into her husband's death. Furthermore, her consuming hatred of Cluentius prompted her to demand that the slave Nicostratus, who had been examined on the former occasion, should be subjected to examination all over again. At first, Oppianicus Junior refused. Later on however, after she had threatened to take her daughter Auria away from him and to change her will, he agreed to surrender his devoted slave to this utterly brutal woman. The result could hardly be called an examination at all. It was sheer slaughter.

That, then, is the story of how the question of Oppianicus' death was revived by a fresh inquiry, three years after the event. You will no doubt want to ask which slaves were examined on this second occasion. You will assume that some new facts about the death of Oppianicus must allegedly have come to light, some new persons brought under suspicion. Not at all! The slaves selected for examination were Strato and Nicostratus. They, however, you will point out with surprise, were the identical two who had been examined on the previous occasion at Rome. Yes: though it is certainly hard to credit, I agree. There had been that earlier inquiry at Rome. There had been the conclusion by the witnesses Titus Annius, Lucius Rutilius, Publius Satureius, and all those other excellent men, that the first inquiry had gone every bit as far as it could go. And yet, in spite of all that, is it really credible that this woman was so completely off her head, so utterly deranged – not indeed by any mental ailment, but by all the terrible crimes on her conscience – that after a lapse of three years she could still make yet another attempt to strike a fatal blow at her son, by launching a second inquiry into precisely the same facts and in the presence of exactly the same people – or rather (for I should qualify that statement in case you tell me that her affectionate farmer was there) exactly the same *respectable* people?

I can think of one possible explanation that might perhaps be attempted. True, Attius has not actually produced it, but I am thinking of what *might* be said. Well, it could be suggested that Strato, at some point or other during the investigation of his theft, had happened to come up with some confession about the supposed poisoning of Oppianicus. Gentlemen, there are certain occasions when truth contrives to find a way of its own to the surface, triumphing against all the villainy that has dragged it down; and then the defence of an innocent man, half stifled before, manages to breathe once

again. This happens, for example, when individuals who are
cunning experts in fraudulence lack the audacity to carry
through their designs. It also happens in the opposite circumstances, when creatures who are audacious to the last degree
nevertheless lack the sinister skill to give their audacity full
effect. Whereas if their intelligence had been allied to courage,
or their courage had been supplemented by intelligence, such
criminals would be almost invincible.

Well, here it was Sassia's intelligence that was deficient.[1]
That a theft had been committed was beyond question. Everybody at Larinum knew it had. And it was perfectly obvious
that everything pointed to Strato. After all, he was deeply
incriminated by the saw, and he was also given away by the
boy who had been his accomplice. So this was, in fact, what
the investigation of his activities was all about. There was no
other reason whatever for conducting such an inquiry. But,
as I say, it might also conceivably have been maintained that
Strato, while under examination regarding the theft, was
induced by torture to make some revelation or other about
Oppianicus' death. That, surely, Attius, is what you ought to
have insisted. After all, it was what Sassia said at the time, and
kept on saying. But there you have an example of my very
point. There is no doubt whatever about the woman's
audacity, but she is lacking in judgement and common sense.
For extensive minutes of this second inquiry have been
submitted to the present court. They have been read out aloud,
and have been laid before you for your scrutiny. And she
herself has testified that they are the actual documents which
were sealed by the witnesses at the time. And yet, surprisingly
enough, they contain not so much as one single mention of
Strato's theft![2]

1. This sentence does not appear in the Latin.
2. i.e. Strato's evidence, as recorded, was entirely concerned with
Oppianicus' death. But at no point does Cicero tell us what he (or
Nicostratus) was reported to have said, or try to refute their evidence.

What Sassia could have done – if it had occurred to her, as it did not – was first to record Strato's statement about the theft, and then at some later point insert some statement about the alleged poisoning of Oppianicus, so as to make it look as though the admission had not, indeed, been deliberately elicited from him, but had just come out under the stress of the torture. For the subject of this second inquiry, I repeat, was the theft. Any suspicion that Oppianicus' death was due to poison had been completely eliminated by the previous investigation. And the woman Sassia herself had clearly concurred with this conclusion, since she had accepted the advice of her friends at Rome that the first investigation could not go any farther. Furthermore, during the three years that followed, she had singled out Strato for greater marks of her affection than she had displayed towards any of her other slaves, treating him with exceptional consideration, and loading him with every sort of favour.

You can hardly, therefore, expect us to believe that throughout the entire course of the inquiry into the theft – a theft moreover of which he was guilty beyond the slightest question – Strato completely failed to utter one single word about the matter which was the specific and exclusive subject of investigation. Are you really trying to tell us that, from the very outset of the hearing, he immediately began to talk about Oppianicus' poisoning, and went on about the same subject to the exclusion of absolutely everything else? You might at least admit that he *mentioned* the theft – if not in its proper place, then perhaps at the very end of his examination, or in the middle of it: or at any rate at some stage or other!

It must have become clear to you by now, gentlemen, that the minutes of this second inquiry were fabricated: and that it was this evil woman who was responsible for the fabrication. The hand that perpetrated this fraudulent act was the same hand with which she would be delighted to kill her own son, if only she were given the power. Name me one witness whose

signature and seal are to be seen on this record. You will not
find a single one, except, perhaps, an individual whose low
character is a better argument for my case than if no one had
appeared at all.[1] Here, Attius, is something that simply cries
out for an explanation on your part. It is quite extraordinary
that you should venture to lodge a criminal, capital charge –
an accusation based on a written document upon which the
defendant's entire future hangs – without being able to name
one person who can vouch for the document, one person who
sealed it, one person who witnessed it. You surely cannot
cherish the illusion that a court of this calibre will be impressed
by a document which this mother herself has taken from her
own bosom and handed over to you with the sole intention of
bringing ruin upon her own innocent son. Very well, then:
it is obvious that the minutes of the second inquiry carry not
the slightest weight whatsoever. One feels obliged to wonder
why an authentic complete record was not preserved for the
benefit of the judges, and for the benefit of the friends and
associates of Oppianicus whom Sassia had summoned to the
two investigations, and for the benefit of ourselves who are
engaged upon the present trial.

You will also want to be told the eventual fates of the two
slaves, Strato and Nicostratus. Will you kindly let us know,
Oppianicus Junior, what became of Nicostratus? Since you
were planning to prosecute Cluentius in the not too distant
future, you ought to have brought your slave to Rome, made
him available as a source of information, and kept him safe for
further examination, safe for this court of ours, safe for the
present trial. As for Strato, everyone at Larinum knows what
happened to him. His tongue was torn out and he was crucified.
For Sassia, in her frenzy, paid no heed to her own guilty conscience, disregarded the hatred of her townsmen, cared nothing
for her dreadful reputation far and wide. That all the world
would see her crime meant nothing to her at all. One thing

1. i.e. the farmer Statius Abbius, who was alleged to be Sassia's lover.

only caused her terror: the thought that a poor dying slave, in his last utterances upon earth, might denounce her horrible deeds.

In heaven's name, was there ever such an awful phenomenon as that woman? One would think that in all the world there could be no region capable of producing or harbouring a monstrosity so appalling, a criminality so detestable and unnatural. Surely it must be clear to you by now, gentlemen, that when I referred to my client's mother in the first words of this speech I was absolutely right. For from the very beginning, without cessation, there has been no conceivable kind of evil and wickedness that she has not longed for, and hankered after, and plotted, and perpetrated against her own son.

About the wrong she committed because of that first lecherous passion for her son-in-law Aulus Aurius Melinus, with whom she contracted that unspeakable marriage, I shall say nothing now. Over the mother's infatuation, which drove her own daughter Cluentia away from her husband's arms, I propose to draw a veil. These were things which gravely dishonoured her family; but so far they did not threaten the life of my client. I shall refrain, too, from expressing my full horror about her next marriage, to Oppianicus, though it was a marriage which brought grief on his household and death to her own stepchildren, since he gave her, as security, the corpses of his own dead sons. Nor shall I dwell upon her actions when she learnt that Aulus Aurius Melinus, formerly her daughter's husband and recently her own, had been proscribed and assassinated by Oppianicus' instigation: I mean when she chose to take up residence in the very house where, day after day, she could fasten her eyes upon the evidence of her former husband's death – and upon his estate that had come to her as spoils.

No, all this I pass over: but the first of her misdeeds which I must single out to deplore is that crime which has now been detected at long last, the attempt to poison her son Cluentius through the agency of Fabricius. At the time when the attempt was made there were already widespread suspicions on the subject, but Cluentius refused to believe them. Now, however, they are believed by everybody – because the facts are wholly indisputable. And another thing which is equally certain is that the poisoning attempt was made with the full knowledge of Sassia, his mother. For Oppianicus never planned a thing without her advice. Moreover, if his plot had been entirely his own responsibility, it is surely to be presumed that afterwards, when it had been detected, she would not just have thought of him as a distasteful husband whom it was better to desert! It is only to be supposed that in that case she would have fled headlong from his presence, shunning him as the most horrible of enemies, and abandoning for ever that house which had such dreadfully evil associations.

However, she was preoccupied by quite other matters. For from that time onwards there was no place safe from the incessant intrigues she was directing against her son. Day and night, she devoted all her thoughts to plotting his destruction. First of all, she made certain that Oppianicus Junior should become available for the prosecution of Cluentius. This she ensured by giving him her daughter Auria in marriage: and she promised that he would be her heir. It is quite normal, when a quarrel breaks out between relatives, for the results to include divorce and the rupture of family ties. In this case, however, the result was a marriage, since Sassia took the view that no one could really be relied upon to bring charges against her son unless he married her son's sister first. And then again the general practice, when fresh family relationships are formed, is to allow past quarrels to be forgotten. But she, on the other hand, saw the new marriage bond in the opposite light altogether: to her it was a guarantee that her feud was never going to be dropped, under any circumstances whatever.

Nor did she limit her endeavours to just finding an accuser

against her son and leaving it at that. For once she had found him, she also thought out every possible means of arming him with formidable weapons. That was the purpose of all her threats and promises to the slaves. That was the aim of those brutal and long-drawn-out investigations into the death of Oppianicus, investigations which came to an end not because she herself showed the slightest signs of compassion but because her friends felt obliged to intervene. The same evil designs produced the inquiry at Larinum three years later. The same mad fury impelled her to falsify its record. The same frenzy caused her to take the frightful step of cutting out the slave's tongue. To sum up, the whole elaborate charge against Cluentius is her own purely fictitious concoction.

When Oppianicus Junior, the prosecutor of her son, had been suitably equipped to do the job, she sent him off to Rome. She herself stayed behind at Larinum for a time in order to collect and hire witnesses. But when she heard that my client's trial was on the point of taking place, she arrived here with the utmost speed. She was anxious to put all her endeavours at the disposal of the prosecution – and her money at the disposal of the witnesses. Or perhaps she was overwhelmingly eager not to miss a spectacle that must indeed have been dear to a mother's heart; the mourning clothes and unkempt, woeful appearance of her own son.

And so Sassia herself came to Rome; and I can tell you what her journey was like. Since the people of Aquinum and Fabrateria are my neighbours,[1] many bystanders have told me all the details, and I know exactly how it all happened. You must imagine great crowds of men and women assembling, and a mighty groan issuing from every throat, as they all gazed upon this female, furnished with a vast retinue and loaded with huge sums of money, hastening along the road from Larinum, hastening all the way from the Adriatic coast to Rome itself,

1. These places, now called Aquino and Ceccano, are seven and five miles respectively from Cicero's birthplace, Arpinum.

for the specific purpose of striking down her own son on a capital charge and causing his utter destruction. Among all those spectators, I truly believe that there was not a single one who felt that any place where she had set her foot would ever be clean again until it was subjected to solemn rites of purification: they were convinced, one and all, that the very earth itself, the common mother of every one of us, had become utterly polluted wherever that most abominable of mothers had trod. And so there was not a town which allowed her to tarry, not an inn where the innkeeper did not shrink from the contagion of her baleful eye. No hostelry, no city, could bring itself to receive her; night and solitude were her lot.

And now today, once again, she must not imagine that any detail of her activities, her machinations, her daily plots have escaped our notice. The people whom she has approached with promises of money, trying to corrupt their loyalty with bribes, we can readily identify. We have even found out about the sacrifices she performs every night[1] – though she imagines them to be the darkest of secrets. We know all about those impious prayers and unholy vows, in which she actually dares to call on the immortal gods themselves to sponsor her evil designs. For evidently she fails to understand that what placates their divine hearts is not impure superstition and the sacrifice of victims to further infamous crimes, but duty to god and man, and devotion, and prayer that comes from pious hearts. For it is clear beyond any shadow of doubt that the immortal gods have spurned this woman's rancorous frenzy, and have contemptuously cast it from their altars and shrines.

Gentlemen, you too, by the force of circumstances, have been placed in the position of gods, since the entire future of my client lies wholly within your power today. Protect his life, I implore you, from his unspeakable mother. In times gone

1. Women were generally forbidden to perform nocturnal sacrifices; Cicero, *On Laws*, II, 21. He is suggesting that Sassia was guilty of magic.

by, many a judge has thought fit to dismiss the wrongdoings
of children because he felt sympathy for their parents. What
I am begging you to do is something strangely different: I am
begging you not to sacrifice my client's wholly blameless life
to a mother who is utterly inhuman.

I make this plea all the more confidently because you can
see here before your own eyes the entire population of Larinum
gathered together in my support. For it is clear enough, though
it seems hard to credit it, that every single able-bodied citizen
of the town has come to Rome today, in order to contribute
their great enthusiasm and large numbers to the aid of my
client by any means that they can. I assure you that Larinum,
at this moment, is only being looked after by women and
children: home forces it has none, and there is nothing but the
general peace of Italy to serve as its protection. Yet even those
women and children who have stayed behind, no less than
the men you see here, remain tormented with suspense day
and night until they learn the outcome of this trial. For it is
their firm belief that the verdict you are about to pronounce
is not just a verdict affecting one of their townsmen, but something that vitally concerns their town's standing, honour, and
prosperity for all future time.

Aulus Cluentius, gentlemen, is unique in his dedication to
his native Larinum, his devotion to its individual townspeople,
his fair and just dealings towards all and sundry. The rank he
inherited among his fellow-citizens, the position his ancestors
handed down to him, was exceedingly distinguished. And he
for his part has fully lived up to this inheritance, in no way
falling below their example in his responsible attitude, his
consistently admirable conduct, his gracious accessibility, his
generous munificence. The terms, therefore, which these men
of Larinum have chosen to express their affection for him
reflect not only their strong sincerity, but also a feeling of
profound concern and distress. While this testimonial is being
read aloud, will those who have presented it please stand up?

[The testimonial from Larinum is read aloud]

See, gentlemen, how they are weeping. This will give you some indication of the tears that were pouring down the cheeks of every one of the town councillors of Larinum when they passed this resolution. To see the love Cluentius' neighbours bear him is tremendously impressive. Their goodwill towards him is overwhelming, and so is their present anxiety on his behalf. Not content with merely forwarding the text of the resolution they had passed in his favour, they decided that a great number of their citizens, respected figures who are likely to be well known to everyone of us, should come to Rome in person, and deliver their eulogy of Cluentius from their own mouths.

Many other people have flocked here as well. The Frentani and Marrucini, for example, have sent important dignitaries.[1] You see before you excellent Roman knights from Teanum in Apulia, and from Luceria in the same land; they have all come to do everything they can for our cause. Bovianum and the entire Samnite country have not only transmitted honorific testimonials, but have dispatched their own distinguished and respected representatives in person. But to return to the men who have come from the region of Larinum itself – property-owners, businessmen, stockbreeders, all eminent figures of the finest reputation – their anxious solicitude almost defies description. I can think of few men as greatly loved even by one single individual as Cluentius is loved by his entire community.

I am only sorry that the virtuous and illustrious Lucius Volusienus cannot be here as well. And it is also a disappointment that I am unable to name among those present today Publius Helvidius Rufus, that knight of such exceptional qualities.[2] He spent days and nights with me on the case,

1. Cicero's successful conduct of this case must have won him great goodwill in the territories mentioned here.
2. These men are unknown.

working at it with unremitting diligence. But then he fell seriously and dangerously ill. Yet, even so, his own survival is a matter of much less concern to him than the survival of Cluentius. And pay special attention, please, to the testimonial from the senator Cnaeus Tudicius, for you will find that he, too, is equally determined to speak up for my client. And you, also, Publius Volumnius, will permit me, I hope, to include a reference to your name, though I do so with greater reserve since you are one of the judges who will be called upon to give your verdict in the case.

To sum up, I declare that the entire population of the region where my client lives is unanimously devoted to him and his cause. On the one side, then, we have all these people, and all their dedication, and all the trouble they have so unsparingly taken – in addition, may I add, to all the work I personally have devoted to the case, since in accordance with ancient custom I have conducted the entire defence myself.[1] And then, gentlemen, we also have your own sense of justice, your own humanity, as a strong bulwark and support.

On the other side stands one person only, Cluentius' one real assailant: his own mother. And what a mother she is! Just look how the savagery of her evil designs drives her blindly on her way. Never for a moment has any fear of dishonour availed to curb her lusts. Every ordinance ever devised by mankind has been dragged in the dust by her depravity. She is too brutalized even to seem a member of the human race at all, too ferocious to be recognizable as a woman – too abominably cruel to be thought fit to bear the name of mother! By transforming herself into the wife of her own son-in-law, the stepmother of her own son, the harlot of her own daughter's husband, she has turned the very names of human relationships inside out, reversing the very decrees of nature herself. And now she has sunk to such unprecedented

1. Although in Cicero's time it was customary for a defendant to employ a number of counsel.

depths that, except for the mere outward form, one can no longer see in her the smallest vestige of human likeness at all.

If therefore, gentlemen, you shun evil, I call upon you to deny this mother the blood of her own son. Let her gift be, instead, her son's triumphant deliverance, which will infuriate her more than anything else in the world. Forbid her the extreme satisfaction of ruining her son: send her forth today routed by a verdict reflecting your determination to be just. If, as my knowledge of your characters indicates, you are lovers of honour, high principle and right conduct, then bid this man who is your suppliant, who for all these years has been the victim of unjust prejudice, this man who has been beset by perils on every side, to rise up, at long last, from the ground where he is lying. Today, for the very first time since the villainy and greed of his enemies ignited this blaze of hatred against him, he has begun, deeply encouraged by your known regard for justice, to take heart once again, to feel some blessed respite from all his anxieties. His entire future lies in your hands. Those who deeply desire his salvation are numerous; but the only people who can actually save him are yourselves. Gentlemen, Cluentius implores you, amid his tears, not to sacrifice him to unfair prejudice, which can have no place in any court of law; not to sacrifice him to his mother, whose impious vows and prayers to the gods you should repudiate with utter disgust; not to sacrifice him to the horrible Oppianicus, who was rightly found guilty of the crimes he committed, and is dead.

Should this trial, on the other hand, end in disaster for my innocent client, then indeed will that wretched man, if he succeeds in the hard task of keeping alive at all, regret often and bitterly that the attempt to get Fabricius to poison him was ever thwarted. For had the lethal draught not been detected, it would have seemed to Cluentius no poison at all, but a medicine to heal a multitude of sorrows. And perhaps, who knows, even his mother Sassia herself would then have deigned to walk in the funeral procession of her own son, giving way, at least ostensibly, to maternal lamentations.

If he loses his case, what, I ask you, will his survival on that past day have gained him? He was preserved from that deadly plot, it will then seem, only to lead a life of mourning, only to die, in the end, debarred even from burial in his own family tomb. His miseries, surely, have lasted long enough: long enough has he been the victim of fraudulent prejudice. If there were resentments against him, even the most persistent grudges must now be thought of as appeased – except his own mother's alone. You are fair-minded people, gentlemen, and when a man is brutally assailed it is your custom to grant him your generous help. Save Cluentius, I beg you. Permit his home-town to welcome him back unharmed. Restore him to his friends, his neighbours, his associates, whose devotion you behold. Place him under an obligation to yourselves and your children – an obligation which will last for all time.

That, judges, is what you must do. It is demanded of you by your honour and your humanity. I appeal to you, and I appeal in the absolute confidence of a just cause, to release finally from his misfortunes a truly good and innocent man, a man who is loved and cherished by a whole host of his fellow-citizens. And when you do this, you will also be triumphantly proving something else as well: that whereas the place for prejudice is a public meeting, a court of law is the abode of truth.

III

IN DEFENCE OF
GAIUS RABIRIUS

Introduction to Cicero's Speech

IN *100 B.C. the radical, reformist (*populalaris*)[1] politician Lucius Appuleius Saturninus had posed a great threat to the senatorial establishment. He was a real and unmistakable innovator, seeking a great extension of the powers of the tribunes of the people – and if he had had his way he would have effectively muzzled the senate.[2] He relied on the support of the national hero Gaius Marius, whose army veterans, he hoped, would give him the forceful support, and the protection against assassination, that a tribune could not mobilize on his own. At first Marius supported him. But then, deeply worried by the independent policy the tribune was attempting to follow, and shocked by the murder of an anti-radical consular candidate, Gaius Memmius, he withdrew his assistance. As disorder spread, the senate, with Marius' backing, passed its emergency decree (*senatus* consultum de re publica defendenda *or* ultimum, p. 9) against Saturninus and his henchmen, and shut him and his followers into the senate-house, where they were murdered, probably in breach of a safe-conduct (p. 286 n. 4).*

Thirty-seven years later, in 63 B.C., the elderly senator Gaius Rabirius was prosecuted by the tribune Titus Labienus for killing Saturninus.[3] Cicero, who in this year was holding the consulship

1. See above, pp. 7, 180 n. 1.

2. For a more objective estimate than the hostile Cicero's of the significance of Saturninus see A. N. Sherwin-White in R. Seager (ed.), *The Crisis of the Roman Republic* (reprint of 1956 article), p. 154. Saturninus' fall (however much Cicero might criticize the tribune Labienus, his own contemporary) really meant the collapse of the bogey of 'government by tribunes' (see List of Terms); henceforward the danger to the Republic was government by war-lords.

3. For political charges brought by tribunes, see A. H. M. Jones, *The Criminal Courts of the Roman Republic and Principate*, p. 16.

257

he had so greatly coveted,[1] *spoke in Rabirius' defence, and a translation of his speech is offered here.*

The trial, or rather two successive trials,[2] *possessed strange characteristics which have been the subject of voluminous controversy and are still imperfectly understood. But two of the oddest features are beyond dispute. In the first place, the prosecution was launched an extraordinarily long time after Saturninus had met his violent death. Secondly, the case was not assigned to the court to which, at this time, murder cases were habitually allotted, the court before which Cicero had defended Roscius and Cluentius (p. 17). For behind Labienus' prosecution was the rising* popularis *politician Gaius Julius Caesar, the future dictator, who felt that sufficient publicity would not be attracted by that orthodox procedure; he wanted to attach a peculiar solemnity to the case.*[3] *Instead, therefore, of being brought before the murder court, Rabirius, after undergoing a preliminary prosecution on other and relatively trivial charges (p. 270), was tried on two occasions for high treason, under its antique and almost obsolete name of* perduellio.[4] *Although, that is to say, these were trials for murder, they were not murder trials in the technical sense, but actions for treason. Like parricide (p. 26), this was a crime traditionally incurring a penalty which inspired Cicero with horror. The guilty man was tied to a cross made out of a barren tree (barren because he was a polluted object), and on this he was crucified. These procedures for treason were set in motion against Rabirius in order to stress the national significance of the issue involved; and the revival of this issue, though the incident had taken place so long ago, was deliberately decided upon by the* populares *in order to present Rome with a test case.*

1. He was the first 'new man' (i.e. member of a family which had never held a consulship), with no political background, to become a consul since 94 B.C.

2. Cf. Jones, op. cit., p. 41.   3. ibid., p. 43.

4. *Perduellio* had been generally replaced by the wider concept of *maiestas*, defined by Cicero (*On Invention*, II, 17, 53), established as a crime by Saturninus himself (the *Lex Appuleia* of 103 B.C.), and assigned a permanent court by Sulla in 81.

For the senators and their followers who had attacked and killed Saturninus – because they believed that his radical proposals were endangering the state – did so, as we have seen, after the senate passed its emergency decree.

Radical politicians had never been happy about these emergency decrees, ever since the first such measure had resulted in the death of their hero Gaius Gracchus in 122 B.C. (p. 9). Now, in 63, there were once again rumours of plots, counterplots and coups d'état, and the populares – who were beginning to take more solid shape as an opposition force – felt so worried about the possibility of repressive measures, exercised through some fresh senatorial emergency decree that might already be imminent,[1] that they were eager to bring the whole concept of such decrees into question by a hearing in a public court. Or rather, apart from extremists, they were probably prepared to accept the validity of the concept as such, but wanted to make sure it should never be given too immediate or dictatorial an application. This, then, was the purpose behind the proceedings of Caesar and Labienus.[2]

By insisting on moderate applications only, one of the things which the populares desired to ensure was that no future emergency decree, if there was ever to be one, should come to be regarded as authorizing executions out of hand, without trial. And indeed, such an effort at definition seemed necessary, for the wording of these decrees was (intentionally) vague: they urged the consuls and others 'to defend the state and see that it took no harm'.[3] The likelihood that from time to time the senate would deem it necessary to deliver exhortations of this kind to the principal officers of state was considerable,

1. The withdrawal of a major bill of agrarian reform sponsored by Publius Servilius Rullus, after it had been attacked by Cicero (p. 288 n. 3), had stirred up rumours of conspiracies – and no doubt also of a new emergency decree.

2. Probably this warning demonstration against the conservatives was directed, in the background, by Cnaeus Pompeius Magnus (Pompey the Great), who was still away in the east.

3. This was the wording after the period of the Gracchi at least. The various decrees also contained additional clauses.

since it was so very easy, at Rome, for law and order to collapse (p. 9).

The sort of position that could arise when that happened is by no means irrelevant to our own times, when the Northern Ireland government felt obliged to revive its measures providing for internment without trial. H. M. Last wrote in 1943 that

Society at least tacitly reserves to itself the right, if a situation develops in which its normal means of protection are inadequate, to use abnormal means of any kind whatever which may seem necessary to ensure its survival. Whether such abnormal measures for the defence of society can be described as legal or not depends on the law of the state in which they are taken. They can properly so be called where the law provides an alternative procedure for dealing with various forms of violence, to be introduced when the ordinary procedure is no longer enough (e.g. the Riot Act in Britain). . . . But law is sometimes reluctant to contemplate the event of its own need for reinforcement; and there have been other states (including Rome) where the normal procedure for use against domestic enemies is the only procedure for this purpose recognized by the law. In them, when this one procedure proves incapable of keeping a danger under control, since there is no legal alternative to take its place, law at least partially breaks down. . . . About the action taken by the agents of society during such an interruption it is futile to ask whether it was legal. . . . Nevertheless, there are other questions about such an action which may properly be asked – whether, for instance, it was in fact directed to restore the reign of law, where it was calculated to do so in the shortest possible time and with the least avoidable hardship to individuals, and so forth. But there is one question, prior to the rest, which on such occasions it is essential to ask if the executive is not to run the risk of losing its respect for law – that is, whether the responsible agents of society, when they took non-legal action, had good reason to believe that danger had reached a magnitude at which the procedure prescribed by law was no longer capable of coping with it, and that consequently . . . the reign of law had suffered an interruption.[1]

In view of these uncertainties and hazards, it is important to know what exactly the senate's exhortation to the Roman officers of state, 'to defend the state and see that it took no harm', permitted and

1. H. M. Last, *Journal of Roman Studies*, XXXIII, 1943, p. 94.

implied. A. W. Lintott's recent interpretation is as follows: the conservatives, according to him, 'outflanked the populares *and the* Lex Sempronia *[the law which forbade the execution of a citizen without the confirmation of the Assembly, p. 17], by the effective development of the* senatusconsultum ultimum. . . . *This extends the* provincia *[sphere of action] of the magistrates – to whom alone it is addressed – encourages them to use their existing powers to the full for the maintenance of order, and provides a justificatory testimonial should their action later be challenged in the courts. It did not contain an indictment of named persons as* hostes publici *[enemies of the state] or a declaration of* tumultus *[war emergency], though these were made on occasion by separate decrees.'[1] The normal reaction of officials addressed by the* senatusconsultum ultimum *was to arm the people and to suppress by force the cause of the disturbance.[2]*

The tribune Titus Labienus, who was entrusted with the presentation of this test case, had a personal motive for attacking Rabirius, since his own uncle Quintus Labienus had been one of the associates of Saturninus, killed at the same time as Saturninus himself. It was Titus Labienus, therefore, who took the necessary measures to resuscitate the old treason court – no doubt in consultation with Caesar, who was very fond of such antiquarianisms. Labienus did this by proposing a law that appointed the board of two which had, in the past, sometimes been entrusted with the investigation of such offences.[3] The two were selected by lot from a panel drawn up by a

1. A. W. Lintott, *Violence in Republican Rome*, O.U.P., 1968, summarized by A. N. Sherwin-White, *Journal of Roman Studies*, LIX, 1969, pp. 286f. In certain respects they amend Last's interpretation of this clause.

2. This is somewhat ambiguously stated by Cicero, *In Defence of Milo*, XXV, 70; cf. T. N. Mitchell, *Historia*, XX, 1971, p. 53 and n. 31, in an article discussing Cicero's relation to these decrees.

3. It would, however, also have been in keeping with tradition to have appointed quaestors (see List of Terms) to deal with a case of *perduellio*, but this was not done on the present occasion because Caesar wanted to handle the case himself; cf. Jones, op. cit., pp. 35, 43.

praetor who was evidently in the plot.[1] *By a more than suspicious coincidence the lot fell on Caesar himself and on an obedient distant cousin, Lucius Julius Caesar, who had been consul in the previous year.*

This duet, then, conducted the first trial; however, Cicero, by imposing his veto as consul, succeeded in getting it stopped. The exact course of events has been disputed,[2] *but what apparently happened next was that, in spite of Cicero's efforts to prevent this, Rabirius then came up for trial once again, this time on an ordinary capital charge (p. 17): and this second trial was the occasion of Cicero's present speech. The case was heard in the Assembly.*[3] *Titus Labienus was both the accusing magistrate and the Assembly's presiding officer (being a tribune, he had the power to exercise capital jurisdiction himself; p. 12).*

Adopting what he describes as his lofty style[4] *and an emotional manner which would not have been so appropriate in an address to a lawcourt or the senate, Cicero begins by stressing that he is speaking not only as counsel but as consul: for behind the attack on Rabirius he detects a revolutionary plot against the government and constitution of Rome. Then he emphasizes that the tribune Titus Labienus, so far from being the democrat that* populares *claimed to be, had advocated an archaic, barbarous procedure and penalty, unworthy of a free country. Next Cicero turns back nearly four decades to the*

1. Not, as is generally supposed, the senior praetor (*praetor urbanus*), Quintus Caecilius Metellus Celer (p. 263 n. 3).

2. See especially W. E. Heitland (ed.), *Cicero: Pro Rabirio*, C.U.P., 1882; T. Rice Holmes, *The Roman Republic*, O.U.P., 1923, pp. 452ff.; E. G. Hardy, *Some Problems in Roman History*, 1924, pp. 27ff., 99ff.; J. Lengle, *Hermes*, LXVIII, 1933, pp. 328ff.; A. Boulanger, *Cicéron: Discours*, Tome IX, 1960, pp. 117ff.; G. C. Giardina (ed.), *Cicerone: Pro Rabirio*, Milan, 1969; Jones, op. cit., pp. 40ff.

3. The Comitia Centuriata (see List of Terms: Assembly). By this time the employment of the Assembly as a court of jurisdiction (*iudicium populi*, as opposed to the *quaestiones* [p. 12] which were *iudicia publica*) had become very much rarer than in previous times; cf. Jones, op. cit., pp. 4ff.

4. Jones, op. cit., p. 40.

circumstances in which Saturninus met his death. Rabirius, he declares, did not kill Saturninus – though if he had done so, added the orator, he would have good reason to boast of such a deed. The blame, or rather in Cicero's view the credit, needs rather to be assigned to the great Marius himself – Caesar's own kinsman and hero – who, as consul in the year 100 B.C., had been largely responsible for the moves against Saturninus. The name of the actual killer, Cicero went on to say, was known – he was a slave called Scaeva – but all the noblest leaders of the time had shared the responsibility, and it was something they were entitled to be proud of. Then followed a rousing peroration, of which only part has survived.

The conclusion of the trial proved as astonishing as anything that had gone before. There was a venerable custom, obsolete for many hundreds of years, according to which, at times when the Assembly was in session, a red flag was flown upon the Janiculum hill (Mt Gianicolo) across the Tiber: and this flag was lowered whenever it became necessary to warn the Assembly that the enemy – in those distant days the Etruscans – were at hand. Now, this antique custom was suddenly revived: for according to the historian Dio Cassius the senior praetor (praetor urbanus), Quintus Caecilius Metellus Celer,[1] suddenly hauled down the flag: and so, according to the law, the proceedings of a trial of this kind had come to an end.[2]

Although many have argued that Metellus Celer must have been in collusion with the prosecution this does not seem to have been the case. Dio Cassius represents him as objecting to the whole proceedings (or at least to the first trial) as illegal, and indeed his record indicates that he was a conservative who must have sympathized with Rabirius and Cicero.[3]

It was open to Labienus to renew the prosecution; but he did not.

---

1. See Genealogical Table, I, and List of Terms.
2. Dio Cassius, XXXVII, 27. If no other tribune was willing to use his veto and no evil omen occurred, this was the only way to stop a tribunician trial; cf. Jones, op. cit., p. 42. Dio Cassius causes confusion by conflating the two trials of Rabirius.
3. Cf. Jones, op. cit., p. 42.

This cannot have been because he was daunted by the flag episode. As M. Cary remarks,

it is incredible that Labienus and the People [Assembly] should have allowed themselves to be put off by the flag trick, if they had been in grim earnest. A judge and jury at the Old Bailey would not throw up an important case at the news that the Spanish Armada flares had been lit on Hampstead Heath.[1]

So Labienus' failure to persevere must have been due to a different cause. That is to say, he felt he had done enough. The radicals had already achieved what they desired: they had given the whole issue of the senate's emergency powers a good airing. Dio Cassius believed that, if the trial had continued, Cicero would have lost his case. That may be so,[2] and could well have been the reason for Metellus Celer's dramatic intervention – since Rabirius' innocence of the murder was by no means generally accepted.[3] However, the exaction of vengeance upon the aged Rabirius was not an aim particularly dear to Caesar and his friends. What they wanted was to issue a warning that the senate should only use its emergency decree (if at all) in wholly defensible and invulnerable conditions.

Later in the same year, the matter became a live issue: and it was seen that Cicero's speech for Rabirius, defending the senate's employment of such decrees, had been the theoretical prelude to a very real and concrete situation. For when it became increasingly clear that the aristocratic revolutionary Lucius Sergius Catilina was preparing a rebellion against the government,[4] the senate once again passed an

1. M. Cary, *Cambridge Ancient History*, IX, 1932, p. 490 n. 1.

2. Suetonius, *Divus Julius*, 12, is probably wrong in implying that Rabirius would have been acquitted.

3. Rabirius was said to have displayed the head of the dead man at dinner-parties; Pseudo–Victor, *On Illustrious Men*, 73, 12. According to one account, he had played the leading part in the senate's display of force in 100 B.C.; Suetonius, op. cit. For the strength of Labienus' case, cf. A. W. Lintott, *Violence in Republican Rome*, p. 169.

4. *Cicero: Selected Political Speeches*, pp. 71–145.

emergency decree.[1] *Catilina himself fled (he was later killed in battle),
but Cicero, as consul – the post which Marius had occupied in 100 B.C.
– arrested six of his fellow-conspirators, including men of very high
rank, and had them put to death. He did not order these executions
until after the senate had voted that this should be done. Nevertheless,
his action raised a number of urgent questions. Although he had
enjoyed the senate's backing, the senate itself was, technically speaking, an advisory body, and, whether it had previously passed an
emergency decree or not, was it entitled to order the execution of
Roman citizens? Moreover, could such executions really be justified
when the men had already been taken into custody, as Catilina's
associates had been, so that they could not be said to present any
immediate danger to the state?*

*Cicero, who believed that his suppression of the plot was the
greatest achievement of his life, bringing a new and glorious Harmony
of the Orders into being,*[2] *continued for the rest of his days to insist
that the executions were justified and necessary, since if the men had
been imprisoned they would only have escaped. At first he was overwhelmed with compliments by the senate; but soon both public and
senatorial feeling began to turn against him. Moreover, his boasting
about the defeat of the Catilinarian conspirators*[3] *alienated Pompeius,
who, returning from the east after conclusive victory over King
Mithridates VI of Pontus, was by far the most important man in the
state.*

1. For this, see J. Ungern-Sternberg von Puerke, *Untersuchungen zur
spätrepublikanischen Notstandsrecht*, Vestigia XI, Munich, 1970, pp. 86ff.

2. Already before the end of 63 the newly elected tribune Quintus
Caecilius Metellus Nepos (the brother of Quintus Metellus Celer, but
much less favourably inclined to Cicero) declared at a public meeting
that Cicero ought not to be allowed to deliver the usual valedictory
address of a consul leaving office, since he had executed citizens without
trial. Early in 60 B.C. – the year in which his Catilinarian speeches of 63,
with adjustments, were published – Cicero wrote, 'I am abandoned on
all sides – my grand connexions are no real friends at all!' (*Letters to
Atticus*, I, 18, 1.)

3. For an explanation of Cicero's self-praise, see *Cicero: Selected
Political Speeches*, pp. 11ff.

This failure to gain the support of Pompeius proved decisive, since in 60–59 B.C. he, Caesar and Crassus formed the informal First Triumvirate, which concentrated all political power in their own hands. Caesar suggested to Cicero that he might join them, but he refused to sacrifice his independence in this way. His refusal meant, however, that legal proceedings against him because of his action against the Catilinarians had become inevitable. And so, in 58 B.C., his political enemy Publius Clodius Pulcher, now tribune, enacted a law that anyone who had executed a citizen without trial should be outlawed. Without awaiting prosecution, Cicero fled to Macedonia, where he spent the most miserable year and a half of his life. The case for wider authority in the hands of the senate and officers of state, the case which he had attempted to outline in his defence of Rabirius and had brought into practical effect against the Catilinarian plotters, had finally gone against him.

CICERO'S SPEECH

CITIZENS OF ROME:

I do not usually begin my speeches explaining why I am defending a particular individual, since I have always felt that, when a Roman citizen is imperilled by a trial, that is a good enough bond for me. Nevertheless, in speaking as I am today, in defence of the civil rights,[1] reputation and fortunes of Gaius Rabirius, I do feel I owe you an explanation of the service I am trying to render him. And I feel this especially strongly because the very reasons which seemed to me to make it imperative to defend him should make you feel it to be equally necessary to acquit him.

Well, the motives that have induced me to speak for Rabirius are varied. They include the long-standing friendship between us, his important position in Roman life,[2] the demands of common humanity, and my lifelong practice as counsel for the defence. But there are also quite special reasons why I have felt particularly keen to do everything I possibly can to defend him successfully. For one thing the public interest demands it. And secondly, there is my particular duty as a consul: for I know very well that you entrusted me with this consulship precisely in order that the public interest should be my constant care.

Why has Gaius Rabirius been put on trial on a capital charge? Certainly not because he is guilty of any crime. Not because his way of living has incurred the slightest disapproval. Not even because of the ancient, serious grievances which some of

1. For this Roman concept of a capital charge (*caput*), see above, p. 17.
2. Rabirius was a senator, but had been a knight at the time of Saturninus' death. In a fragment from a lost passage of the speech Cicero describes him as 'exceptionally beloved by the entire Roman people, and most of all by the order of knights' (Servius, *Commentary on Virgil's Aeneid*, I, 13).

his fellow-citizens, for reasons of which I am aware, have harboured against him.[1] No, this onslaught upon my client, in his infirm and friendless old age, has been prompted by quite other purposes. It is nothing less than an endeavour to deprive Rome's constitution of the greatest of all the bulwarks of our national dignity, handed down to us by our ancestors.[2] And, by means of the abolition of this bulwark, it is an attempt to ensure that the authority of the senate, the power of the consuls, the united endeavours of right-minded men, shall in future be so greatly weakened that they will no longer be able to stand up against the pestilent scourge which threatens the very existence of our nation.

A good consul, when he sees the entire defences of the state undermined and torn apart, is surely under a solemn obligation to come to its rescue. He must protect the lives and interests of the people, appeal to his fellow-citizens' patriotic instincts, and, in general, set the welfare of the community above his own. And it is equally the duty of every sound and resolute citizen – and that is what you Romans have shown yourselves to be, in every emergency of our national history – to block all attempts at revolution, strengthen the national defences, recognize the position of the consuls as the country's sovereign executive power, and accept the senate as the supreme deliberative authority. And today, in particular, you have a special duty to perform. It is to proclaim, by your votes, that any citizen whose conduct has been in harmony with these principles which I have mentioned, far from meriting retribution and punishment, deserves all praise and honour. That is why, although the task of defending Rabirius falls primarily upon myself, it is essential that you should wholeheartedly share my earnest desire for his deliverance.

1. It is uncertain if this alludes to the resentment felt against him for his part in the riots resulting in the deaths of Saturninus and his associates, or if it refers to other acts of violence by Rabirius.

2. The senate's power to declare an emergency decree; see above, p. 259.

I, 4 IN DEFENCE OF GAIUS RABIRIUS

Fellow-citizens, may I suggest to you how this trial ought to be interpreted? It should be regarded as dealing with the most significant and perilous design – a design demanding the most vigilant rejection from every one of you – that has ever within human memory been launched by a tribune of the people, and resisted by a consul, and referred to this Assembly. For the present trial, gentlemen, constitutes nothing less than an attempt to contrive that there shall never again be a national council of state, never again a patriotic union against evil revolutionary agitators, never again a refuge for our country in times of grave emergency, never again a guarantee of its secure survival. In a crisis of such dimensions, and most of all when a man's life, honour and fortunes are at stake, I know very well where my own duties lie!

As I start, then, I offer a prayer for the grace and favour of Jupiter the Best and Greatest and all the other immortal gods and goddesses, whose succour and aid, far more than the counsels and decisions of human beings, bestow such sound governance upon this state of ours. I beseech that they will permit this day, before dusk has fallen, to cast its beneficent light upon the salvation of my client and the prosperity of our country. And next, citizens, I address a prayer and plea to yourselves, whose power stands second only to the supreme authority of the immortal gods. Remember that it is not only the life of the unhappy, innocent Gaius Rabirius which is committed into your hands, and depends upon your verdicts, but the welfare of our entire country as well. So you must display, I implore you, two qualities: your customary compassion in determining the fate of the defendant, and your habitual wisdom in protecting the security of our nation.

You have restricted my efforts, Labienus, by cutting down the time at my disposal;[1] the duration regularly and habitually

1. Labienus was apparently able to do this in his capacity as presiding officer; Jones, op. cit., p. 40.

allotted to a defence counsel is curtailed to the narrow space of half an hour. I have no alternative but to submit, yet it is a great injustice that I should have to bow to conditions the prosecutor has himself laid down, and a great misfortune that I should find myself subjected to the will of a hostile opponent. In thus limiting me to a mere half-hour you have, it is true, not quite deprived me of my function as defending counsel. But my role as consul you have abolished. For the time now at my disposal, though almost long enough for the actual purpose of my defence, will be much too short for the strong protest which it is incumbent upon me to lodge in my consular capacity.

As to the secondary charges, you surely cannot expect me to reply at any length to your revival of the allegation that my client profaned holy places and graves.[1] Indeed, even you yourself had nothing to say in support of this smear except to record that it was originally owed to Gaius Licinius Macer.[2] And when you recalled this alleged incident, it seems surprising that you were perfectly well able to remember the accusations brought against Rabirius by Macer, who hated him, whereas the fact that an impartial board of judges, on their oaths, had completely cleared him of the offence apparently slipped your memory.

Or am I required to deliver a long speech about that prosecution of Rabirius for embezzlement and the alleged burning of public archives? Now, on this charge Gaius Curtius,[3] a kinsman of Gaius Rabirius, appearing before a very

1. Sulla may have established a special court to hear religious offences of such a kind.

2. Democratic politician and historian. He brought this action against Labienus when he himself was tribune of the people in 73 B.C., but he was convicted of extortion and committed suicide in 66.

3. Eminent financier, and leader among the knights. He was apparently the brother-in-law of Rabirius, and adopted Rabirius' son, the financial speculator Gaius Rabirius Postumus.

distinguished court, was acquitted without a stain on his name: just what one would have expected in view of his excellent character. And as for Rabirius, he was never even brought to trial at all. There was not the slightest question of such a thing. For not one single word has ever been spoken which could make him liable to even the smallest suspicion in connexion with these supposed crimes.

Your allegations about Rabirius' sister's son, too, do not seem to me to deserve very careful answers. You pretend that my client murdered the man so as to secure an adjournment of the legal proceedings against Curtius on the grounds of family bereavement.[1] But to suggest that he preferred his sister's husband Curtius to her son – and, indeed, preferred him so greatly that he was prepared to assassinate her son just in order to get her husband's trial postponed for a mere two days – is the reverse of plausibility.

Nor, surely, need I say very much about earlier charges that Rabirius detained another man's slaves in contravention of the Fabian law, or that he broke the Porcian law by scourging or killing Roman citizens.[2] Of a man who remains so extremely popular in every part of Apulia, and is greatly loved by the people of Campania as well,[3] this surely cannot be true. Indeed, in order to give him support in his ordeal, not only individuals but virtually the entire populations of whole territories in these areas have converged upon Rome; and their emotional

1. Family bereavement exempted a man from the need to perform any public act.

2. The date and authorship of the *Lex Fabia* on kidnapping slaves (and apparently, later, Roman citizens) is uncertain; cf. P.A. Brunt, *Italian Manpower*, O.U.P., 1971, pp. 292ff. The *Lex Porcia de tergo civium*, passed by Marcus Porcius Cato the Censor (probably in 198 B.C.), had prohibited the scourging of Roman citizens without appeal. The incident in question probably occurred while Rabirius was holding a military command.

3. Presumably these were both regions in which Rabirius possessed estates.

attachment to his cause was far too deep to be explained just as a manifestation of neighbourly feeling. And I see no reason, either, to offer a lengthy refutation of the point which was introduced to support the proposal that Rabirius should be punished by a fine. I refer to the allegation that he was sexually promiscuous, and inflicted a similar promiscuity on others.[1] Actually, I suspect that this charge was one of the reasons why Labienus limited my time to half an hour. I can quite see why he would have good cause not to want me to enlarge on the subject of sexual promiscuity.[2]

Well, then, so far as the charges which require my attention as counsel are concerned, you can see that the half-hour you allowed me was actually more than I needed. But the part you were really anxious that I should curtail and abbreviate was my proposed discussion of the death of Lucius Appuleius Saturninus. And that, citizens, is a subject which demands something more than the talents of an advocate. For it also stands in need – in imperative need – of the intervention of a consul.

You keep on insisting that what I am after is the abolition of the ancient court of high treason.[3] If so, however, that is a charge against myself, and not against Rabirius. Furthermore, gentlemen, if I could claim the credit, or better still the sole credit, for finally abolishing that court, I should indeed be proud. Labienus censures me for my efforts in this direction. But I can assure you I would be only pleased if the responsibility for such an achievement could be regarded as my own.

1. This was one of a number of charges introduced to initiate the proceedings; cf. Jones, op. cit., p. 40.

2. A coarse sexual nickname in the poet Catullus might also be intended for Labienus (though it is not usually attributed to him); cf. T. Frank, *American Journal of Philology*, XL, 1919, pp. 407ff.; R. Syme, *The Roman Revolution*, 1939, p. 63 n. 1.

3. See above, p. 258.

Nothing in the world could give me greater satisfaction than the knowledge that I myself, during this present consulship of mine, had succeeded in expelling the executioner from the Forum, in ejecting the cross from the Field of Mars.[1] But instead the glory belongs in the first place, citizens, to our ancestors who, at the time when they drove out the kings, expunged every trace of their cruel ways from among the Roman people that had now become free.[2] And, secondly, the credit belongs to a whole host of courageous men – the men who were determined that this freedom of yours should not be tainted by barbarous punishments, but should instead rely on the very leniency of its laws for its protection.

Tell me, then, Labienus; are you the people's friend, or am I? What *you* think right is that Roman citizens, here in the middle of their own Assembly of Tribes, should be handed over to the executioner in chains. What you choose to ordain is that in the Field of Mars, at the sacred spot itself where the Assembly of the Centuries[3] holds its meetings, a cross should be erected and planted for the crucifixion of Roman citizens! What I, on the other hand, assert is that the presence of an executioner must never, come what may, pollute the places where the Assembly meets. The Forum of the Roman People must be kept undefiled, its Assembly untainted, by even the suggestion of such a horrible abomination. The sanctity of the Field of Mars must never be besmirched. The person of every Roman citizen must remain inviolate. The rights that stand for the liberty of the individual must never, under any circumstances, be tampered with.

Labienus is a tribune of the people. But what sort of a people's friend is this, what sort of a guardian to protect the

1. Crucifixions always took place in the Field of Mars (Campus Martius) outside the city walls.

2. The expulsion of the last king (Tarquinius Superbus), and foundation of the Republic, were traditionally ascribed to 510 B.C.

3. For these Assemblies, see List of Terms.

people's freedom and rights? The Porcian Law[1] ordained that no Roman citizen should be flogged: here is the merciful man who wants to bring the whip back again. The Porcian Law protected the liberty of citizens from the lictor: Labienus, who loves the people, has given this liberty over into the executioner's hands. Gaius Sempronius Gracchus passed a law exempting citizens from prosecution on capital charges unless and until the consent of your Assembly were first ordained:[2] yet this democratic Labienus, without your consent, has forcibly secured that the board of two which he himself has created[3] should not merely place Roman citizens on trial, but should even be able to condemn them to death, without the slightest attempt to hear their cases at all.

I cannot believe that you have the nerve to talk to me about the Porcian Law, or the law of Gaius Gracchus, or the liberties of Roman citizens, seeing that you yourself, by the introduction of unheard-of punishments and the employment of unprecedentedly brutal language, have shown such persistent determination to violate these liberties, and to test the Roman people's endurance of such abuses, and to overthrow its cherished traditions. Considering that you are such an indulgent man and such a friend of the people, it is strange indeed to see how greatly the order, *Go, lictor, and bind his hands*, seems to appeal to you.[4] For that is an order which is entirely alien to the leniency and clemency of our own time. Indeed, it was alien even to the distant ages of Romulus and Numa Pompilius. Those torturers' formulas which your gentle, democratic heart so delights in pronouncing, like *Veil his head, hang him on a barren tree*, emanate rather from Tarquin, that

1. See above, p. 271.
2. See above, p.17.
3. See above, p. 261.
4. If Cicero had not put a stop to the previous trial conducted under the archaic procedure (p. 262), this formula would have been pronounced immediately after the sentence; cf. Livy, I, 26.

most arrogant and brutal tyrant.[1] Such phrases, citizens, as I say, disappeared from our community an enormously long time ago, obliterated by the dusk of antiquity and the rising sun of freedom.[2]

Besides, if this procedure you are supporting were so democratic, if it could be described as containing the smallest element of justice or fairness, surely it would inevitably have been adopted by Gaius Sempronius Gracchus. You cannot expect us to believe that the death of your uncle[3] caused you greater sorrow than the death of his brother Tiberius caused Gaius Gracchus,[4] or that the loss of this uncle you had never set eyes upon distressed you more profoundly than Gracchus was distressed by the loss of his brother, to whom he had been so exceptionally close. If you are trying to tell us that the means by which you chose to avenge this uncle of yours is a means which Gracchus would have been quite content to use in order to avenge his brother if this had only occurred to him, then I beg you to spare us such excessively feeble arguments! And do not waste time pretending that your uncle, that other Labienus whoever he may have been, was more deeply mourned by the people of Rome than Tiberius Gracchus ever was.

1. According to Livy, loc. cit., this formula would have been pronounced after a subsequent appeal to the Assembly had proved unsuccessful.

2. These formulas allegedly went back to a law of quasi-mythical regal times. Livy, I, 26, 8 and 11, attributes them to the fourth king, Tullus Hostilius, but Cicero here ascribes them to the wicked last king, Tarquinius Superbus. The mythical Romulus and Numa Pompilius were believed to have been the first and second kings. The 'barren tree', consecrated to the gods of the underworld, was the executioner's gallows.

3. Quintus Labienus, one of the followers of Saturninus who perished with him. 'Your' is plural (vester), suggesting that Titus Labienus was associated in this trial of Rabirius with one or more of Quintus' sons.

4. Tiberius Gracchus had been killed on the Capitol in 133 B.C. (p. 7). Usually, Cicero did not favour the memory of the Gracchi.

Or are we going to be told that you are more dutiful than Gaius Gracchus, or braver, or cleverer, or richer, or more influential, or more eloquent? Even if he had possessed only the tiniest fraction of the qualities in question, they would still have appeared substantial in comparison with your own. As it was, however, Gaius Gracchus possessed a larger share of these assets than any other man. So the gulf between you and him is immeasurable. Furthermore, Gaius Gracchus would have died a thousand horrible deaths rather than allow an executioner to appear in any Assembly he had convoked. For the rules of the censors forbid these individuals not only to set foot in the Forum, but even to breathe the same air as we do, or to live inside our city.[1]

So this is the man who has the nerve to pronounce himself the people's friend, and to declare that I, on the other hand, am inimical to your interests. And yet it is he, not I, whose researches have hunted out all these brutal punishments and brutal phrases. Nor, in his anxiety to track them down, has he been content to draw upon the customs you yourselves practise, or even the customs of your fathers. Instead he has gone all the way back to the chronicles of antiquity, the acts of the ancient kings.[2] I, on the other hand, have devoted all my resources, all my ideas, every word that I utter and every action that I perform, to resisting and contesting his cruel endeavours.

Citizens, you surely cannot accept a situation which even slaves would find unendurable unless some hope of liberation were held out to them. Compare setbacks of other kinds that

1. It was part of the responsibility of the censors (see List of Terms) for public works to allocate quarters to the public slaves, who included the executioners.

2. Cicero may be referring to the mythical trial of Horatius, foe of the Curiatii (M. Grant, *Roman Myths*, p. 147), which was the occasion of Livy's description of the grim formulas (cf. pp. 274 n. 4, 275 n. 1; Jones, op. cit., p. 43). The right of appeal was believed to go back to this precedent; ibid., p. 10.

may come a man's way – dishonour inflicted by a public court
of law, or banishment, or a fine. When those disasters befall
us, at least some trace of our freedom is still retained. Even if
death is to be our fate, we can at least, usually, die free. But the
executioner, the veil that covers the condemned man's head,
the cross of crucifixion, these are horrors which ought to be
far removed not only from the person of a Roman citizen but
even from his thoughts and his gaze and his hearing. It is
utterly wrong that a Roman citizen, a free man, would ever
be compelled to endure or tolerate such dreadful things.
Indeed, it ought never even to occur to him that there could
be the faintest possibility of his experiencing them; he never
ought to be called upon to expect them or even hear them
mentioned. If a slave has a kind master, he has the power, by
a single act,[1] to ensure that the liberated man is exempted from
every one of these punishments. It would therefore be outrageous if we citizens of Rome, after all the services we have
rendered, the careers we have followed, the honours we have
acquired, are to be none the less liable to the scourge, the
executioner's hook,[2] the dreaded cross.

And so Labienus, I admit freely and boastfully, indeed I
glory in making the admission: mine was the initiative, mine
the determination, mine the authority which compelled you
to drop that cruel, brutal procedure, so much more appropriate
to a tyrant than a tribune.[3] In seeking to enforce its imposition
you were content to ignore all our ancestral traditions and
laws; the prestige of the senate, the principles of our religion,
the ordinances of our national auspices, were totally without
meaning in your eyes.[4]

1. The freeing (manumission) of the slave, whom his master touched
with a rod, the *vindicta*.
2. Condemned criminals were dragged along by a hook fastened to
their necks.
3. See above, p. 262.
4. For the auspices, see List of Terms.

Nevertheless, since the time at my disposal is so brief, I do not propose, at the present juncture, to go into these matters any further. We shall have ample opportunity to discuss them on another occasion.[1]

What I want to speak about now is the charge against Gaius Rabirius relating to the deaths of Lucius Appuleius Saturninus and your eminent uncle.

You maintain that Rabirius killed Saturninus. But Rabirius himself, eloquently defended by Quintus Hortensius Hortalus[2] with the support of a host of witnesses, proved that the accusation was false. I, on the other hand, if the case could be heard all over again with myself as his advocate, would admit to the deed, and confess it, and revel in it. Nothing would please me more, if the nature of this present action permitted such a thing, than to proclaim that the hand which struck down Lucius Saturninus, the enemy of the Roman people, was the hand of my client!

I hear cries of protest. However, they do not disturb me. Indeed, I find the sound comforting, because it shows that, although ill-informed citizens exist, they do not appear to be very numerous. If the Roman people, who stand here without associating themselves with these protests, had believed I was the sort of man to be worried by an outcry of this kind, they would never, believe me, have elected me consul. And in any case the uproar seems to be dying down. It was a noise indicative of stupidity and nothing more, and revealing because it showed how few the protesters were; I am not surprised that these sounds are no longer to be heard.

I would gladly admit, then, I repeat – if I could truthfully

1. Cicero hints at some further unspecified proceedings–either a new hearing of the case of Rabirius, or a prosecution of Titus Labienus. Neither materialized.

2. Quintus Hortensius Hortalus (114–50 B.C.) was the leading orator in Rome until Cicero eclipsed him.

do so or if the case could be revived – that my client was the man who killed Saturninus. I should consider it a truly splendid achievement. But since this particular avenue is closed, I propose to make another admission instead. It reflects less glory upon my client – but it has just as strong a bearing on the charge you are bringing against him. For I confess, here and now, that Rabirius took up arms with the intention of killing Saturninus.

Well, Labienus, you could not expect me to volunteer a more significant admission than that, or to concede a weightier charge. For there is surely no difference between the man who kills and the man who takes up arms for the purpose of killing. If it was a crime to kill Saturninus, then to take up arms against him could not fail to be a crime as well. But if you agree that the taking up of arms was lawful, then you are obliged to agree that the killing was lawful as well.[1]

On the occasion in question, the senate had passed a decree that the consuls, Gaius Marius and Lucius Valerius Flaccus, should summon any tribunes of the people and praetors whom they chose, and should take measures to protect the sovereign authority of the Roman people.[2] So the consuls called upon all the tribunes with the single exception of Saturninus, and all the praetors except Gaius Servilius Glaucia:[3] and they ordered every citizen who had the welfare of the state at heart to take up arms and follow their lead. Everyone obeyed. Weapons were taken from the temples[4] and the public arsenals, and Gaius Marius distributed them among the populace.

1. At this point a page is missing in the oldest manuscript.

2. The emergency decree; see above, p. 257.

3. Glaucia was Saturninus' chief collaborator; he hoped to be consul in the following year (the rival candidate, Gaius Memmius, having been murdered; p. 257).

4. According to an alternative reading, there is a reference to the temple of Sancus (Semo Sancus Dius Fidius, a god associated with oaths and treaties) on the Quirinal hill.

Now, at this point, setting all other aspects aside for the moment, there is one question, Labienus, which I have to put to you. Let us remember that Saturninus had seized the Capitol by force. With him were Gaius Glaucia, and Gaius Saufeius,[1] and that so-called Gracchus, fresh from his prison chains.[2] And since you insist, I will add that your uncle Quintus Labienus was also in their company. In the Forum, on the other hand, were both the consuls. Behind them was assembled the entire senate – and it was a body which even you yourself are in the habit of praising, if only in order to depreciate the senate of our own day. The knights, too, had taken up arms in their support. And, by heaven, what men they were! They were our fathers. They were the generation which played such a great part in political life, which carried the weighty responsibility of providing all the judges for our lawcourts.[3] But, in addition to them all, every single other Roman citizen who existed, if only he held the conviction that his welfare was bound up with the welfare of the state, now proceeded to take up arms in the same cause. So tell me: what do you consider that Rabirius ought to have done?

And remember what the circumstances were. It was the consuls themselves, in pursuance of a decree of the senate, who had issued the call to arms. Marcus Aemilius Scaurus himself, the president of the senate, had taken up his position in the Assembly, weapon in hand.[4] He was so lame that he could hardly walk, but his lameness, as he saw it, would only

1. Gaius Saufeius took office as urban quaestor on 5 December 100 B.C., five days before the probable date of the rioting; cf. H. B. Mattingly, *Classical Review*, 1969, p. 267.

2. A man named Equitius who pretended to be the son of Gaius Gracchus.

3. See above, p. 13.

4. It was Scaurus (consul 115, censor 109 B.C.) who had moved the emergency decree against Saturninus and his supporters. He was one of the principal heroes of the conservative (*optimate*) cause. See Genealogical Table, I.

prevent him from fleeing, not from pursuing. And there stood
Quintus Mucius Scaevola Augur, too, leaning upon his spear.
A very old man, incurably ill, one-armed, disabled and crippled
in every limb, he made it clear enough that for all his bodily
weakness there was no lack of vigour in his heart. Lucius
Caecilius Metellus Delmaticus, Servius Sulpicius Galba, Gaius
Atilius Serranus, Publius Rutilius Rufus, Gaius Flavius Fimbria,
Quintus Lutatius Catulus, and all others who at that time
held consular rank,[1] had armed themselves to protect our
country in its peril. And all the praetors, all the nobility, every
citizen of military age, had hastened to join them – men like
Cnaeus and Lucius Domitius Ahenobarbus, Lucius Licinius
Crassus, Quintus Scaevola Pontifex, Gaius Claudius Pulcher,
Marcus Livius Drusus. If a man's name was Octavius, Metellus,
Julius, Cassius, Cato, Pompeius, then he was certain to be
there. Lucius Marcius Philippus was present, and Lucius
Cornelius Scipio Asiagenus,[2] and Marcus Aemilius Lepidus,[3]
and Decimus Junius Brutus. Publius Servilius Vatia here,[4] the
general under whose command you yourself, Labienus,
served, was also to be seen; and others in attendance were
Quintus Lutatius Catulus Junior, who is with us today and at
that time was still a very young man,[5] and Gaius Scribonius
Curio who is likewise in our company. Indeed, there was
not one single Roman of any distinction who failed to put in
an appearance.

1. i.e. who had held office as consul. For Delmaticus, see Genealogical
Table, I.
2. Consul in 83 B.C.
3. Consul in 78 B.C. (when he led a revolutionary movement).
4. Consul in 79 B.C.: assumed the name of Isauricus. See Genealogical
Table, I.
5. Consul in 78 B.C., and leader of the conservative party (*optimates*).
In the year of the present speech, 63 B.C., he and Publius Servilius Vatia
Isauricus were defeated by Caesar in a competition for the chief priesthood, left vacant by the death of Quintus Caecilius Metellus Pius
(consul 80 B.C.; see Genealogical Table, I).

So what, I ask you once again, was Gaius Rabirius to do? Should he have remained hidden and skulking in some secret place, concealing his cowardice behind the protection of darkness within the four walls of his house? Or should he, perhaps, have proceeded to the Capitol and joined your uncle and his comrades who were seeking death as a refuge from the degradation of their lives? Or was it not, surely, a great deal better that he should unite with Marius, Scaurus, Catulus, Metellus and Scaevola, in fact with every good citizen of Rome, in order to find, along with them, salvation or death?

And as for you, Labienus, I should like to know what decision you yourself would have taken had you been there at that critical time. Your cowardly instincts would have prompted you to take refuge in some dark spot. Your attraction towards the evil frenzy of Saturninus would have tempted you to the Capitol. Yet at the same time you would have heard the consuls calling upon you to defend your country and your freedom. Which authority, then, which voice, which party, would you have chosen to follow, which set of orders would you have decided to obey?

'My uncle,' he says, 'was with Saturninus.' But your father was on the other side, was he not? The knights who were your kinsmen, all the inhabitants of your prefecture,[1] your district, your neighbourhood, the entire population of Picenum, did they see fit to back that maniac tribune, or was it not a fact, instead, that every one of them preferred to support the authority of the senate? It seems to me that what you are attributing to your uncle is a course of action which nobody has ever yet dared to admit even for himself. For no man on earth, however vile and depraved, however lacking in decent feelings or even in the pretence that he possessed

1. A *praefectura* was the designation of assize-towns in Roman territory. The family of Labienus probably came from Cingulum (Cingoli) in Picenum (Marche, eastern Italy).

them, has ever been found willing to confess that he was on the Capitol with Saturninus.

Yet your uncle was there, you say. Well, suppose that he was. And let us even suppose that he was there not under the compulsion of his desperate personal affairs or some domestic trouble, but because his intimate connexion with Saturninus induced him to place his friend before his country. Even so, your uncle's decision was no reason why Gaius Rabirius, too, should desert his patriotic duty, and fail to join the ranks of all those good citizens in arms, and reject the controlling authority of the consuls. As we have seen, the circumstances offered three choices. He could join Saturninus, or he could join the consuls, or he could go away and hide. To hide would have been no better than to die an ignominious death. To associate himself with Saturninus would have been both sinful and lunatic. Honour, principle, and decency alike all demanded that he should enrol with the consuls. And that is what he did, espousing the cause which it would have been the height of madness to oppose, and the height of shame to abandon. So how can you continue to maintain that he committed a crime?

The name of Gaius Appuleius Decianus is often on your lips.[1] Well, while Decianus, enthusiastically backed by all right-minded people, was engaged in bringing a charge against the infamous Publius Furius,[2] he ventured, in the course of his speech, to lament the death of Saturninus: and because of that, he himself was taken to court and convicted. Sextus Titius, too, was found guilty, because he had a portrait of Saturninus in his house.[3] By this verdict against Titius, the

1. Nothing more is known of him except that Valerius Maximus (VIII, 1, 2) praised his integrity.

2. Publius Furius had ventured to oppose the honorific recall, from the war against Jugurtha king of Numidia (north Africa), of the senate's hero Quintus Caecilius Metellus Numidicus (see Genealogical Table, I).

3. Sextus Titius, tribune of the people in 99 B.C., tried to introduce agrarian legislation. The term *imago*, 'portrait', was properly used for the wax masks of distinguished Romans which were kept in cupboards

Roman knights who served as his judges were condemning as a bad citizen, unfit to retain his citizen rights, anyone who possessed a portrait of that man whose seditious conduct had made him an enemy of the state. For the retention of Saturninus' portrait could be interpreted not merely as a pious commemoration of his death, but also as an attempt to stir up the emotions of the ignorant populace, so that they would look back on the dead man with regret. Or the possession of such an object might even be seen as the manifestation of a desire to imitate his deplorable activities.

That is why I am very curious to know, Labienus, where you managed to find the portrait of Saturninus that is in your possession.[1] For ever since Sextus Titius was condemned, no one has ever been rash enough to possess one. If you had ever heard about Titius' fate, I feel sure you would never have felt inclined to parade another likeness of Saturninus on the platform of a public meeting. Why, it brought ruin and banishment to Titius, even inside his own house. And surely you would not want to drive your ship against the rocks on which you saw the craft of Titius smashed, and the fortunes of Gaius Appuleius Decianus reduced to wreckage.

Your trouble all through this action has been ignorance. After all, you were bringing into court a case which was before your time, a case which was dead before you were born. You would have been involved in it, certainly, if you had been old enough, but you were not. Nevertheless, you ought to realize the character of the men, very eminent men, whom you are accusing, now that they are dead, of an extremely grave crime. You ought also to appreciate the large number of citizens still living today whom you are rendering liable, by your charge,

(with inscriptions beneath them) in private houses, but was also employed for painted portraits or portrait busts.

1. Labienus had evidently produced it at one of the earlier sessions of the present trial; cf. Jones, op. cit., p. 41.

to the possible danger of a capital accusation against themselves as well.

For if Gaius Rabirius had committed a capital crime in taking up arms against Saturninus, at least he could have urged his youthful years in extenuation. But consider Quintus Lutatius Catulus the elder, our own Catulus' father, that man who united so many qualities – powerful intellect, noble character, real goodness.[1] Consider Marcus Aemilius Scaurus, famous for his determination, sagacity, and judgement. Consider the two Scaevolas,[2] and Lucius Licinius Crassus, and Marcus Antonius: at that time Antonius was actually stationed with a military force outside the city.[3] These personages stood out among all our other leading public figures of the time, in wisdom and ability alike – but with them were other men of comparable calibre. They were the guardians and helmsmen of the state; and how, now that they are dead, can we ever give them their due? Or how can we ever praise sufficiently those Roman knights, honourable men and excellent citizens, who in that crisis combined forces with the senate for the protection of our country – those tribunes of the treasury,[4] and those men of all other ranks and society as well, who on that day took up arms to defend the freedom of every one of us?

Nor need we speak only of the men who followed the consuls' lead: for the reputation of the consuls themselves is also being judged today. Lucius Valerius Flaccus, throughout his political career, in all his offices of state, in his priesthood and his religious duties, never once failed to prove himself a

1. Consul in 102 B.C., and Marius' colleague in the defeat of the German (Cimbrian) invaders of Italy at Vercellae (Vercelli) in 101.
2. Quintus Mucius Scaevola Augur (consul in 117 B.C.) and his brother Quintus Mucius Scaevola Pontifex (consul in 95 B.C. and chief priest), both eminent jurists. See *Cicero On the Good Life*, p. 232.
3. For Lucius Licinius Crassus and Marcus Antonius, see above, p. 211.
4. See List of Terms.

meticulously conscientious man.[1] Now that he is dead, are we really expected to pronounce him guilty of the appalling crime of killing a fellow-citizen?[2] And Gaius Marius, shall his name also be polluted with this dreadful taint of murder? We can justly describe Gaius Marius as the father of his country, the parent of our entire nation and its liberty.[3] Now that he is no longer with us, must he, too, incur our condemnation for this horrible crime of murder? Since Labienus proposes to erect a cross on the Field of Mars on which to crucify Gaius Rabirius because he took up arms, we are obliged to ask him what punishment he proposes to devise for the man who summoned Rabirius to arm himself. You keep on protesting that Saturninus' safety was guaranteed. But if so, the safe-conduct was given not by Rabirius but by Marius, and if it was broken, it was Marius who broke it. In fact, however, how could any such guarantee possibly have been offered at all, without a previous decree of the senate?[4] If this comes as news to you, you must be a stranger to this city, completely ignorant of our traditions and customs: a stranger in an alien community, and assuredly not an office-holder in your own.

Well, assign part of the responsibility to Marius, then, says Labienus, and what harm can it do him anyway, since he is

1. He became president of the senate in 86 B.C.

2. Cicero uses the term *parricidium*; see above, p. 16.

3. The appeal to Marius had special point because his memory was cherished by Caesar (one of the board of two in charge of the present case), who had ostentatiously restored his monuments two years earlier.

4. Faced with the weakest part of his case – the probability that a safe-conduct was given by Marius, and broken – Cicero denies this on the ground that even after the senate, by its emergency decree, had given the consuls wide powers, it still continued to be their active director and source of authority. This may well have been theoretically correct (cf. T. N. Mitchell, *Historia*, XX, 1971, pp. 50ff.), but all the same it seems scarcely likely that an additional decree would have been necessary before a safe-conduct could be given by one of the consuls.

dead and nothing affects him any longer?[1] But there is more
to it than that. For Gaius Marius, we can be sure, would never
have lived a life full of labours and perils if he had not conceived the hope and expectation that his glory would extend
far beyond the bounds of his mortal life. When he routed
the numberless invaders of Italy,[2] when he delivered our
beleaguered land, is it credible that he could have imagined
that, when he died, his achievements would perish with him?
No, citizens, that he cannot have supposed. For there is not
a single one of us, when he confronts his country's perils with
honour and distinction, who does not feel buoyed up by the
hope that posterity will grant him his reward. And so, although
to my mind there are many reasons for believing that the
souls of good men are divine and immortal, the principal
reason is this, that the greatest and wisest of our national
leaders, when they look forward into the future, invariably
do so with the conviction that they are gazing upon eternity.

That is why I call confidently upon the spirit of Gaius
Marius, and the spirits of all other Roman citizens of outstanding wisdom and excellence, to bear witness on my behalf. For
after they departed from this mortal life, I am convinced that
they were raised to the holy and revered condition of the gods.
And I declare to these noble spirits that I feel it my duty to
protect the ancestral temples and shrines of our city. If it
became needful to take up arms to defend the glory of their
memories, I should wield such weapons as vigorously in such
a cause as they employed theirs in the service of our country.

Nature, gentlemen, has confined our earthly lives within
narrow bounds. But the fame we have it in our power to win
knows no such limits. If we do honour to those who have
departed from this life, we are ensuring that we ourselves,
after we have died, shall be able to enjoy a more glorious
destiny as well.

1. Marius died during his seventh consulship in 86 B.C.
2. See above, p. 285 n. 1.

But it may well be, Labienus, that you care nothing about the figures of the past, who are no longer before our eyes. You will surely agree, however, that we cannot be equally indifferent to those who are still alive. Well, I insist that out of the entire population of Rome on that day, the day you are arraigning in the dock, there was not one male citizen of military age who failed to take up arms and rally to the consuls: which means that every single survivor of that day, whose activity in those critical hours you can deduce from a calculation of his age, is included in the capital charge you are bringing against Gaius Rabirius.

You declare that Rabirius killed Saturninus. I say I only wish he had. For, if that were so, I would not be protecting him him from punishment: I would be demanding a reward! Actually, however, the man who killed Saturninus was Scaeva, a slave of Quintus Croton. The deed earned him his freedom. Now, if that was the reward gained by a mere slave, one can try to imagine what a Roman knight would have deserved. And if Gaius Marius, because he ordered that the pipes which supplied water to the temple and precinct of Jupiter the Best and Greatest should be cut,[1] and because of the Capitoline hill . . . of the disloyal citizens . . .[2]

The senate, when it dealt with the affair at my instance, acted with appropriate sternness and zeal.[3] But so did you yourselves when, expressing your sentiments unmistakably by word and gesture alike, you turned down the proposal that

1. According to Appian, *Civil Wars*, I, 32, it was not Marius who took this initiative.

2. There is a gap in the manuscripts here. Cicero no doubt went on with his defence of the senate's policy, and urged the Assembly to support it as in the past.

3. Cicero is probably referring to the support he obtained from the senate, as from the Assembly, when he opposed the agrarian law of the tribune Publius Servilius Rullus in this same year 63 B.C., the occasion of his three (originally four) speeches *On the Agrarian Law: Against Rullus* (p. 259 n. 1).

the whole world should be divided up, and refused, specifically, to accept those well-known lands of Campania.[1]

The man responsible for this present trial[2] has made an assertion with which I associate myself actively; I should like to publish it abroad with my passionate support. In the whole of the world, he has declared, there is no king left, no people, no nation, for which you, citizens of Rome, need feel the slightest fear. From outside, from foreign parts, there exists not a trace of any menace capable of offering a threat to this commonwealth of ours. But if you want immortality for our country, if it is your desire that our empire and our glory shall be everlasting and eternal, then what we have to resist is the savagery of our own passions, the violence of men who long for revolution: we have to fight against perils arising within the nation itself, plots devised here in our very midst.

Yet against all these evils your forefathers have bequeathed you a splendid defence, and that is the consul's proclamation which begins with the words *Let those who desire the safety of the state*.[3] Uphold this proclamation, I implore you, gentlemen! And never employ your votes to prevent me, as consul, from having recourse to it! For if ever you took such action, you would be banning from this land of ours all future hopes of freedom, deliverance and honour.

If Titus Labienus were ever to model himself on Lucius Saturninus, if he organized a massacre of our fellow-citizens, if he forced open the prison gates,[4] if he seized the Capitol with a band of armed men, what action would I take? I would do exactly as Gaius Marius did. I would bring a motion before

1. Rullus (see last note) proposed to invest a board of ten with special powers to purchase land in Italy, and especially in Campania, for the settlement of veterans.

2. Cicero may be referring either to Titus Labienus or to Caesar.

3. Appeal to arms in pursuance of the senate's emergency decree (*senatusconsultum ultimum*); see above, p. 261.

4. This may be a reference to the violent activities of Equitius who masqueraded as Gaius Gracchus' son; see above, p. 280.

the senate, I would bid you to come to the defence of our
government, and then, backed by every one of you, I would
take up arms against the arms of the foe.

Today, in present conditions, arms are not what we need
to be afraid of. There are no weapons in sight, no signs of
violence or massacre, no sieges of the Capitol and its citadel.
What we have to face instead, however, is a pernicious prosecution, a venomous trial. The entire proceedings are launched
by a tribune of the people; and they are designed as a deliberate
attack upon the state. In these circumstances, I conceived it to
be my duty not indeed to summon you to arms, but to urge
that you repel, by your votes, this assault upon your sovereign
authority. And so now I beg and beseech you all. It is not our
custom . . . a consul . . .[1]

. . . is afraid. My client upon whom a foreign foe has
inflicted these frontal wounds, these marks of valour in defence
of our national cause, is anxious that his honour shall remain
unwounded. No onslaught of the enemy has ever compelled
him to yield ground. Yet now it is the attacks of his own
fellow-citizens that he is compelled to dread – for he is deeply
anxious that he will not have the power to resist them. To be
granted a happy life is more than he dares ask. All he prays for
is an honourable death. To be allowed to enjoy his home is
beyond his ambitions: all he begs for is to be permitted burial
among his own ancestors. His one appeal, his one petition,
is this: do not deprive him of a proper funeral; do not forbid
him to die in his own home! On behalf of his country he has
never shunned the perils of death. Suffer him, at least, to die
within that country's bounds.

And now I have spoken for the duration the tribune allowed
me. I hope with all my heart you will feel that my speech has
not fallen short of my duty – my duty as an advocate to a friend
in his need, and my duty as a consul to the welfare of Rome.

1. There is a gap in the manuscripts here. When they resume, Cicero
has just been speaking of the distinguished military service of Rabirius.

IV

NOTE ON THE SPEECHES
IN DEFENCE OF
CAELIUS AND MILO

After Cicero had gone into exile in 58 B.C., Pompeius came belatedly to his support – with the assistance of the rabble-rouser Titus Annius Milo, who became tribune in the following year. Cicero was recalled to Rome, but his moment of political influence was over, since the First Triumvirate was in complete control. However, he resumed his advocacy in the courts, and delivered numerous speeches. Two of them, during the years immediately following, were related to charges of murder.

In April 56 B.C., the defendant was a clever and fashionable young friend of the orator named Marcus Caelius Rufus; his advocates included not only Cicero but also the triumvir Crassus.[1] Caelius was prosecuted on five charges. The first three, dealt with by Crassus, included an allegation that Caelius, at Puteoli (Pozzuoli), had been a party to attacks upon a visiting Egyptian deputation, sent to Italy by the Alexandrian governing class in order to protest against Cleopatra's father King Ptolemy XII Auletes.[2] Many of the envoys met their deaths at Puteoli, though the absence of the speeches relating to the matter makes it impossible to say exactly how prominent a part Caelius was accused of playing in their deaths. The two remaining charges related to further allegations of murder which Cicero tries to refute in his oration In Defence of Caelius.[3] *The leader of the Egyptian delegation, Dion, had escaped death at Puteoli and then made his way to Rome, only to be assassinated in his turn. His murderer, employed by Ptolemy XII, was said to be a certain Publius*

---

1. There was also a third advocate. The case involved a covert attack on Pompeius, whose relations with his fellow-triumvir Crassus were strained at this time; cf. R. G. Austin (ed.), *Pro M. Caelio*, 3rd edn, 1960, p. viii n. 1. Crassus spoke second, and Cicero last, according to his practice when he was working with other advocates.

2. Cf. M. Grant, *Cleopatra*, Weidenfeld & Nicolson, 1972, p. 16.

3. *Cicero: Selected Political Speeches*, pp. 165ff.

Asicius, but the prosecution declared that once again Caelius was involved. He was also accused of attempting to poison his own former mistress the notorious Clodia, sister of Publius Clodius Pulcher[1] (p. 266), and that gave Cicero, who hated both her and her brother, a splendid opportunity to blacken her moral reputation. Indeed, this procedure, which distracted the judges' attention from awkward speculations about Caelius' own conduct, occupies two thirds of the entire speech.

*The case was heard by a court established to deal with violence (*quaestio de vi*). The law which created the court was a* Lex Lutatia *proposed by the conservative leader Quintus Lutatius Catulus (the younger) in order to deal with collective sedition (78 B.C.).[2] This law had been supplemented by a* Lex Plautia *(before 63 B.C.) creating an additional court to deal with any form of violent behaviour which could be construed as contrary to the public interest.[3] These measures showed that the senatorial leadership, faced with increasing turbulence, had at last conquered its aversion to measures of this kind, which it had hitherto shunned because they could so easily be turned against itself (p. 8). It would have seemed more proper for the charges against Caelius involving murders or attempted murders to come before the murder court which tried Roscius and Cluentius. Two reasons have been suggested for the selection of the court relating to violence instead. First, trials for violence received priority, so that unlike other actions they could even be held during a national holiday, for example while Games were proceeding (as they were now). Secondly, there was a growing tendency to extend the scope of the laws against violence, since this was so greatly on the increase.[4]*

Whether Caelius was guilty of any or all of these charges we

---

1. See Genealogical Table 1.

2. Cf. A. H. M. Jones, *The Criminal Courts of the Roman Republic and Principate*, p. 59; cf. p. 57.

3. A. W. Lintott, *Violence in Republican Rome*, pp. 109ff.; cf. A. N. Sherwin-White, *Journal of Roman Studies*, 1969, p. 286.

4. R. G. Austin, op. cit., p. 153.

cannot say; but the old adage that there is no smoke without fire comes to mind. However, his later career shows that he was acquitted. The combined effect of Crassus' triumviral position and of Cicero's brilliant and amusing oratory carried the day.

Later in the same month the triumvirs met at Luca (Lucca) to renew their compact and decide upon their future activities. Crassus was to proceed to the east, where Rome's only powerful neighbour, the Parthians, who ruled over Mesopotamia (Iraq) and Persia, killed him three years later at the battle of Carrhae. Caesar was authorized to finish off the conquest of Gaul and make an attempt upon Britain, and Pompeius, among other duties, was to look after the capital. This last task was made very difficult by the activities of Publius Clodius Pulcher, who harnessed working people and shopkeepers of the city as a political team, and organized effective gang warfare. Against him, in the streets, fought Titus Annius Milo, who had helped to secure Cicero's return from exile.

In 52 B.C. Clodius and Milo, each with his gang of ferocious followers, encountered one another, possibly by chance, on the Appian Way outside Rome, and the subsequent scuffle resulted in Clodius' death. The savage and destructive rioting which this event caused at Rome, including the burning of the senate house, impelled the senate to pass another emergency decree, and Pompeius was made consul, indeed for the time being sole consul.[1] Since the existing courts concerned with crimes of violence did not seem capable of dealing with the crisis, Pompeius created a new tribunal altogether, and Milo came up for trial before it. Cicero spoke in his defence, and the published version of his speech survives.[2] The speech he actually delivered, however, was apparently less eloquent than this version which has come down to us, since the court was packed with Clodius' thugs, in addition to the soldiers of Pompeius. Consequently, Milo was

1. A few months later he took Quintus Caecilius Metellus Pius Scipio (see Genealogical Table I) as his colleague.
2. Translated in *Cicero: Selected Political Speeches*, pp. 215ff.

convicted,[1] and went into exile at Massilia (Marseille). When Cicero sent him a copy of the speech he had meant but failed to deliver, Milo said he was glad matters had turned out otherwise, since he would not have wished to lose the opportunity of enjoying the excellent mullets of Massilia.[2] Whether he had really given orders for the murder of Clodius we do not know; but it is far from improbable.

1. He was also condemned (*in absentia*) in two other courts (on three other charges), but left Rome a few days after these cases were heard; cf. Jones, op. cit., p. 77.

2. In 48 B.C., however, when Caesar was away, Milo responded to an appeal by Caelius to create disorders in Italy. Both were captured and executed, Caelius at Thurii (Sibari) and Milo at Cosa (Ansedonia).

V

IN DEFENCE OF
KING DEIOTARUS

Introduction to Cicero's Speech

In the end, Pompeius overcame the wave of turbulence at Rome. Soon afterwards, however, he and Caesar found the empire too small to hold them both, and in 49 B.C. civil war broke out between them. Cicero, who had spent an unhappy year as governor of Cilicia (S. Asia Minor, 51–50 B.C.) was afflicted by paralysing hesitations, but finally went to Greece to join Pompeius, whom in spite of all the ups and downs in their relationship he had always liked a good deal better than he liked Caesar.

After Pompeius' defeat at Pharsalus and subsequent death (48), Cicero despondently returned to Italy. Caesar, now dictator, pardoned him for having taken the other side in the war, and they became ostensible friends once again;[1] though Cicero, in fact, deplored his dictatorship, and could never regard it as anything more than a transitional stage towards the restoration of the Republic, which he refused to believe was defunct. During the years 46 and 45 he delivered three speeches before Caesar himself, all seeking to exonerate men who had fallen foul of the dictator during the civil war. One of these speeches, In Support of Marcus Claudius Marcellus, is translated in an earlier volume of this series.[2] The translation of another follows now.

It is a defence of Deiotarus. One of the numerous foreign dependants of Rome who were allowed to rule in semi-autonomy around the fringes of its eastern provinces, he was a Celtic prince of Galatia in central Asia Minor,[3] enjoying the title of king by virtue of his

1. Caesar even went to stay with Cicero at Puteoli (Pozzuoli) in December 45 B.C., as the orator described in *Letters to Atticus*, XIII, 52 (translated in *Cicero: Selected Works*, pp. 89ff.).

2. *Cicero: Selected Political Speeches*, pp. 279ff.

3. The Galatians were Celts who had burst into Asia Minor in the third century B.C. and had finally been confined to the central plateau, where they organized their territory in three tribes (the Tolistobogii, Tectosages and Trocmi), each divided into four parts.

control of certain neighbouring territories.[1] In 45 B.C. Deiotarus was accused of an exceedingly grave offence – or rather of the intention to commit such an offence on an occasion in the past. For it was alleged that, on a certain day two years earlier, he had planned to assassinate Caesar himself. The king's family was at all times convulsed by murderous domestic disputes, and the present charge was lodged by his own grandson Castor, who had fled to Rome in order to tell his melodramatic story.

In 47, when the plan was supposedly formed, Asia Minor had been plunged in chaos. Pharnaces II, a monarch of Iranian origin who was the son of Rome's famous enemy Mithridates VI of Pontus,[2] had taken advantage of the Roman civil war to seize huge areas of the peninsula, including much of Deiotarus' own kingdom. In 48 B.C. Pharnaces defeated Caesar's General Cnaeus Domitius Calvinus at Nicopolis (Purk) in Pontus, and in the following year Caesar himself, released from a state of siege in Cleopatra's palace at Alexandria, moved north into Asia Minor and overwhelmed Pharnaces at Zela (Zile). Deiotarus' role in all these events was a tricky one. In the first place, he had taken what proved to be the wrong side in the Roman civil war, having sided (as most of the eastern potentates were obliged to) with Pompeius against Caesar. But when, thereafter, large areas of his principality were occupied by Pharnaces, Deiotarus showed his anxiety to regain these territories (and at the same time to rectify his mistaken choice in the civil war) by assisting first Calvinus and then Caesar in Asia Minor. True, it was unfortunate that he was reported to have rejoiced at an erroneous report of Calvinus' death (p. 317). Nevertheless, Caesar, after his victory at Zela, consented to be entertained by Deiotarus at his royal residence in Galatia.

It was at this point, according to the allegation of Castor, that Deiotarus had planned to murder Caesar; and the plot, said the young Galatian, only went astray since the dictator did not, as it

1. See below, p. 310 n 2.

2. Pompeius, when he finally defeated Mithridates in 63 B.C., had given Pharnaces the kingdom of the Cimmerian Bosphorus (Crimea).

happened, go into the room where the soldiers lay in ambush to kill him. This was the allegation that Cicero had to answer; and he delivered his speech at a private hearing before Caesar in Caesar's own house¹ – where Cicero, incidentally, complained that the absence of his customary audience was a handicap to his oratorical efforts. It seems unlikely that his client was guilty of the particular intention attributed to him,² though he was a sinister old fox, capable of almost anything else; and Cicero's protestations of Deiotarus' deep affection for Caesar, and of his saintly advanced age, have an unconvincing ring. He was on safer ground when he recalled that the king could point to a long record of loyalty to Rome against its foreign foes.³ But later on, Cicero himself wrote about the speech, in a letter to his son-in-law Publius Cornelius Dolabella, in agreeably modest terms.⁴

Caesar adjourned the hearing without giving a decision. As Cicero had reminded another man he defended in the same place, Quintus Ligarius, the dictator's indignation at the continued resistance of his Roman enemies, supporting the sons of Pompeius in north Africa (46), had made him feel inclined to keep political suspects in anxious suspense; and yet another subsequent campaign against Pompeius' sons in Spain (45) was hardly likely to have made him feel any more indulgent.⁵ Besides, he was planning to return to the east in the following year for a vast military operation against the Parthians, and that would be a better moment than the present for dealing with the princelings of Asia Minor. Probably, when the time came, Caesar would have exonerated Deiotarus, believing that it had been

1. i.e. his residence as chief priest beside the Forum; cf. M. Grant, *The Roman Forum*, 1970, p. 70.

2. Cf. M. Lob, *Cicéron: Discours*, Tome XVIII, 1952, p. 93. But the suggestion that the charge was a put-up job on the part of Caesar to secure Deiotarus' removal is probably wrong; cf. N. H. Watts, *Cicero: Pro Milone* etc., Loeb edn, 1931, pp. 498ff.

3. See below, p. 325 n. 2.

4. Cicero, *Letters to his Friends*, IX, 12.

5. ibid., VI, 13, 3. His decisive victories in these two countries were at Thapsus and Munda respectively.

salutary to keep him on tenterhooks and that henceforward he would be too frightened to be disloyal.

But the time never came, because when the dictator was on the verge of setting out for the east he was assassinated by his own compatriots at Rome. Deiotarus, no doubt delighted with Caesar's death, plunged back into militant life,[1] and Cicero too, who was equally pleased, returned to active politics, delivering his fourteen superb Philippics *against the man who aspired to take over Caesar's mantle, Marcus Antonius.*[2] These speeches cost the orator his life. For Antonius and his allies in the Second Triumvirate, Octavian (the future Augustus) and Marcus Aemilius Lepidus (son of the consul of 78 B.C.), included him among the victims of the proscriptions which inaugurated the new regime, and on 7 August 43 B.C., courageously, Cicero died.

1. See below, p. 326 n. 2.

2. For translations of the first and second of these speeches, see *Cicero: Selected Political Speeches*, pp. 295ff., and *Selected Works*, pp. 101ff. (p. 100 for his death).

CICERO'S SPEECH

In any action of more than usual importance, Caesar, the beginning of my speech generally causes me greater anxiety than my experience and years would seem to warrant. And this present trial, in which my client is king Deiotarus, is one in which I have so many special reasons for anxious emotion that all the enthusiasm I derive from my absolute confidence in his cause is counterbalanced by the nervousness I cannot help feeling.

In the first place, I am speaking for a king: I am defending his life[1] and fortunes. True, a capital charge must be inevitable when what is at stake, Caesar, amounts to nothing less than your own personal security. Nevertheless, for a king to be standing trial for his life is something quite unheard of. Indeed, I can think of absolutely no precedent throughout the whole of human history. Furthermore, this is a king whom I, and the entire senate with me, have repeatedly honoured in earlier years, because of his untiring services to our country.

And yet now it has become my task to defend him against the most dreadful of all possible allegations. And the prosecutors make the whole matter more shocking still: for one is brutal, the other contemptible. Brutal is the word for Castor – unless you prefer to call him criminal and unnatural; seeing that the target of his lethal threats is no one other than his own mother's father![2] Castor has chosen to employ a juvenile terrorist's methods of intimidation against the very person whom it was his duty to shield and protect in his old age. And in this attempt to win support for his entry into public life, the

1. For the meaning of *caput*, in so far as it applied to Roman citizens, see above, p. 17. Deiotarus was not a Roman citizen, and the results of conviction on such a charge would presumably have been fatal.

2. Castor was the son of Saocondarius (Tarcondarius) Castor (p. 320 n. 1) and of Deiotarus' daughter.

young man had recourse to an abominable act of family disloyalty. For he has actually corrupted his grandfather's slave, and detached him from the other servants attending the Galatian envoys,[1] and bribed him to bring an allegation against his own master.

When I saw the expression on the face of this runaway slave, when I heard the terms in which he accused his master – a master who was not there to hear him, and is a profound lover of Rome – I sadly lamented the king's grave misfortune. But the sorrow I felt for the king was nothing to my dread of the troubles that this sort of thing was likely to bring down upon everyone of us here in Rome. For our ancestors ruled that in examining a slave under torture, a form of investigation in which pain elicits the truth even from those most unwilling to comply, it is illegal to extract evidence against the slave's own master. And yet here we have a slave who is prepared, even without such coercion, to bring a charge against a personage whom he would not even be allowed to accuse while being tormented on the rack.

There is also another matter, Caesar, which from time to time causes me anxiety. Yet when I reflect deeply upon your character, it no longer disturbs me after all: since your wisdom is so outstanding that it experiences no difficulty in transforming an unfavourable factor into a favourable one. In itself, the task of defending a man accused of murder before the very person whom he is accused of murdering seems a formidable proposition, since few people could judge a threat to their own lives without showing greater favour to themselves than to the defendant. But in the face of your remarkable and indeed unique qualities, this thought ceases to cause me alarm after all. I cease entirely to fear what your verdict about king Deiotarus is likely to be, because I know very well the verdict you want others to pass upon yourself!

1. The envoys sent by Deiotarus to Rome (p. 312 n. 1). The slave was Deiotarus' physician Phidippus.

But there is another point which does trouble me, I confess –
and this I cannot help. I refer to my embarrassment because
this trial is being held in such an unfamiliar place. Here is a
more important case than any that has ever been debated
before, and yet I am pleading it within the four walls of a
private house,[1] far from any court of law, far from the crowded
audiences which generally provide speakers with their inspira-
tion. Instead, Caesar, it is your own eyes, your regard, your
expression that I have to rely upon to give me assurance. My
whole speech is directed to you and you alone. Certainly, this
is a situation which gives me the strongest possible reason to
hope, with complete confidence, that the truth will prevail. As
incentives to oratorical passions, however, and as stimulants to
the fire and fervour of eloquence, such circumstances are
considerably less effective!

If only I was pleading this case in the Forum – with you
listening to me as my judge – just imagine the presence of that
great audience of Romans, and how it would spur me on! For
when those assembled turned their thoughts to the king, who
had spent his whole life fighting the wars of the people of
Rome, there would be a surge of universal sympathy in his
favour. I should be able to raise my eyes to heaven itself, and
call it to witness. In such an environment the favours of the
immortal gods, the favours of the people and senate of Rome –
which King Deiotarus has so deservedly enjoyed – would be
ever present in my mind. And my speech would surely rise
to the occasion! As it is, however, the whole scale is circum-
scribed by these four walls. The cause I am defending is of
the utmost significance, and yet my advocacy is crippled by
our surroundings. You have often defended law-suits yourself, Caesar. Your own experiences will tell you how I am
feeling. However, I also know very well that they will guarantee me your careful, impartial attention, which alone can have
the power to dispel my anxieties.

1. Caesar's own residence; cf. above, p. 301.

Before I come to the actual accusation against Deiotarus, I want to tell you a little about what the accusers are hoping to achieve. They are not very gifted men, and they seem to be short of experience and practice as well. Yet, even so, they cannot have embarked on this case with a total lack of expectations and plans.

It did not, for example, escape their notice that King Deiotarus had angered you: and they remembered that your resentment had already cost him setbacks and losses.[1] They knew also that, in contrast with your irritation with Deiotarus, you were well disposed towards themselves. And since this was a case in which your life was actually said to have been in danger, they imagined that your exasperation with Deiotarus would mean that a fraudulent charge against him was likely to receive a ready welcome. So at the very outset, Caesar, I call upon you to give a demonstration of your impartiality and your lofty principles and your clemency, by freeing us from all fear on this particular score: reassure us that there is no longer any remnant of anger in your heart.

I appeal to the right hand of mutual hospitality which you yourself, in the past, have extended to Deiotarus, that hand, I would stress, which has ever been firmly extended, not only so as to bring you victory in every war and battle, but also to honour every promise and undertaking you have ever given in all your life. It was at your own desire that you entered the home of Deiotarus, in order to renew the ties of hospitality that had been formed in earlier days.[2] You were welcomed by his household gods: the altars and hearths of

1. Caesar had curtailed Deiotarus' territory by removing the region of the Trocmi which he had seized (p. 301 n. 1: the easternmost of the three Galatian tribes), and lands the king had owned in Lesser Armenia (north-eastern Asia Minor).

2. Caesar had been in Asia Minor in 81–80 and 76–74 B.C., and Cicero is presumably referring to one of these periods.

king Deiotarus saw you as a friend, whose resentment had been placated.

You are a man who is accessible to appeals, Caesar, and once you have responded to an appeal that is always the end of the matter. Once you are reconciled to an enemy, he finds that you have banished every trace of animosity from your heart. Now, the grievances you harboured against Deiotarus are common knowledge. It is true that you never accused him, in the terms you would employ against an enemy. You remonstrated with him, rather, as a friend who had fallen short of his duty, because he had laid more emphasis upon his friendship with Cnaeus Pompeius than upon his friendship with yourself. And even this you would have been prepared to overlook, you declared, if he had not done more than just send aid to Pompeius, or even if he had only sent his son, excusing his own personal presence on grounds of his advancing years. In this way you exonerated him of the main ground of offence. All that remained was the imputation of a not too serious fault, which might be described as a lapse in the duties of private friendship.

You did not punish him, therefore, and you went further still, for you recognized him as your host and left him as king, thus releasing him from all apprehension. For the step to which I was referring had not been in the slightest degree motivated by ill-will towards yourself. He had only made the same mistake as everyone else. A king, whom in the past the senate often addressed by his royal title in a whole series of highly complimentary decrees, a king who from his earliest youth saw that body as the very model of august dignity, had become the victim – foreigner as he was, in a far-off country – of the same circumstances which we ourselves proved unable to escape, even though we were born and had spent our lives in the very heart of the Roman state itself.

For the information that reached him from Rome indicated that the civil war had been launched with the senate's unanimous support, and that the consuls and praetors and tribunes of the people, and we who were generals,[1] had been entrusted with the defence of the state. This could not fail to move Deiotarus. Devoted as he is to the interests of our commonwealth, he felt sorely afraid for the safety of the Roman people, with which he deemed that his own safety was inseparably united. Yet, in spite of his profound anxiety, he still felt it best to take no action. But his perturbation reached its height when he heard that the consuls and all the ex-consuls had fled from Italy – for that is what he was told – and that the entire senate, every Italian, was scattered and dispersed far and wide.[2] For the road to the east lay wide open to all such reports and rumours, and no accurate accounts ever followed in their wake. About the terms you yourself proposed, about all your efforts towards reconciliation and peace, about the intrigues formed by certain individuals against your authority, Deiotarus heard nothing at all.

Nevertheless, in spite of this lack of information, he still remained inactive until envoys and letters arrived for him from Cnaeus Pompeius. Pardon Deiotarus, pardon him, Caesar, if he yielded to the prestige of the man we all followed, the man on whom every possible distinction had been heaped by gods and men alike, and by no one more generously and abundantly than yourself. For if your own great exploits have eclipsed the achievements of everyone else, that does not mean that we have forgotten all about Cnaeus Pompeius. His mighty name, his abundant wealth, his renown in every branch of war, the tremendous honours showered upon him by the Roman people, by the senate, by yourself, these are

1. Cicero had been hailed 'Imperator' by his troops in 51–50 B.C. (the traditional reward for a victory) for some trifling successes over tribes in Cilicia.

2. Pompeius, with the greater part of the senate, fled to Greece in 49, soon after the outbreak of the civil war between himself and Caesar.

matters of common knowledge. His glory surpassed everyone who came before him as completely as your own has surpassed the whole world. Admiringly we counted up all the wars, all the victories, all the triumphs, all the consulships of Cnaeus Pompeius. Yours are beyond our power to count.

And so in that miserable, ill-fated war, King Deiotarus went to join the man whom in earlier days he had helped in legitimate wars against Rome's foreign foes – the man to whom he was bound by ties of hospitality and friendship. He went at the request of his friend, at the summons of his ally, at the call of the senate he had learned he must obey. And, when he went, it was no pursuer of defeated foes that he was going to join, but a fugitive. He went not to share victory, but peril. Afterwards, once the battle of Pharsalus had been fought, Deiotarus dissociated himself from Pompeius.[1] Expectations that were doomed to disappointment did not appeal to him. He felt that he had satisfied the demands of duty, if duty it had been, or that he had gone far enough along a path of delusion, if delusion it was. So he withdrew to his own home, and while you were fighting the Alexandrian War he dedicated himself to your interests.[2] Your distinguished general, Cnaeus Domitius Calvinus, was given quarters and supplies for his army by Deiotarus,[3] and he also sent money to Ephesus, to the man you had singled out as your most loyal and trusted supporter.[4] By holding two public auctions, and then a third, he raised funds for the expenses of your campaign.[5] He risked his own life in the front line, and fought by your side against

1. After the defeat at Pharsalus (48 B.C.) Deiotarus fled from Greece on the same ship as Pompeius.
2. Caesar was besieged in Alexandria (in the company of Cleopatra) for six months (48–47 B.C.).
3. But in the battle of Nicopolis in 48, in which Calvinus was defeated by Pharnaces (p. 300), Deiotarus' troops were routed.
4. Unidentifiable.
5. In fact, however, Deiotarus' auctions were probably held to raise a fine which Caesar had imposed on him for joining Pompeius.

Pharnaces, deeming your enemy his own.[1] And the spirit in which you accepted these services, Caesar, was revealed when you bestowed upon him the noble title of king.[2]

And now this man, whom you yourself preserved from peril, whom you honoured with the most glorious distinctions, is actually accused of having planned to assassinate you inside his own home!

It is something you cannot even begin to suspect him of, unless you regard him as out of his mind. The monstrous wickedness of a host murdering his guest under the very eyes of his own household gods, the barbaric brutality of wrenching from mankind the most brilliant light that has ever vouchsafed illumination to the human race, the crude impudence of failing to revere the conqueror of the entire world, the inhuman ingratitude of acting like the most brutal despot towards the very man who had granted him the name of king – leave all these terrible thoughts aside, if you can, and just reflect, purely and simply, upon the insane stupidity of such an action. For at one single blow Deiotarus would have stirred up, in alliance against himself, all the kings of every realm that exists upon the earth – many of them his own neighbours – and all the great array of free peoples, allies, and provinces of Rome. In fact there would not have been a single weapon in the entire world which was not pointed at his own throat. If he had even so much as dreamt of such an appalling crime, much less committed it, he himself, and his whole kingdom, and his wife, and his beloved son, would all have been torn asunder into shreds.

1. After Caesar had defeated Pharnaces at Zela, Deiotarus seized the territory of the Trocmi, thus causing the other tetrarchs to complain to Caesar, who removed it from him (p. 306 n. 1).

2. Deiotarus had first been given the title by Pompeius – not because of his Galatian territories, of which he remained prince (tetrarch), but as ruler of his territorial gains in Pontus and Lesser Armenia. Caesar, as consul in 59, confirmed the title, adding further lands.

Do not tell me he is so impetuous and hot-headed that all this failed to occur to him. On the contrary, a more shrewd and cautious and circumspect man would be impossible to find. Yet in the present context it is not so much Deiotarus' shrewdness and brain-power that need to be cited in his defence, as the principles of good faith and conscience that govern his whole life. You know he is an honourable man, Caesar. You know how good he is, and how reliable. Anyone and everyone who has so much as heard of the name of Rome itself will have heard also of the integrity, and high-mindedness, and moral strength, and firm loyalty, of Deiotarus.

Yet the dreadful misdeed he is accused of would have been an action which even a complete fool could not have thought of committing, because his own instant annihilation must inevitably have followed. To perpetrate such a crime would not have occurred to the most abominable criminal in the world, unless his wits were totally deranged. Yet Deiotarus' intelligence was in no respect less outstanding than his character. How on earth, therefore, can his accusers pretend to believe that he could ever have been such an idiot as to plan a deed like that?

Not only does your charge totally fail to carry conviction, but it does not even manage to kindle the smallest ray of suspicion. Listen to the story the prosecutor tells. 'After you, Caesar, had arrived at the fortress of Peium,[1] and had taken up your residence in your royal host's mansion, there was a room in which the presents the king had set aside for you were placed on view.[2] After you had finished your bath, and before

1. Reading uncertain. But Strabo, XII, 5, 2, says that Deiotarus' royal treasure was at Peium (east of Gordium, the modern Yassihüyük), and his palace was at Blucium (the modern Karalar, between Gordium and Ancyra, which is the modern Ankara).

2. It is to be hoped that the presents were of better quality than the gifts of Deiotarus mentioned in a private letter of Cicero (*To his Friends*, IX, 12), who describes them as 'coarse homespun' – the description he also applies to the present speech.

you took your place at dinner, he intended to accompany you to this room. Inside it lurked armed men determined to strike you down and stab you to death.' This, then, is the charge, this is the pretext which induces a renegade to accuse his king, a slave to denounce his master. When I was first entrusted with this case, I must tell you, Caesar, that my immediate reaction was to suspect that this young Castor had bribed Phidippus, one of the king's slaves who was attending the Galatian delegates at Rome as their physician.[1] Castor, I thought, had suborned Phidippus to give false evidence, and was obviously going to concoct some allegation of poisoning. In fact, this conjecture, although it came close to the sort of thing that people wanting to bring charges invent, did not correspond with what happened. As it turned out, the doctor did not say anything about poisoning at all. And yet poison could have been introduced into his drink or food with very much less danger of detection than the violent methods which were actually alleged. Besides, it would have offered a better chance of escaping retribution, because when poison has been administered it can be denied.

If, on the other hand, Deiotarus had killed you openly, as they pretend that he proposed to do, he would have made himself the victim not only of the hatred of the entire world, but also of its overwhelmingly forcible reprisals. Had he, on the other hand, employed poison, he could not, it is true, have hidden the deed from Jupiter the god of hospitality, but he might well have concealed it from his fellow human beings. You, Phidippus, were an expert doctor, and he regarded you as a loyal slave. Nevertheless, he did not see fit to entrust you

1. Deiotarus had probably sent these envoys to Rome (as well as a previous deputation to Tarraco [Tarragona] in 45 B.C., during Caesar's final campaign against the sons of Pompeius, culminating in his victory at Munda), in the hope of getting back the territory of the Trocmi, whose prince, Mithridates of Pergamum, granted these lands when they were taken away from Deiotarus in 47 (p. 306 n. 1), had died.

with this course of action, which could have been organized with so much greater secrecy and carried out so much more discreetly. But are we really supposed to believe, Phidippus, that, instead of doing any such thing, there were these violent men lurking in an ambush and brandishing their daggers – and that Castor apparently had no hesitation in telling you all about them? The whole charge is really the most totally fictitious flight of fancy.

'You were saved by the good fortune,' says the prosecutor to Caesar, 'which so often keeps you company. For at this point you indicated that you did not want to inspect the presents just then.' Yes, but what happened next? Are we really to suppose that Deiotarus, having failed to achieve his purpose at that particular juncture, would immediately proceed to disband his army? After all, was there really no other place where he could equally well station an ambush? Besides, you had already expressed the intention of returning to that same room after you had dined, and that is precisely what you did. Surely, it would not have been such an insuperable problem to keep the armed men in their original place of concealment for just an hour or two.

Instead, you ate your meal, in good, cheerful spirits, and afterwards you went to your room, as you had said you would. And there was Deiotarus treating you just as King Attalus treated the younger Scipio Africanus. For Attalus, we have read, sent Scipio sumptuous gifts all the way from Asia to Numantia, and Africanus accepted them in front of a parade of his entire army.[1] Deiotarus, on the other hand, did not just send you his gifts, but presented them to you in person, with kingly generosity and courtesy. And then you retired to your bedroom.

1. Cicero's memory is at fault. According to Livy, *Epitome*, 57, it was not Attalus III of Pergamum but Antiochus VII Sidetes of Syria who sent these gifts to Scipio Africanus the younger (Aemilianus) while he was besieging Numantia in northern Spain (134–133 B.C.).

May I invite you, Caesar, to cast your mind back to the occasion? Review the events of that day once again, and try to recall the expressions on those faces which were turned towards you so admiringly. I am sure you cannot remember the slightest trace of consternation or agitation. And, as for Deiotarus, I am equally sure you did not note the very smallest departure from the tranquil decorum of a man who is always a model of dignity and impressiveness.

But in any case it is quite impossible to conceive of any reason why he should have decided to kill you after you had taken your bath, but *not* after you had eaten your dinner! 'Ah, but he put it off until the next day,' explains the prosecutor. 'His intention was to wait until they came to the fortress of Blucium, and then carry out his plan there.' What on earth was the reason for the change of scene? However, for the sake of argument, let us imagine just for a moment that this theory of the postponement contains points that are worth discussing. Then how do they explain it? Well, on that first evening, they say, when you expressed a desire to vomit after dinner,[1] they proposed to take you to the bathroom, because that is where the ambush had been posted. However, your famous good fortune saved you as so often before, since you expressed a preference to retire for the purpose to your own bedroom instead. But let me tell this runaway slave, curse him, that not content with showing himself an iniquitous scoundrel, he must be an absolute fool as well. For we are presumably asked to suppose that the men the king had posted in the ambush were made of solid bronze, and that it was out of the question to *move* them from the bathroom to the bedroom.

Well, that is the sum total of the ambush charge. For that was all Phidippus said. 'I was involved in the plot myself,' he declared. But you cannot surely mean that Deiotarus was

---

1. Cicero, *Letters to Atticus*, XIII, 52, implies that Caesar followed this habit on medical advice; see *Cicero: Selected Works*, p. 90.

lunatic enough, first to let someone into the secret of such an atrocious crime, and then to allow him freely out of his sight and indeed actually to dispatch him to Rome, the place where he knew his grandson Castor happened to be, who hated him so bitterly – and where Caesar was, too, the very person against whom the king had supposedly been plotting! The improbability increases still further when you reflect that Phidippus would have been the only man in the world able to take advantage of his absence from Deiotarus in order to denounce him. Phidippus himself says that the king threw his brothers into prison 'because they too were in the know'. So you are trying to tell us that, whereas Deiotarus imprisoned the people who stayed with him, you yourself, who possessed the same inside knowledge that you attribute to them, were left entirely free and even allowed to go to Rome!

The remaining part of the accusation, Caesar, was divided into two sections. According to the first part, the reason why the king watched incessantly for an opportunity to kill you, as they claim he did, was because he hated you. Secondly, he raised a powerful army against you.

The question of the army I shall deal with as briefly as I have dealt with the previous matter. Never at any time did king Deiotarus dispose of troops strong enough to attack a Roman formation. His soldiers were only just numerous enough to defend his own frontiers against raiders and brigands, and to send help to our own generals. It is true that at one time he was capable of mobilizing larger forces. Yet now he can barely maintain the small numbers that he has. 'But he sent reinforcements to someone or other called Caecilius,[1] and when they didn't want to go he threw them into prison.' Now, I will not trouble to

1. Quintus Caecilius Bassus was a Roman knight of Pompeian sympathies who submitted to Caesar after Pharsalus but subsequently, in 46, incited the legions in Syria to revolt, and had still not been put down when Caesar was killed.

point out how unlikely it is that the king disposed of men to send, or that if he sent them they would have disobeyed him. I will not even stress the improbability of the story that, having rebelled against his orders on so very important an issue, they were merely imprisoned instead of being put to death. But this I really have to ask: is it in the slightest degree plausible to suppose that Deiotarus sent this contingent to Caecilius when he must have been perfectly well aware that Caecilius represented a lost cause? Surely he cannot have believed that Caecilius was really a great personage. On the contrary, Deiotarus, with his profound understanding of Roman affairs, must have taken a peculiarly low view of the man – either because he knew nothing about him or because he did! However, the prosecutor adds a further allegation against the king as well. When Deiotarus sent cavalry to help you, Caesar, they were no good, we are told. I can well believe, Caesar, that they were nothing like as good as yours. But he did send you the very best he had. Castor also claims that one member of the force was identified as a slave.[1] I doubt very much if this was true. I never heard it. But even if it was true, I would not suppose that Deiotarus personally was to blame.

And how did he show his alleged hostility towards yourself? I suppose we shall be told that he hoped and expected you would find it difficult to extricate yourself from Alexandria because of the nature of the country and position of the river.[2] Yet that was the very time when he was supplying you with funds, and helping to maintain your army, and doing everything in his power to assist Cnaeus Domitius Calvinus whom you had placed in charge of the affairs of Asia Minor. Later, too, after your victory in that country,[3] Deiotarus not only

1. In Rome, in ordinary circumstances, it was forbidden to enrol slaves in the army.

2. Caesar did get out of the city in the end and fought a decisive victory against the generals of Ptolemy XIII in March 47 B.C.

3. See above, p. 300.

offered you his hospitality, but actually shared your dangers in the field.

Next came the war in Africa.¹ There were grave rumours about your life – the same sort of rumours that had excited the maniac Caecilius. But the attitude the king adopted was beyond reproach, as you can very clearly see from the public auctions that he held. He was obviously prepared to sacrifice everything he had rather than fail to supply you with funds. The prosecutor, on the other hand, has produced quite another story. 'At this very time,' he says, 'Deiotarus was sending agents to Nicaea and Ephesus to pick up the rumours from Africa and pass them on to him as quickly as they could. Among the reports the king heard was a story that Domitius Calvinus had perished in a shipwreck, and that you yourself were besieged in a fortress.² On being told this, Deiotarus made a reference to Domitius by quoting a Greek tag which we also have in Latin: *Perish our friends, so long as our enemies perish too.*'³ Yet even if Deiotarus had been your bitterest enemy he would never have said a thing like that. For he is a kindly man, and the sentiment is brutal. And how could he have called himself a friend of Domitius if he was no friend of yours? Besides, it was in any case a practical impossibility for him to act in an unfriendly fashion towards yourself, since by the rights of war you could have put him to death. But you did nothing of the kind. Indeed, as he remembers very well, you gave him and his son⁴ the title of king.

And let us see where this gallows-bird takes us next. He says that Deiotarus was so glad and excited to hear the news

1. Caesar defeated Quintus Caecilius Metellus Pius Scipio and the sons of Pompeius at Thapsus (Ras Dimas in Tunisia) in April 46 B.C.

2. Probably Ruspina.

3. Author unknown. Calvinus was in court at the present hearing; see below, p. 322. Nicaea is the modern Iznik.

4. Deiotarus junior, to whom Cicero, when he was governor of Cilicia in 61–50 B.C., had entrusted his son and nephew (*Letters to Atticus*, V, 17, 18).

about Calvinus and yourself that he got drunk and danced naked at a party. Crucifixion is too good for a runaway slave who tells that sort of story. I defy anyone to say they have ever seen Deiotarus either dancing or drunk. The king is a man of the highest character, and you, Caesar, I believe, are extremely well aware of this. And conspicuous among his merits is an admirable sobriety. I know this is a quality not often praised in kings. To be called sober does not seem an especially glorious compliment for a royal personage. People are more accustomed to acclaim kings as brave, just, upright, dignified, magnanimous, open-handed, philanthropic, munificent. Those are the qualities that we describe as royal. Sobriety, on the other hand, is a private characteristic. Yet in my view – for what it is worth – sobriety, that is to say moderation or temperance, is an extremely valuable and significant virtue. Moreover, it has figured prominently in the character of Deiotarus from his very earliest years, as was noted and recognized by everyone throughout the entire province of Asia,[1] and particularly by our own officials and commanders, and the Roman knights who are engaged in business in the province.

Deiotarus has won his present title of king because of a long series of services to our country in the field of public affairs. In addition, whenever he was able to find a little leisure from fighting Rome's wars, he liked to devote it to developing friendly relations and business connexions with individual Romans. By this means he became well known to a great many of us, and we were able to learn that he was not only an illustrious prince[2] but also an excellent head of a family, and

1. Western Asia Minor.
2. The word *tetrarches* is used. Although this term had originally been used for rulers of the fourth part of a country, Deiotarus had initially been one of twelve Galatian princes. Then, however, he was made sole ruler of the tribe of the Tolistobogii (western Galatia) by Pompeius, and granted certain supervisory powers over the other two tribes of Galatia – whose territories he encroached upon whenever possible.

at the same time a hard-working farmer and stockbreeder. Moreover, even when he was still only a youth, before he had gained the successes of his later life, his every action was already serious and dignified. Surely, then, we are not to suppose that such a man, after he had attained mature years and renown, could bring himself to take the floor and give a performance as dancer!

As for yourself, Castor, you would have done far better to model yourself on your grandfather's character and conduct than to use a runaway slave as your mouthpiece, and malign a great and good man. Indeed, even if your grandfather did happen to have gone in for dancing, instead of being the model of high principle and upright behaviour that he in fact is, such an imputation could scarcely be applied with any plausibility to a person of his advanced years. For, by the time we are speaking of, he was already in the evening of his days, and the occupations he had practised from his earliest years onwards – not dancing at all, but skilful swordsmanship and horsemanship – had all become things of the past for him. In these later days, it took more than one man to lift him into his saddle. All the same, we admired a man of his age for being able to stay in it at all!

But take this grandson of his on the other hand, this Castor. He soldiered under me in Cilicia,[1] and we served together in Greece.[2] His father had sent him to Pompeius with a picked unit of cavalry, and how well I remember him prancing about in our army at the head of his squadron, showing off in the most boastful and ostentatious fashion, outbidding everyone in his enthusiasm and ardour for the cause. Later on, when the battle of Pharsalus had been fought and our army was destroyed, I, who had always advocated peace, urged that it was not enough to lay our weapons aside: they ought to be thrown away altogether. But I was entirely unable to convert

1. When Cicero was proconsul there in 51–50 B.C. (see also p. 299).
2. For the Pharsalus campaign in 48 B.C.

Castor to such a view. Full of keenness for the war, he believed that this was the way he ought to live up to his father's expectations.[1]

That royal house has been privileged indeed! For not only has it managed to remain unpunished, but it has even been given a free hand to incriminate other people! Deiotarus, on the other hand, is peculiarly unfortunate, because he actually finds himself prosecuted by a man who was on the same side as himself. It is bad enough for him, Caesar, to be brought before you yourself for trial. But he has also suffered the additional calamity of prosecution by his own flesh and blood. Will you not be prepared, Castor, to accept the good luck that has already come your way, and leave it at that? Will you never be content until you have brought total destruction upon your own family?

All right, then, there was a feud between you and Deiotarus. Certainly there ought not to have been a feud, since it was thanks to the king that your family, which had previously been quite obscure, emerged from darkness into light. For who had ever heard of your father until he had a father-in-law to his credit? But feud or no feud, and however ungratefully and unnaturally you chose to repudiate your family ties, you could at least have carried on your quarrel humanely, instead of persecuting your victim with a fabricated accusation, and thirsting after his life, and menacing him with a capital charge. However, let us go so far as to allow, if we must, that you felt obliged to carry your bitter hatred to lengths as extreme as these. Even so, it remains impossible to excuse the

1. Castor's father Saocondarius (Tarcondarius) Castor, who married Deiotarus' daughter, was perhaps tetrarch (prince) of the Tectosages (central Galatia); cf. D. Magie, *The Romans in Asia Minor*, II, 1950, pp. 1236ff. It was no doubt he who prompted his son to bring this charge against Deiotarus, who consequently had him murdered after Caesar's death. But Castor, the present prosecutor, survived to succeed his grandfather in 40 B.C.

way you have violated every right of the individual, every right of society, every right of humanity itself.

For to suborn a slave and seduce him by bribes and promises, to abduct him to your house and arm him against his own master, is tantamount to declaring an unholy war not just against one single relative of your own but against every other household that exists! For if your corruption of a slave were allowed not merely to escape punishment, but to win explicit approval from the highest of all authorities, let me tell you that even the most powerful walls, and laws, and legal principles, will never again be strong enough to guarantee the security of any one of us. For when a slave, a possession of our own, our own private property, has gained the freedom to break out with absolute impunity and attack us as if we were his enemy, then the slaves are now the masters, and the masters have become slaves. How times have changed, and customs with them![1] There was a story told about the great Cnaeus Domitius Ahenobarbus, who held office as consul, censor and chief priest when we were boys. While he was tribune of the people, he used his powers to summon Marcus Aemilius Scaurus, the leading Roman of his time, before a people's court.[2] But when one of Scaurus' slaves came secretly to Ahenobarbus' house offering to provide evidence against his own master, Ahenobarbus ordered that the man should be arrested and handed over to Scaurus himself. Certainly it would be very wrong to compare Ahenobarbus to Castor; what is more instructive, however, is to note the differences between them. Ahenobarbus was the enemy of the slave's master, but he sent the slave back to him all the same. Whereas

1. *O tempora, O mores!* Repeated from Cicero's first speech *Against Catilina*, I, 2.

2. Ahenobarbus, while tribune in 104 B.C., accused Scaurus (see Genealogical Table, I) of the violation of ritual correctness at a ceremony, and brought him to trial (*iudicium populi*) before the Comitia Centuriata (see List of Terms, Assembly).

what you have done, Castor, is to seduce a slave away from your own grandfather. Ahenobarbus refused to listen to a slave, although the man had come of his own free will without anyone bribing him to do so. You, on the other hand, actually bribed the slave to speak. Ahenobarbus spurned the assistance of a slave against his own master. You employed him specifically to bring his master into court.

Ah, you may protest, you only bribed Phidippus on one single occasion. However that may be, you will recall that after he had been with you, and after you had produced him as a witness, he refused to stay in your company any longer, and escaped back to the delegates he was attached to.[1] And then he sought out Cnaeus Domitius Calvinus, who is with us today. The eminent Servius Sulpicius Rufus[2] happened to be dining with Domitius, and in the hearing of Sulpicius, and of our excellent young friend here Titus Manlius Torquatus,[3] Phidippus admitted openly that you had bribed him, and that yours were the promises which had induced him to tell all those lies.

The attack you launched against Deiotarus, Castor, was sheer unbridled malice, plain wanton inhumanity. One sees why you came to Rome. Your purpose was nothing less than to overthrow the laws and traditions of our city, to besmirch our humane society with the savage habits to which you were accustomed at home.

All the same, Castor's charges have been scratched together cunningly enough. 'Blesamius,' he says – for in order to slander you he took in vain the name of this reputable man with whom you, Caesar, are very well acquainted[4] – 'Blesamius constantly wrote to King Deiotarus, declaring that

1. See above, p. 312.
2. Famous jurist and orator, and friend of Cicero.   3. Unknown.
4. Blesamius was a member of the deputations sent by Caesar to Tarraco and Rome (p. 312 n. 1).

you were unpopular, that you were regarded as a tyrant,
that Roman popular feeling had been deeply offended by the
erection of your statue among those of the kings,[1] that your
public appearances were not being greeted with any applause.'
But it must be clear enough to you, Caesar, that this is just
street-corner gossip; my opponents have been listening to
disaffected elements round the city, and that is where they have
been able to pick up these rumours. I ask you, can you
possibly imagine Blesamius describing Caesar as a tyrant?
You are trying to tell us, I have to suppose, that Blesamius has
been seeing, on all sides, the severed heads of murdered
citizens, that he has witnessed people persecuted and flogged
and murdered by Caesar's orders, families plunged in ruin and
desolation, soldiers bristling with arms all over the Forum!

No: when you won your victory, Caesar, this time the
experiences we have so often suffered in past civil wars did not
recur. You are the only victor we have known whose triumphs
did not cost a single non-combatant life. And if we who are
free men, who were born the freest of the free, do not find
you a tyrant in any way whatever, but see you as the most
merciful of victorious commanders, it is hardly likely that you
will seem a tyrant to Blesamius, who lives under the autocratic
government of a monarchy! As to your statue, who worries
about that, one single statue when there are so many around?
When we do not resent a man's trophies, we surely do not
need to resent his statues either. And if the location of the
statue is what they are protesting about, Caesar has got another
on the Rostra as well, which is quite as splendid a position,[2]

1. Caesar's statue was placed on the Capitol with those of the seven
kings of Rome and Lucius Junius Brutus, who had allegedly overthrown
the monarchy (Dio Cassius, XLIII, 45, 3).

2. Cicero deliberately misses the point: on the New Rostra (M. Grant,
The Roman Forum, pp. 110ff.) Caesar's statue was only one of a number
of statues of generals, whereas on the Capitol it was with statues of the
ancient kings, whom many regarded as the symbols of a hated autocracy
(p. 328 n. 1).

so why complain about the other one? With regard to the applause, my answer is this: never once have you deliberately sought any such thing, and if on occasion your reception has been muted, this was because people were overawed by the strength of their admiration; or perhaps they abstained because nothing so commonplace as mere applause came anywhere near what you deserved.[1]

Well, I do not believe I have left anything out. But one point I deliberately held back until the end. I refer to my hope, Caesar, that this speech of mine will result in your complete reconciliation with Deiotarus. It is not that I am any longer worried in case you have a grudge against him. What I am afraid of is that you may suspect that *he* harbours a grudge against *you*. But believe me, nothing could possibly be farther from the truth. He remembers what you have allowed him to keep, not what he has lost. He does not think of himself as penalized by you at all. As he sees the matter, you had numerous supporters to whom you felt obliged to give numerous rewards – and if these rewards had to be taken from himself, who had after all been on the other side, it was not for him to object. When Antiochus the Great, king of Asia, after his defeat by Lucius Cornelius Scipio Asiaticus,[2] was ordered to withdraw the frontiers of his kingdom to the Taurus mountains, he forfeited, among other possessions, the whole of what is our province of Asia today. Yet he repeatedly expressed the view that Rome had treated him kindly. For he had been released from an excessive administrative burden,

1. In a letter of July 45 B.C., to his friend Atticus, Cicero noted (with approval) that the populace had refrained from applauding a statue of Victory in a procession because it was accompanied by a statue of Caesar (*Letters to Atticus*, XIII, 44).

2. Antiochus III, the monarch of the Seleucid empire which centred upon Syria and Mesopotamia but temporarily included much of Asia Minor, was defeated in 190 by Scipio Asiaticus (aided by his brother Scipio Africanus the younger) at Magnesia ad Sipylum (Manisa) in western Asia Minor.

he declared, by his confinement to a kingdom of reasonable proportions. And Deiotarus is far more justified than Antiochus in offering himself the same consolation, since the latter was suffering punishment for a mad undertaking, whereas Deiotarus was only expiating a mistake.

You showed how willing you were, Caesar, to give Deiotarus his full due, when you granted him and his son the designation of king.[1] Retaining and cherishing that title, he feels that the benefactions he has received from the Roman people, and the high opinion he has earned from the Roman senate, are still his proud possessions, of which nothing has been lost. He is a man of nobility and courage, and neither his enemies nor the blows of fortune will ever bring him down. He has many assets, he believes, that can never be taken away from him. He has earned them by his deeds in the past – and his valiant spirit has kept them intact.

For many a complimentary resolution in praise of Deiotarus has been decreed by many a Roman general,[2] and no evil stroke of fortune, no vicissitude, no unjust blow, could ever erase these commendations. Ever since Deiotarus was old enough to serve in the field, no Roman commander who has ever fought a war, whether in Asia or Cappadocia or Pontus or Cilicia or Syria, has failed to cite his services in honorific terms. And the honours which the senate, too, has repeatedly lavished upon him, honours recorded in the official archives and public memorials of Rome, will never be effaced throughout all the centuries of future time. If everything else that has

1. See above, p. 310 n. 2.
2. Deiotarus had remained faithful to the Romans during the first and second wars against Mithridates VI of Pontus (fought by Lucius Cornelius Sulla in 88–85 and Lucius Licinius Murena in 82–81 B.C.), during the expedition of Publius Servilius Vatia Isauricus against the Isaurian pirates (78–75), and during the third war against Mithridates VI fought by Lucius Licinius Lucullus and then Pompeius (74–63). He assumed the title 'Roman-Lover' (*Philoromaeus*); *L'année épigraphique*, 1936, 110. For Vatia and Lucullus, see Genealogical Table, I.

ever happened was consigned to total oblivion, those glorious citations would still be remembered. And his personal bravery, his noble heart, his moral strength, his unfailing integrity, what can I say about these? They are the qualities of character which wise and learned men, without exception, have pronounced to be the highest virtues of all. Indeed, some have even declared that they are the only true virtues that exist, and have asserted that if a man possesses them he has everything he needs, not only to lead a good life, but to lead a happy life as well.[1]

Deiotarus spends his time, night and day, engaged in philosophical reflections of precisely this kind. And so far removed is he from feeling any grievance against yourself – for it would be ingratitude and madness to do anything of the kind – that, on the contrary, he feels deeply grateful to your clemency for all the peace and quiet he is able to enjoy during the evening of his life.[2] His feelings of this kind are nothing new. But as things are now, I am very sure that the letter which, at Tarraco, you gave Blesamius here to deliver to him – I have read a copy of it – has reassured him still further, and, indeed, has removed every trace of anxiety from his heart. For in that letter you bade him be of good hope and good courage. Now, I am in a position to know extremely well that you are not in the habit of writing that sort of message without meaning every word of it. For it was in almost exactly the same terms, as I well remember, that you wrote to myself.[3] You told me, too, to be of good hope. And you meant exactly what you said.

1. The Stoics.

2. After Caesar's death, however, Deiotarus plunged back into an active life of politics, fighting, aggression and murder, changing sides in the Roman civil wars several times before his death in 40 B.C.

3. Caesar wrote to Cicero from the east in about July 47 B.C., after Cicero had been with his enemies at the campaign of Pharsalus in the previous year.

I must tell you that I feel a strong sense of personal involve-
ment in King Deiotarus' cause. Public life has brought us
together as friends. The ties of hospitality have been strength-
ened by mutual regard. Our association has developed into
intimacy. The invaluable assistance he provided to myself and
my army has attached me to him with unbreakable bonds.[1]
And yet, in the midst of this concern for Deiotarus, I cannot
help sparing an anxious thought also for the many other
distinguished men to whom you have extended a pardon. For
the forgiveness they received at your hands ought to be a
single act of mercy, granted once and for all. It would be
terrible if they had to feel that there was something imperm-
anent about your generosity. That people's apprehensions
should have to linger on and on surely cannot be right. When
you have once freed a man from his fears, it would be quite
wrong if he then had to start being afraid all over again.

There is one method, Caesar, which is quite commonly
practised when people are being tried on grave charges; but
I certainly do not need to adopt it today. I refer to the attempts
by advocates to find the best ways of arousing compassion. In
the present case, that is wholly unnecessary. For when a man
is down, and is begging for mercy, his fate arouses compassion
spontaneously, unbidden by the words of any speech. All the
same, I do just ask you to give sympathetic thought to these
two kings, Deiotarus and his son.[2] They are not here for you
to see, but I urge you to imagine the terrible nature of their
predicament. And then, having already refused to give way
to your anger, you will assuredly not refuse to yield to pity.

There are many memorials of your mercifulness, Caesar,

1. When Cicero was governor of Cilicia in 51–50 B.C., he and Marcus
Calpurnius Bibulus, governor of Syria, were greatly afraid of a Parthian
invasion, and Deiotarus offered to place the whole of his forces, 12,000
infantry (2 legions organized on the Roman model) and 2,000 cavalry,
at the disposal of Cicero, whose army was thus doubled in size.
2. See p. 317.

but none are more glorious than the lives that you have seen fit to spare. Such deeds of generosity are significant enough when private persons are concerned. But when the beneficiary is a king, the renown won by this graciousness is more impressive still. The name of king has always been respected in this country,[1] and the titles of the kings who are allies and friends of Rome are revered most of all. This was the designation which Deiotarus and his son feared your victory would take away from them. But now they have the happy knowledge that you have allowed them to keep it, since you have confirmed that it shall still be theirs, so that they will be able to hand it on to later generations.

These delegates who are here today offer themselves as hostages for the deliverance of their two kings. They are Hieras and Blesamius and Antigonus, men who have long been known to yourself and to us all. And with them is Dorylaus, an equally loyal and excellent personage who, as you will remember, was recently dispatched to you on a mission in Hieras' company. Every one of these delegates is a close friend of the kings, and I am sure that they enjoy your own confidence as well. Ask Blesamius if he has ever written Deiotarus one single word that could be considered derogatory to your dignity. As for Hieras, he takes upon himself the entire responsibility of deputizing for Deiotarus in this action. He is even ready to offer himself as defendant, in substitution for his king. Appealing to your excellent memory he reminds you that while you were staying in Deiotarus' principality he, Hieras, never left your side. He joined you, he recalls, at the moment you passed over the frontier to enter his country, and he stayed with you until you had crossed the opposite frontier and departed. When you came into the dining-room after

---

1. This was not by any means always true of the *Roman* kingship (p. 323 n. 2), but Cicero is flattering Caesar, who traced his descent from the mythical Aeneas and his son Iulus, and from the mythical or quasi-mythical Ancus Marcius; cf. M. Grant, *Roman Myths*, pp. 94, 151ff.

your bath, when you were inspecting those presents after dinner, when you retired to your bedroom, Hieras declares that he was in your company all the time. And he adds that on the following day he once again was in attendance upon you continuously. That being so, if any of these allegations could be construed as reflecting the existence of a real, authentic plot, Hieras gives you unreserved permission to put the entire blame upon himself!

So I beg you to bear in mind, Caesar, that your verdict upon the two kings today will mean either their utter destruction and irreparable disgrace, or their salvation; the salvation of their lives and of their honour alike. Our opponents are cruel: what they are after is the ruin of Deiotarus and his son. But you are a clement man, and I implore you to come to their rescue!

APPENDIXES

Appendix A
LIST OF TERMS

AEDILES. Two curule (representing the whole people), and two plebeian (representing the *plebs*, q.v.): officials ranking above quaestors and below praetors (q.v.), concerned with the care of the city of Rome, its corn-supply, and its Games. If a sufficient number of praetors was not available, ex-aediles served as chairmen of criminal courts (*quaestiones*).

ALLIES (*socii*). Term applied not only to allies of Rome outside the empire but also to 'free' treaty-bound communities within the empire, e.g. the Italian communities that revolted in the Social or Marsian War (91–87 B.C.), and the subjects of Rome in the provinces.

ASSEMBLY OF THE ROMAN PEOPLE (*Comitia*). The sovereign executive body of Rome. The citizens were summoned by a senior official in groups, i.e. *curiae*, centuries, or tribes. The *comitia curiata*, the most ancient form of Assembly, were purely formal by the time of Cicero, their competence having been progressively limited by the *comitia centuriata* which met in the Field of Mars (Campus Martius) and enacted laws, elected the most important state officials, and declared war and peace. In ancient times trials and appeals were held before the *comitia centuriata*, but by Cicero's time this practice had become obsolete: it was revived against his client Rabirius (p. 262). There were also two sorts of Assemblies of Tribes (q.v.), of which one (*concilium plebis tributum*) – not strictly *comitia* – elected tribunes of the people and plebeian aediles (qq.v.) and held trials for non-capital offences, while the other – *comitia* created in imitation of the *concilium* – elected quaestors, curule aediles, and military tribunes (q.v.), and held minor trials. The essence of the political struggles of the late second and first centuries B.C. was the desire of radical reformist politicians (*populares*) to deal direct with the Assembly over the heads of the senate.

AUSPICES (*auspicia*). Certain types of divination – particularly from birds – officially practised at elections, inaugurations of office, entrances into a province, and the conduct of wars. The diviners (*auspices*) also still possessed a formal role in marriage rites.

CAPITAL CHARGES. For the meaning of *caput* in this connexion, see above, p. 17.

CENSORS. Two in number, appointed every five (earlier every four) years at Rome, for eighteen months, to draw up and maintain the list of citizens (*census*) and revise the list of members of the senate. As guardians of public morals, they were entitled to place a mark of disapproval against (i.e. to strike off) the names of both senators and knights (q.v.) who had in their opinion acted improperly. Italian municipalities imitated the institution by giving their chief officials censorial powers every five years (*duoviri quinquennales*).

CHIEF PRIEST (*Pontifex Maximus*). Head of the Pontifices, one of the four orders of priesthood; and head of the whole state clergy.

CONSULS. The supreme civil and military officials (magistrates, q.v.) of Republican Rome, two in number, holding office for one year, and giving their names to that year. Ex-consuls (*consulares*) traditionally formed an inner ring of the senate.

DICTATOR. Originally a temporary, extraordinary, supreme office for an emergency, restricted to six months. Sulla retained the power for two years, and Caesar, after three renewals, assumed it permanently at the end of his life.

FREEDMEN. Liberated (manumitted) slaves. The law bound a freedman in certain ways to his former owner, now his *patronus*, whose status, even to the extent of Roman citizenship, they normally acquired. They were not, however, eligible for the higher state offices or (until the first century B.C.) for service in the legions.

GAMES. Annual or occasional formal sports and representations, generally of religious origin.

GOVERNORS of Roman provinces, usually former consuls or praetors (qq.v.), were normally sent to them for one year; but their tenures could be renewed.

JUDGES. The permanent *quaestiones* (q.v.) were composed of panels of judges, each under the presidency of a praetor or former aedile. These judgeships became the major bone of contention between the senate and knights (q.v., and see pp. 13f.).

KINGS. Traditionally the earliest rulers of Rome, beginning with the mythical Romulus (753 B.C.) and concluding with the semi-mythical Tarquinius Superbus who was believed to have been expelled in 510 B.C.

KNIGHTS (*equites*). The order in the state second to the senate, with a minimum property qualification of 400,000 sesterces (q.v.). They did not engage in the official career but, apart from the powerful pressure group of *publicani* (who purchased tax contracts from the state), were not so exclusively devoted to business as has often been supposed (p. 13). Their coherence as an order owed a great deal to their conflict with the senate for judgeships (q.v.).

MAGISTRATES. The leading civil and military officials of the state. Only the Tribunes of the People (q.v.) were not technically magistrates, though they had become indistinguishable from them.

NOBLES (*nobiles*). By the first century B.C. the title of *nobilitas*, though not a strict term of law, was reserved for families which had held a consulship (q.v.). Members of families which had never produced a consul (such as Cicero's) were described as 'new men' (*novi homines*). When Cicero speaks of the 'cause of the nobles' he is referring to the side led by Sulla in his victorious civil war against the successors of Marius (83–82), resulting in his appointment as dictator (q.v.).

PLEBS. The name given to the general body of Roman citizens, as distinct from the patricians. The functions performed by its Assembly (q.v.), the *concilium plebis tributum*, included the election of its special representatives, the Tribunes of the People (q.v.).

PRAETORS. The annually elected state officials, eight in number from the time of Sulla, who were next in importance to the consuls. They were largely concerned with the administration of justice, and acted as chairmen of the permanent criminal courts (*quaestiones*, q.v.). Their senior member was the city praetor (*praetor urbanus*), who compiled the roster of judges.

PREFECTS. Military commanders of contingents of allies (q.v.), especially cavalry.

PROSCRIPTIONS. A *proscriptio* was the publication of a list of Roman citizens who were declared outlaws and hunted down and executed, their property being confiscated. In the present book the term relates mainly to the proscriptions of Sulla, who, partly as an act of revenge for the massacres by Marius (87) and his successors (82), was said to have named 4,700 persons, including over 40 senators and 1,600 knights (q.v.).

QUAESTIONES. The term was originally used for special criminal inquiries. Then, from 149 B.C. onwards, permanent courts (*quaestiones perpetuae*) were gradually set up for individual crimes of frequent occurrence (p. 13). For their membership, see above, s.v. Judges.

QUAESTORS. The quaestorship was a junior state office (tenable in Rome or the provinces) which from the time of Sulla, who fixed the total number of quaestors at twenty and the minimum age at thirty, entitled its holders to membership of the senate (q.v.). (*Quaestores parricidii*, prosecuting certain capital cases before the Assembly, had become obsolete by the second century B.C.)

SENATE. The chief council of the state, technically an advisory body, but with great traditional influence (contested by reformist and radical politicians) over the Assembly (q.v.). The senate's decree, the 'advice' it offered to the state officials (all of whom were among its members), was the *senatus consultum*. In a crisis, it could issue a declaration of public emergency, the *senatusconsultum de republica defendenda* or *senatusconsultum ultimum*, but the scope of such decrees was intensely controversial (pp. 259ff.).

SESTERCE (*sestertius*). A unit of currency, containing four *asses*. At this time, however, neither sesterce (earlier a tiny silver coin) nor *as* (a bronze piece which had declined in weight from one Roman pound to half an ounce in 89–86 B.C.) was issued, the principal coin being the silver *denarius* of 16 *asses* or 4 *sestertii*.[1]

TRIBES, GALATIAN. The Celtic Galatians who occupied a large region of central Asia Minor in the third century B.C., and were subsequently ruled over by Cicero's client Deiotarus (p. 299), retained their organization in three tribes, the Tolistobogii, Tectosages and Trocmi.

TRIBES, ROMAN. All Roman citizens were registered in one of the thirty-five territorial tribes (four urban and thirty-one rural) which were the units for voting on certain matters in the Assembly (q.v.).

TRIBUNES, MILITARY (*tribuni militum*). The senior officers of the

1. Modern equivalents are impossible: but for an attempt see M. Grant, *Nero*, p. 257.

legions. Those of four legions were elected by the Assembly; the remainder were nominated by commanders-in-chief.

TRIBUNES OF THE PEOPLE (*tribuni plebis*), ten in number, were traditionally charged with the defence of the lives and property of the people (*plebs*), which swore to uphold their inviolability (*sacrosanctitas*). The tribunes summoned the *plebs* to the Assembly (q.v.) of Tribes and asserted a right of veto (*intercessio*) against any act performed by state officials. Long after they had been muzzled by the senate, the Gracchi and Saturninus (p. 257) sought to revive their powers – which were then sharply curtailed by Sulla, though Labienus subsequently tried to exercise them against Cicero during the latter's consulship.

TRIBUNES OF THE TREASURY (*tribuni aerarii*), originally collectors of the war tax, became a class somewhat similar to, but less wealthy than, the knights, with whom (together with senators) they were associated on panels of judges (q.v.) from 70 to 46 B.C.

TRIUMPH. The processional return of a victorious Roman general, when he sacrificed to Jupiter on the Capitol. Triumphs were awarded by the senate.

TRIUMVIRS (*tresviri*). The First Triumvirate, informally but effectively controlling the government, was established by Cnaeus Pompeius Magnus, Marcus Licinius Crassus, and Gaius Julius Caesar in 60–59 B.C. The Second Triumvirate of 43 B.C., with formal autocratic powers, comprised Marcus Antonius, the younger Gaius Julius Caesar – i.e. Octavian, the future Augustus – and Marcus Aemilius Lepidus. (The *tresviri capitales* performed police functions at Rome and assisted the praetors [q.v.] in their judicial functions.)

Appendix B
GENEALOGICAL TABLES

I. THE FAMILY OF THE CAECILII METELLI[1]

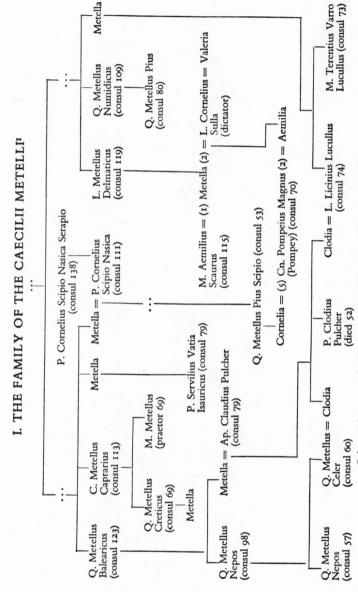

1. Other eminent members of the family, not mentioned in this book, are omitted.

II. THE FAMILY OF CLUENTIUS[1]

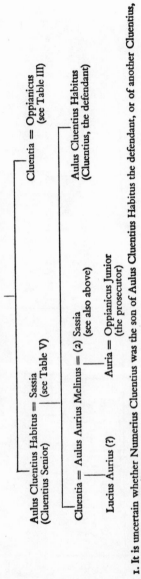

Aulus Cluentius Habitus = Sassia
(Cluentius Senior)   (see Table V)

Cluentia = Aulus Aurius Melinus = (2) Sassia
                                    (see also above)

Lucius Aurius (?)

Auria = Oppianicus Junior
        (the prosecutor)

Cluentia = Oppianicus
           (see Table III)

Aulus Cluentius Habitus
(Cluentius, the defendant)

1. It is uncertain whether Numerius Cluentius was the son of Aulus Cluentius Habitus the defendant, or of another Cluentius, or of Aulus Aurius Melinus.

III. THE FAMILY OF OPPIANICUS[1]

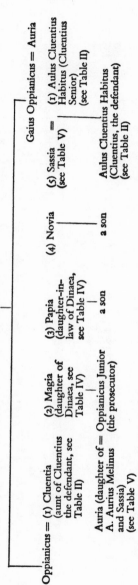

Gaius Oppianicus = Auria

Oppianicus = (1) Cluentia (aunt of Cluentius the defendant, see Table II)

    (2) Magia (daughter of Dinaea, see Table IV)

    (3) Papia (daughter-in-law of Dinaea, see Table IV)

    (4) Novia

    (5) Sassia = (see Table V)

(1) Aulus Cluentius Habitus (Cluentius Senior) (see Table II)

Auria (daughter of A. Aurius Melinus and Sassia) (see Table V) = Oppianicus Junior (the prosecutor)

a son [under (2) Magia]

a son [under (3) Papia]

a son [under (4) Novia]

Aulus Cluentius Habitus (Cluentius, the defendant) (see Table II)

1. It is uncertain how Statius Abbius the farmer, Sassia's alleged lover, was related to Oppianicus.

IV. THE FAMILY OF DINAEA[1]

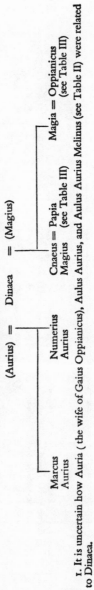

(Aurius) = Dinaea = (Magius)

Marcus Aurius

Numerius Aurius

Cnaeus = Papia
Magius   (see Table III)

Magia = Oppianicus
          (see Table III)

1. It is uncertain how Auria (the wife of Gaius Oppianicus), Aulus Aurius, and Aulus Aurius Melinus (see Table II) were related to Dinaea.

V. THE FAMILY OF SASSIA

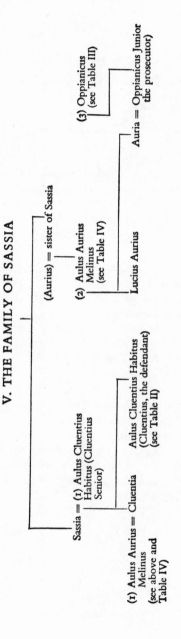

Appendix C
TABLE OF DATES

106 B.C.	Birth of Cicero
102, 101	Marius repels German invaders
100	Murder of Saturninus
91–87	Marsian or Social War
82–80	Dictatorship of Sulla (d. 78)
80	*In Defence of Sextus Roscius of Ameria*
70	*Against Verres*
66	Praetorship of Cicero
	In Defence of Aulus Cluentius Habitus
63	Consulship of Cicero
	In Defence of Gaius Rabirius
	Cicero's *Catilinarian Orations*
60–59	Formation of First Triumvirate (Pompeius, Caesar, Crassus)
58–57	Exile of Cicero
56	*In Defence of Marcus Caelius Rufus*
52	*In Defence of Titus Annius Milo*
51–50	Cicero's governorship of Cilicia
49–44	Dictatorships of Caesar, victorious over Pompeius (d. 48) and his sons in the Civil War
45	*In Defence of King Deiotarus*
44	Death of Caesar
44–43	Cicero's *Philippics* against Marcus Antonius
43	Formation of Second Triumvirate (Marcus Antonius, Octavian [the future Augustus] and Lepidus)
43	Death of Cicero

Appendix D
SOME BOOKS ABOUT CICERO[1]

D. R. Shackleton Bailey, *Cicero*, Routledge & Kegan Paul, 1971.

P. A. Brunt, *Social Conflicts in the Roman Republic*, Chatto & Windus, 1971.

K. Büchner, *Cicero*, Heidelberg, 1964.

Cambridge Ancient History, Cambridge University Press, volume IX, 1932.

Cicero, *Letters to Atticus* (ed. D. R. Shackleton Bailey), Cambridge University Press, vols. I–VII, 1965–71.

Cicero: Selected Political Speeches (ed. M. Grant), Penguin Books, 1969.

Cicero: Selected Works (ed. M. Grant), Penguin Books, 1960 (reprint 1971).

T. A. Dorey (ed.), *Cicero*, Routledge & Kegan Paul, 1964.

A. E. Douglas, *Cicero*, 'Greece and Rome' (New Surveys in the Classics, no. 2), 1968.

M. Gelzer, *Cicero: Biographischer Versuch*, Wiesbaden, 1969.

M. Gelzer, *The Roman Nobility*, Blackwell, Oxford, 1969 (translation by R. Seager of German essays of 1912 and 1915).

E. S. Gruen, *Roman Politics and the Criminal Courts, 149–78 B.C.*, Harvard University Press, 1968.

A. H. M. Jones, *The Criminal Courts of the Roman Republic and Principate*, Blackwell, Oxford, 1972.

J. M. Kelly, *Roman Litigation*, Oxford University Press, 1966.

G. Kennedy, *The Art of Rhetoric in the Roman World*, Princeton University Press, 1972.

W. Kunkel, *An Introduction to Roman Legal and Constitutional History*, Oxford University Press, 1966 (translation by J. M. Kelly of fourth German edition).

A. W. Lintott, *Violence in Republican Rome*, Oxford University Press, 1968.

1. Articles, editions of speeches, and other specialized works are referred to in the footnotes to the introductions and texts of the individual speeches.

Marco Tullio Cicerone: Scritti commemorativi pubblicati nel bimillenario dell morte, Florence, 1961.

T. Peterson, *Cicero,* New York, 1919 (reprint by Biblo & Tannen, 1963).

G. Radke (ed.), *Cicero: ein Mensch seiner Zeit,* Berlin, 1968.

E. Rawson, *Cicero: A Portrait,* Allen Lane, 1975.

G. C. Richards, *Cicero: A study,* Chatto & Windus, 1935.

H. H. Scullard, *From the Gracchi to Nero,* Methuen, 1959 (paperback 3rd edn, 1970).

R. Seager (ed.), *The Crisis of the Roman Republic* (reprints of articles), Heffer, Cambridge, and Barnes & Noble, New York, 1969.

R. E. Smith, *Cicero the Statesman,* Cambridge University Press, 1966.

D. Stockton, *Cicero: A Political Biography,* Oxford University Press, 1971.

R. Syme, *The Roman Revolution,* Oxford University Press, 1939 (paperback reprint, 1960).

L. R. Taylor, *Party Politics in the Age of Caesar,* California University Press (Berkeley), 1949.

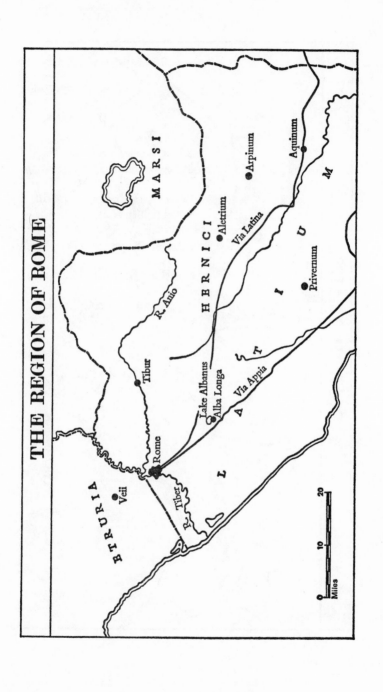

THE REGION OF ROME

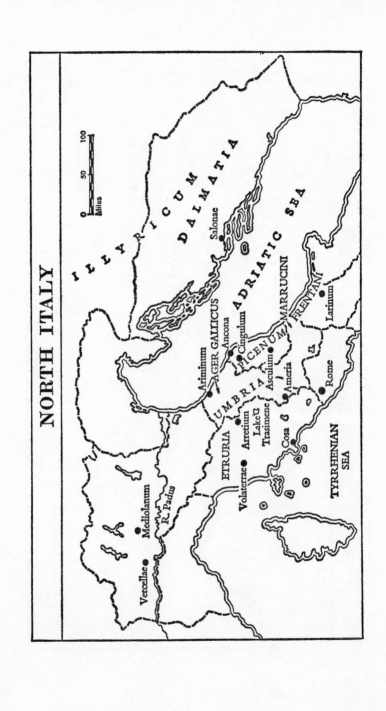

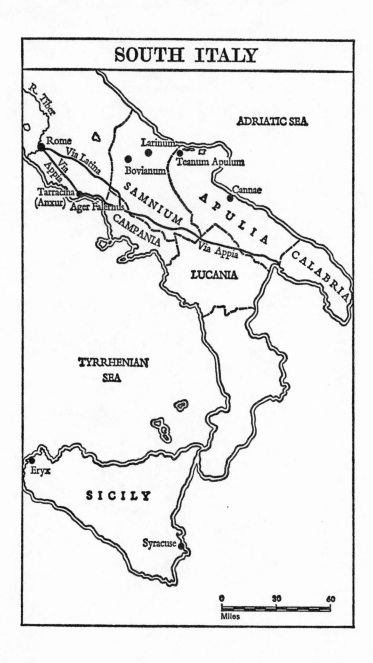

SOUTH ITALY

R. Tiber

ADRIATIC SEA

Rome
Via Latina
Via Appia
Tarracina (Anxur)
Ager Falernus

Larinum
Bovianum
Teanum Apulum
Cannae

SAMNIUM
CAMPANIA
APULIA
Via Appia
CALABRIA
LUCANIA

TYRRHENIAN SEA

Eryx

SICILY

Syracuse

0   30   60
Miles

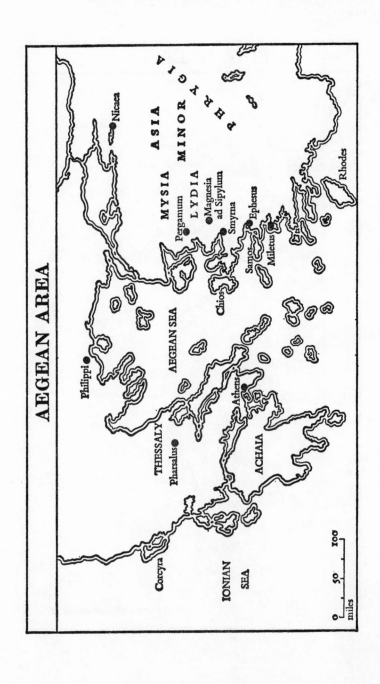

AEGEAN AREA

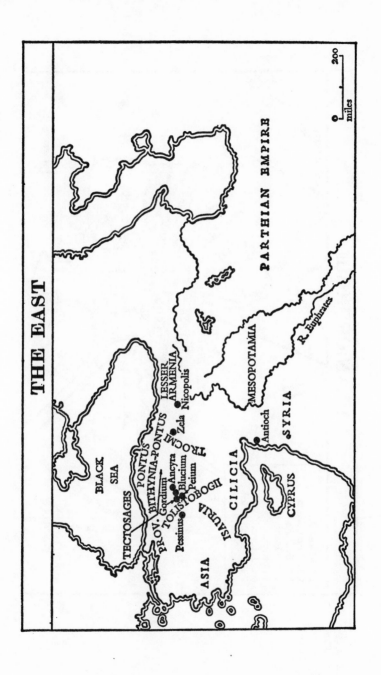

THE EAST

BLACK SEA

TECTOSAGES

PONTUS

PROV. BITHYNIA-PONTUS

TROCMI

Gordium

Pessinus

Ancyra

TOLISTOBOGII

Blucium

Peium

Zela

LESSER ARMENIA

Nicopolis

ASIA

ISAURIA

CILICIA

Antioch

CYPRUS

SYRIA

MESOPOTAMIA

R. Euphrates

PARTHIAN EMPIRE

0
miles
200

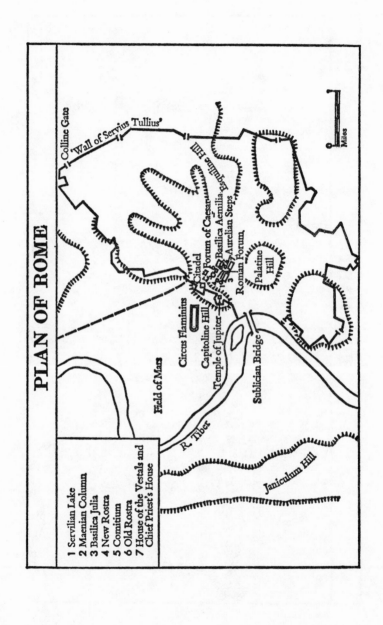

PLAN OF ROME

Colline Gate

"Wall of Servius Tullius"

Forum of Caesar
Basilica Æmilia. 356
Aurelian Steps
Roman Forum

Citadel
Circus Flaminius
Capitoline Hill
Temple of Jupiter

Palatine Hill

Field of Mars

Sublician Bridge

R. Tiber

Janiculum Hill

Miles

1 Servilian Lake
2 Maenian Column
3 Basilica Julia
4 New Rostra
5 Comitium
6 Old Rostra
7 House of the Vestals and
  Chief Priest's House

INDEX

The following abbreviations are employed:
A. = Aulus; C. = Gaius; Cn. = Cnaeus; Dec. = Decimus;
L. = Lucius; M. = Marcus; Mam. = Mamercus;
Man. = Manius; Num. = Numerius; P. = Publius; Q. = Quintus;
Ser. = Servius; Sex. = Sextus; St. = Statius; T. = Titus;
Ti. = Tiberius.

INDEX

INDEX